The Routledge Handbook of Attachment: Theory

D1520053

The Routledge Handbook of Attachment: Theory provides a broadly based intro-duction to attachment theory and associated areas, written in an accessible style by experts from around the world. The book covers the basic theories of attachment and discusses the similarities and differences of the two predominant schools of attachment theory.

The book provides an overview of current developments in attachment theory, explaining why it is important not only to understanding infant and early child development but also to adult personality and the care we provide to our children. *The Routledge Handbook of Attachment: Theory* provides detailed descriptions of the leading schools of attachment theory as well as discussions of this potentially confusing and contentious area, and includes a chapter on the neuropsychological basis of attachment. The book also examines other domains and diagnoses that can be confused with issues of attachment and considers contexts when different approaches may be more suitable.

Providing a comprehensive yet accessible introduction to the theories of attach-ment, *The Routledge Handbook of Attachment: Theory* is an indispensable guide for professionals working with children and families in community and court-based settings, clinical psychologists, psychiatrists and social workers, clinicians in training and students.

Paul Holmes is a child and adolescent psychiatrist who also trained as an adult psychotherapist. He worked in community child and adolescent mental health teams for many years, and with specialist services for fostered and adopted chil-dren. He has increasingly applied his long-standing interest in attachment theory to his work in providing expert psychiatric opinions to the British courts in child care proceedings.

Steve Farnfield is a Senior Lecturer and established the MSc in Attachment Stud-ies at the University of Roehampton, UK. He is a social worker and play therapist with many years' experience and a licensed trainer for the Dynamic-Maturational Model of Attachment Infant CARE-Index, Preschool Assessment of Attachment and Adult Attachment Interview developed by Patricia Crittenden.

The Routledge Handbook of Attachment: Theory

Edited by
Paul Holmes and Steve Farnfield

Routledge
Taylor & Francis Group

LONDON AND NEW YORK

First published 2014
by Routledge
27 Church Road, Hove, East Sussex, BN3 2FA

and by Routledge
711 Third Avenue, New York, NY 10017

Routledge is an imprint of the Taylor & Francis Group, an informa business

British Library Cataloguing in Publication Data
A catalogue record for this book is available from the British Library

Library of Congress Cataloging in Publication Data
The Routledge handbook of attachment : theory / edited by PaulHolmes and
Steve Farnfield.
    pages cm
    1. Attachment behavior. 2. Psychotherapy. I. Holmes, Paul, editorof compilation.
    II. Farnfield, Steve, editor of compilation.
    BF575.A86R685 2014
    155.9'2—dc23
    2014019637

ISBN: 978-1-138-01672-9 (pbk set)
ISBN: 978-1-315-76509-9 (ebk set)
ISBN: 978-0-415-53826-8 (hbk)
ISBN: 978-0-415-53827-5 (pbk)
ISBN: 978-1-315-76209-8 (ebk)

Typeset in Times New Roman
by Swales & Willis Ltd, Exeter, Devon

Printed and bound in the United States of America by Publishers Graphics,
LLC on sustainably sourced paper.

This book is dedicated to all the children and families with whom we have had the privilege to work and who have contributed significantly to our understanding of the importance of attachment.

Contents

Notes on contributors   ix
Preface   xiii
PAUL HOLMES AND STEVE FARNFIELD

Overview: attachment theory, assessment and implications   1
PAUL HOLMES AND STEVE FARNFIELD

1   **ABC + D of attachment theory: the Strange Situation procedure
    as the gold standard of attachment assessment**   11
    LENNY VAN ROSMALEN, MARINUS H. VAN IJZENDOORN AND
    MARIAN J. BAKERMANS-KRANENBURG

2   **Why are we interested in attachments?**   31
    PETER FONAGY, NICOLAS LORENZINI, CHLOE CAMPBELL AND
    PATRICK LUYTEN

3   **The Dynamic-Maturational Model (DMM) of attachment**   49
    STEVE FARNFIELD AND MARTIN STOKOWY

4   **Similarities and differences between the ABC + D model
    and the DMM classification systems for attachment:
    a practitioner's guide**   73
    PRACHI E. SHAH AND LANE STRATHEARN

5   **Disorganised attachment and reactive attachment disorders**   89
    DAVID SHEMMINGS

6   **Mentalising in attachment contexts**   107
    PATRICK LUYTEN AND PETER FONAGY

7   **Attachment, our brains, nervous systems and hormones**   127
    GRAHAM MUSIC

8   **All the A's and an O: attachment is not everything**   148
    CORNELIA GUTJAHR

9   **Other dimensions of developmental influences: not everything
    can be explained by attachment theory**   166
    MARGARET DEJONG

    Index   181

Contributors

Marian J. Bakermans-Kranenburg is Professor at the Centre for Child and Family Studies, Leiden University, the Netherlands. She is interested in parenting and parent–child relationships, with a special focus on neurobiological processes and the interplay between genetic and environmental factors. Intervention studies and adoption studies as (quasi-) experimental manipulations of the environment have their natural place in this line of research. She was awarded the Bowlby-Ainsworth award of the New York Attachment Consortium (2005) and was VIDI (2004) and VICI (2009/2010) laureate of the Netherlands Organization for Scientific Research. She is a Fellow of The Royal Netherlands Academy of Arts and Sciences and a Fellow of the Association for Psychological Science, both since 2012.

Chloe Campbell is a Research Associate at the Psychoanalysis Unit, University College London, UK.

Margaret DeJong is a Consultant Child and Adolescent Psychiatrist and Head of the Department of Child and Adolescent Mental Health at Great Ormond Street Hospital for Children, UK, as well as Honorary Senior Lecturer at the UCL Institute of Child Health. She runs the Parenting and Child Service, an assessment and therapeutic service for children with a background of abuse, neglect and trauma. This includes multidisciplinary expert witness work in complex child protection cases, in which she has many years' experience. She also provides a psychiatry liaison service at Great Ormond Street. She has a background in general child and adolescent mental health and paediatric liaison work, a diploma in advanced family therapy from the Tavistock Clinic and a longstanding interest in parenting difficulties relating to child protection issues. She has published in the fields of maltreatment and paediatric liaison.

Steve Farnfield is a Senior Lecture in Attachment Studies and convenor of the MSc in Attachment Studies at the University of Roehampton, UK. He is a social worker and play therapist with over 40 years' experience in the field of child and family welfare and formerly taught on the Social Work and Post Qualifying Child Care Programmes at the University of Reading, UK. Steve is a licensed trainer for the Dynamic-Maturational Model of Attachment Infant

CARE-Index, Preschool Assessment of Attachment and Adult Attachment Interview developed by Dr Patricia Crittenden. He has also developed a system for analysing attachment and mentalising using narrative story stems with pre-school and school aged children.

Peter Fonagy is Freud Memorial Professor of Psychoanalysis and Head of the Research Department of Clinical, Educational and Health Psychology at University College London (UCL), UK, and Chief Executive of the Anna Freud Centre, London, UK. He is also Director of UCL Partners' Mental Health and Wellbeing Programme and National Clinical Lead of Improving Access to Psychological Therapies for Children and Young People. He is a Senior Investigator for the National Institute of Health Research and a Visiting Professor at Harvard University, USA. His clinical interests centre around issues of borderline psychopathology, violence and early attachment relationships. He has published over 500 chapters and articles and has authored or edited a large number of books.

Cornelia Gutjahr is a child and adolescent psychiatrist working in the Child and Adolescent Mental Health Service in Brighton, UK. She trained as a doctor at the University of Freiburg in Germany and as a child psychiatrist at St George's Hospital and at the Maudsley Hospital in London. She now has a specialist interest in clinical problems associated with attachment and with neuro-developmental disorders.

Paul Holmes is a Consultant Child and Adolescent Psychiatrist with extensive clinical experience in community child mental health teams and in specialist services working with looked-after and adopted children, their families and their carers. In his private practice he undertook over 500 child psychiatry assessments for the courts in children's proceedings where he has used his expertise in attachment theory to inform his work. He has trained both as a psychoanalytic and psychodrama psychotherapist and is the author of the *Inner World Outside: Object Relations Theory and Psychodrama* and is the editor of three other books on psychodrama.

Marinus H. van IJzendoorn is a Professor of Child and Family Studies at Leiden University and a Research Professor of Human Development at Erasmus University Rotterdam in the Netherlands. His major research interests include attachment across the life-span and in various contexts; gene-by-parenting interventions and differential susceptibility; neural and hormonal concomitants of parenting and emotional development. He was awarded the Aristotle Prize of the European Federation of Psychologists Associations (2011), the Bowlby-Ainsworth Founder Award of the New York Attachment Consortium (2011), an Honorary Doctorate of the University of Haifa, Israel (2008), the Distinguished International Contributions to Child Development Award of the Society for Research in Child Development (2007), and the Spinoza Prize awarded by the Netherlands Organization for Scientific Research (2004). He is a Fellow of The Royal Netherlands Academy of Arts and Sciences (elected in 1998).

Nicolas Lorenzini is a clinical psychologist and is conducting his doctoral research at University College London, UK, and the Anna Freud Centre, London, UK.

Patrick Luyten is Associate Professor at the Faculty of Psychology and Educational Sciences, University of Leuven, Belgium, and Senior Lecturer at the Research Department of Clinical, Educational, and Health Psychology, University College London, UK. His main research interest focuses on the role of personality, stress and interpersonal processes in depression, chronic fatigue syndrome and fibromyalgia. In this context, he is also interested in the processes involved in the intergenerational transmission of these disorders, and in the role of early adversity in particular. He is currently also involved in studies on mentalisation-based treatment of patients with borderline personality disorder. He is a member of the editorial board of several scientific journals, including *Psychotherapy: Theory, Research, Practice, Training*, *Psychoanalytic Psychotherapy*, and *Personality Disorders: Theory, Research*. He is in private practice in Leuven, Belgium.

Graham Music is Consultant Child and Adolescent Psychotherapist at the Tavistock and Portman Clinics, London, UK, and an adult psychotherapist in private practice. His publications include *Nurturing Natures: Attachment and Children's Emotional, Sociocultural and Brain Development* (2011) and *Affect and Emotion*. He has a particular interest in exploring the interface between developmental findings and clinical work. Formerly Associate Clinical Director in the Tavistock Child and Family Department, he has worked therapeutically with maltreated children for over two decades, has managed a range of services concerned with the aftermath of child maltreatment and neglect and organised community-based therapy services, particularly in schools and in GP practices alongside health visitors. He has recently been working at the Portman clinic with forensic cases. He organises trainings for therapists in the Child and Adolescent Mental Health Service (CAMHS), leads on teaching on attachment, the brain and child development, and teaches and supervises on the Tavistock Child Psychotherapy Training and other psychotherapy trainings in Britain and abroad.

Lenny van Rosmalen studied education and is working as assistant professor at the Department of Child and Family Studies of the University of Leiden, the Netherlands. She is interested in advice books on parenting and in the history of attachment theory. Currently she is writing a doctoral dissertation on the early work of Mary Ainsworth.

Prachi E. Shah is an Assistant Professor of Pediatrics at the University of Michigan, USA, and a board-certified developmental pediatrician whose clinical and research focus centres on developmental outcomes of infants at biological risk, including infants born preterm, and infants with a history of prenatal alcohol exposure. She is currently the medical director of the Fetal Alcohol Spectrum Disorders Diagnostic Clinic and Neonatal Follow-up Program at the University of Michigan. Her clinical and research interests focus on the developmental and behavioural outcomes of high-risk infants, and how those outcomes are shaped by the quality of parenting.

David Shemmings is Professor of Child Protection Research and Visiting Professor of Child Protection Research at Royal Holloway, University of London, UK. He has spent the past 15 years undertaking research into attachment theory in close relationships and its implications, especially in the field of child protection. David is the author of over 60 articles, books and chapters on relationally based theory, research and practice. He is the co-author of *Understanding Disorganized Attachment: Theory and Practice of Working with Children and Adults* (JKP Books, 2011) and *Working with Families and Disorganised Attachment* (JKP Books, 2014). David leads the Advanced Child Protection stream in the West London Alliance Post-qualifying Initiative (involving eight London boroughs). David also co-directs the Assessment of Disorganised Attachment and Maltreatment (ADAM) project in over 30 child protection organisations across the UK and Europe. Finally, he is co-Director of the Centre for Child Protection at the University of Kent, UK, which has established a multi-disciplinary and international distance-learning MA in Advanced Child Protection as well as 'serious, interactive games' to enhance practitioners' skills.

Martin Stokowy, MD, is Assistant Medical Director of a Psychiatric Hospital in Cologne, Germany. He is trained as a psychiatrist, psychotherapist and neurologist. His fields of interest are psychoanalytic treatment in the psychiatric field, attachment theory, and parent–infant treatment. He also works as a supervisor in various public health institutions. He has published a few articles in German about the treatment of psychotic patients and a book about the DMM in German, together with Nicola Sahhar. He is a member of the International Association for the Study of Attachment (IASA), and was the venue chair of the 3rd IASA conference in Frankfurt, Germany, in 2012.

Lane Strathearn is a developmental paediatrician at Texas Children's Hospital, USA, and an Associate Professor in the Department of Paediatrics and the Menninger Department of Psychiatry and Behavioral Sciences, Houston, USA. His clinical work encompasses a range of neurodevelopmental disorders such as autism. He is also a neuroscientist and Director of the Attachment and Neurodevelopment Lab at Baylor College of Medicine, with his research focusing on the neurobiology of mother-infant attachment, and long-term effects of child maltreatment on cognitive and emotional development. This includes longitudinal studies of women and infants, examining maternal brain and hormonal responses to infant face and cry cues, using functional MRI and behavioral observation. His most recent grants support research into maternal brain responses of drug addicted mothers, and the potential role of intranasal oxytocin to enhance maternal caregiving responses. He also uses fully automated eye tracking technology to examine visual fixation preferences in children and adolescents with autism, testing whether intranasal oxytocin alters these developmental preferences. A native of Brisbane, Australia, Dr Strathearn is married with 7 children.

Preface

This volume is a companion to *The Routledge Handbook of Attachment: Assessment* (Farnfield & Holmes 2014) and *The Routledge Handbook of Attachment: Implications and interventions* (Holmes & Farnfield 2014) in which our authors address three linked areas: theory, assessment and interventions.

We have both had a long-standing professional interest in child welfare, child protection and therapeutic services: Paul Holmes as a child psychiatrist and adult psychotherapist, Steve Farnfield as a social worker, play therapist and university lecturer. Like many professionals involved in these fields, in recent years we have become increasingly interested in using attachment theory and the associated evidence-based assessments, presented in these books, to underpin our work as therapists, supervisors and (for Paul Holmes) as an expert witness in children's legal proceedings. These three books were designed to cover the areas of expertise we draw on in this work.

Attachment theory and assessments can be used to assist in making decisions about the possible social or therapeutic interventions that might assist families and children. Changing attachment strategies, in particular reorganising towards security or balance, is actually hard, particularly when a child or adult has been traumatised by abuse, and professionals have to decide if the problems are better worked through or worked around (Moran *et al.* 2008). Put another way, our knowledge about attachment often informs our thinking about a client's problems, but in some cases we might decide to leave their attachment strategies alone. These issues are discussed in Holmes and Farnfield (2014).

In recent years most formal instructions given to child mental health experts in children's court proceedings have contained questions on attachment. Evidence on attachment and also parenting which is used in court proceedings concerned with family and child welfare has been usually provided by expert witnesses (often child psychiatrists or psychologists) specifically instructed to address these matters in assessment reports. However, these books were written at a time of great change in the processes in children's proceedings in England and Wales in both public law (care proceedings) and private law (contact and residence proceedings). There have been both debate and challenges in the press and elsewhere about the lack of openness in the proceedings of the family courts and the role of social workers and experts and the way life-changing decisions are made about children's welfare and future care. In our opinion the increased use of research and evidence-based assessments should provide some reassurance about the objectivity of at least part of this process.

There has also been increasing concern about both the time-scale and cost consequent upon the instruction of independent experts. As a consequence, at least in England and Wales, an increasing number of assessments of attachment in individuals (adults and children) together with the ability of some parents to care for their children will be undertaken by other professionals, in particular social workers.

This book has been written to help these professionals, and others working in the child care system such as lawyers and judges, with these complex tasks. Each chapter has been written by experts often discussing their own research in this field. As a consequence some of the important topics covered in this book are considered more than once from the perspectives of each author.

References

Farnfield, S. & Holmes, P. (2014) *The Routledge Handbook of Attachment: Assessment*, London and New York: Routledge.

Holmes, P. & Farnfield, S. (2014) *The Routledge Handbook of Attachment: Implications and interventions*, London and New York: Routledge.

Moran, G., Bailey, H. N., Gleason, K., DeOliveira, C. A. & Pederson, D. R. (2008) 'Exploring the mind behind unresolved attachment: Lessons from and of attachment-based interventions with infants and their traumatized mothers', in H. Steele & M. Steele (eds), *Clinical Applications of the Adult Attachment Interview*, New York: The Guilford Press, pp. 371–398.

Overview

Attachment theory, assessment and implications

Paul Holmes and Steve Farnfield

This book considers attachment theory from its roots in the work of John Bowlby to the most recent developments by leading figures in the field. Taken together these theories provide a powerful evidence-based way of understanding personality development and human interactions.

However, despite its popularity, attachment theory cannot explain everything about human development and emotions. Therefore, this book also considers other ways of understanding human behaviour. For example, the 'medical model' considers behaviour and symptoms in a way that may lead to psychiatric diagnoses and possible treatment (see Chapter 8) and parent–child interactions can also be considered under various 'domains' of behaviour which are not core aspects of attachment such as parenting tasks which include providing physical care, boundary setting and appropriate social experiences (see Chapter 9).

Attachment theory

Bowlby started to develop attachment theory after the Second World War, his early ideas being laid out in his report for the World Health Organization, published in a popular form as *Child Care and the Growth of Love* (1953). His view was that theory always needed to be supported by research rather than just clinical observations, as was the practice of his fellow psychoanalysts at the time.

In this book Bowlby described children's reaction to separations from their mothers, many of them following periods of hospitalisation. He observed four types of response:

1. a hostile reaction to the mother on reunion with her, which sometimes takes the form of a refusal to recognise her;
2. an excessive demandingness towards the mother or substitute mother, in which intensive passiveness combined with insisting on his own way, acute jealousy and violent temper tantrums;
3. a cheerful but shallow attachment to any adult in the child's orbit;
4. an apathetic withdrawal from all emotional entanglements, combined with monotonous rocking of the body and sometimes head banging.

(Bowlby 1953: 27)

Bowlby established research projects on the responses of infants to separation with his colleagues James Robertson and Mary Ainsworth (Ainsworth & Bowlby 1991). Robertson studied the behaviour of children hospitalised with tuberculosis and then returned to the care of their families. Ainsworth worked in London with Bowlby before continuing her research studying infant/mother separations using home-based observations of children and their mothers in Uganda and subsequently in Baltimore in the USA.

Her research culminated in the development of her classic laboratory assessment the Strange Situation procedure (SSP) (Ainsworth *et al.* 1978) designed to assess the attachment of infants to their mothers. The SSP involved, under controlled circumstances, a series of stressors of the child's attachment system culminating in a three-minute separation from their mother. The procedure was video-recorded and the child's reactions were subsequently coded by the research team. Ainsworth described three types of response in children, which she and Bowlby called A, B & C. The SSP has become the 'gold standard' for all subsequent tools that have been developed to assess attachment across the full age range.

ABC

The classical developments of attachment theory are discussed in more detail in chapters by Van Rosmalen, Van IJzendoorn and Bakermans-Kranenburg (Chapter 1) and Fonagy, Lorenzini, Campbell and Luyten (Chapter 2).

It is interesting that the categories of response of children after separation from their mother described by Bowlby in 1953, above, overlap the three attachment types identified by Ainsworth. Bowlby's second category, in particular, closely resembles Type C (infant behaviour classified as insecure-ambivalent) and his third category children in Type A (classified as insecure-avoidant).[1] It would appear that Bowlby's original clinical observations were supported by subsequent formal research.

The theory Bowlby set in train has developed significantly over the years with, as one might expect, areas of divergence among his successors. This book also provides an update on the conflicting ideas and theories associated with the term 'attachment'.

In Chapter 2 Fonagy and his colleagues discuss the significant advances made in recent years in using attachment theory and modern research techniques to formulate a better understanding of the development of personality disorders, progress that addresses Bowlby's key concern about the 'embryology of personality' and the power of this increasing knowledge to reduce, in Bowlby's terms, mental illness. There is an association between a parent suffering from a personality disorder and the quality of care they can provide to their children. Indeed there may be cycles of emotional disturbance across generations, parents who suffer emotionally and/or who physically maltreat their children are at risk of rearing, potentially, another generation who may also maltreat their children.

Bowlby always hoped that physical studies, such as those made possible in his day by using an electro-encephalograph (EEG), would further studies into attachment (Bowlby 1953: 7). Developments in technology such as magnetic-resonance imaging (MRI) and computerised tomography (CT) scans have more than fulfilled Bowlby's ambitions. The advances in our understanding of the attachment process made possible by new technology are discussed by Fonagy and colleagues in Chapter 2 and more fully by Music in Chapter 7.

ABC + D and the Dynamic-Maturational Model

The Bowlby–Ainsworth theory of attachment has been taken forward by a large number of people usually involved in university research or clinical practice or combinations of both. Two of Ainsworth's research students, Mary Main and Patricia Crittenden, were prominent in the first wave of research.

Review of the early SSP videotapes revealed that not all of them could be classified according to the ABC criteria and a fourth category was added by Main and Solomon to describe the behaviour of children who showed, often momentary, lapses in their organised response to their mothers on reunion. This was designated the disorganised-disorientated or D category which included some children who had been maltreated (Main & Solomon 1986) and combined with Ainsworth's prototypical patterns produced the classificatory system termed here ABC + D. Those classified as D seem to include Bowlby's fourth group of possibly depressed children he described in 1953.

Crittenden provided a different interpretation for these observations. She agreed that not all children assessed using the SSP fitted into the ABC model. However, she differed from Main in seeing these children as, on the whole, having an organised response to the problem of maintaining the availability of an attachment figure who was frightening or frightened. Crittenden went on to develop an alternative explanation termed the Dynamic-Maturational Model (DMM) of attachment. Like the ABC + D model, the DMM is directly descended from Bowlby–Ainsworth but has both different constructs and uses some familiar constructs in different ways (see Farnfield & Stokowy in Chapter 3).

The ABC + D approach has a meticulous research base and has set the standard for assessment in both children (the SSP) and adults with the Adult Attachment Interview (AAI) (Main & Goldwyn 1984). The equivalent to the ABC + D attachment types of childhood in adults are called Dismissing (Ds), Secure/Autonomous or Free (F), Pre-occupied-entangled (E) and Unresolved (U), together with the Cannot be Classified (CC) category (Hesse 1996; Hesse & Main 1999).

A recent meta-analysis compared SSP data of non-clinical Italian infant–mother dyads with normative (non-clinical samples) from the USA and found the coding distributions shown in Table O.1.

The same study compared the AAI data from combined Italian studies of non-clinical populations of mothers, fathers and adolescents with that from American mothers. The results are shown in Table O.2.

Table O.1 SSP four-way ABC + D classifications

	Italian	USA
Avoidant (A)	28%	23%
Secure (B)	44%	55%
Ambivalent (C)	6%	7%
Disorganised (D)	22%	15%

(Cassibba *et al.* 2013)

Table O.2 AAI four-way DFE + U classifications

	Overall Italian	American mothers
Dismissing (Ds)	21%	16%
Secure-autonomous (F)	60%	56%
Preoccupied-entangled (E)	11%	9%
Unresolved (U)	8%	18%

A number of interesting points arise from these figures. In particular, 'normative' populations are neither overwhelmingly secure nor immune from significant experiences of trauma and loss. Only 55–60 per cent of adults and 44–55 per cent of infants are secure. This does not mean that everyone else has significant anxious or dysfunctional attachments. Indeed many people in these types, albeit having insecure attachment patterns, function very well in life and indeed often in relationships. Such individuals are described as 'normative'. On the other hand, approximately 15–20 per cent of a normative, non-clinical population, are likely to show up as disorganised or unresolved, which heightens the likelihood of more serious psycho-social problems (e.g. Moran *et al.* 2008; Stovall-McClough *et al.* 2008). Finally there are cultural differences. Rather surprisingly, given the cultural stereotypes of the two populations, Italian infants are more reserved and inhibited than their American counterparts. The apparent low proportion of AAIs rated U in Italy is also interesting.

The ABC + D model does not always meet the demands of practitioners when trying to understand the complex behaviours of the very troubled people they meet in everyday practice (i.e. those who are not 'normative'). In particular, assessments that conclude a child 'is disorganised' tell us little more than we knew before.

It is for this reason that we, like some other practitioners, have found the DMM useful. It offers a developmental approach to attachment together with a range of strategies that match those met with in practice and looks in more detail at the self-protective function of strategies (and thus differentiates between the normative and psychopathological insecure attachment types). It also focuses on how the individual processes information about attachment-based experiences, which can assist in the selection of the most appropriate treatment.

One of the aims of these handbooks is to give space both to the more widely known ABC + D approach and the one developed by Crittenden, as we believe a dialogue between the two models would be beneficial in both developing theory and, most important, designing more effective interventions. The classical ABC + D model is discussed by Van IJzendoorn and his colleagues in Chapter 1, the DMM is introduced by Farnfield and Stokowy in Chapter 3 and comparison of the two models is given by Shah and Strathearn in Chapter 4.

Disorganised attachment and reactive attachment disorders

While the attachment type 'disorganised' is found within the developments of classical attachment theory, the diagnosis of reactive attachment disorder has its roots in the medical model of the diagnostic process. In our experience professionals often confuse these two terms and, indeed, may at times use them as if they are interchangeable. Shemmings discusses this contentious area in Chapter 5.

Mentalisation

Attachment theory has been further developed by Peter Fonagy and colleagues in their theoretical and research-based studies on the process they call mentalisation. This, uniquely human capacity refers to the ability to think about the contents of our own minds and the likely mental processes of other people. Mentalisation, its association with attachment behaviour and its relevance to personality development together with borderline personality disorders are discussed by Luyten and Fonagy in Chapter 6.

Other explantions for child behaviour and distress

Enthusiasts of attachment theory see it as a powerful way of understanding human interactions and psychological development. However, it is not a 'theory that explains everything'. In our experience there is often great uncertainty about where the boundaries of behaviour influenced by attachment processes should be drawn and what would be better understood using the medical model and the formal diagnoses of psychiatric illness (see Gutjahr, Chapter 8).

Human interactions and behaviour can also be understood in terms of other social or psychological processes (or domains) of human interaction (see DeJong, Chapter 9).

Assessment of attachment

Attachment theory has generated a range of evidence-based and age-appropriate assessment measures that can greatly assist in developing a better understanding of a child's attachment to their carers, in particular birth and foster parents. They also provide good information on adult attachment, the impact of unresolved loss and trauma and the effectiveness of caregiving (parenting). Taken together, the available assessments provide a good set of tools with which to mount a comprehensive assessment of the attachment and caregiving components of family functioning (Farnfield 2008).

It must be stressed, however, that a child's view of their experiences obtained when using an attachment assessment tool must not be confused with that child making, in another context, allegations of neglect, maltreatment or overt abuse. Any such disclosures must be investigated using other tried and tested processes such as taking a good history, medical examinations or a formal video-taped interview (called an Achieving Best Evidence (ABE) interview in England and Wales).

Most of the available assessment measures of attachment were designed initially as academic research tools to test the main constructs of the theory. They are now used increasingly in clinical and social work practice but most of them are difficult to code without trainings which consume a lot of time and money. We believe there is no short cut to this problem. The available assessment tools can be, and are, used to inform clinical practice without formal coding but for high tariff cases involving, for example, decisions about removing children to foster care or adoption, a forensic model of blind coding by reliable raters is preferred (Main et al. 2011; Crittenden et al. 2013). These issues, together with a review of the most widely used assessment measures, are the subject of *The Routledge Handbook of Attachment: Assessment* (Farnfield & Holmes 2014).

Interventions

In *A Secure Base*, Bowlby (1988: 37) quotes Kurt Lewin approvingly with regard to there being nothing more practical than a good theory. Attachment theory is rarely of direct interest, or use, to the recipients of social or mental health services, but it has considerable power to shape and aid the thinking of professionals concerning the problems of their clients. However, such professionals also want interventions that have been shown to be effective and, as a consequence, there is an increasing literature on evidence-based practice and interventions (for psychotherapy research: see Fonagy et al. 2002; Weisz & Kazdin 2010 for children and Roth & Fonagy 2006 for adults; Carr 2009 for children and adults; for mental health treatments for children and adolescents also see Corcoran 2011).

However, in the field of human suffering it is not always easy or in some cases even possible to use only evidence-based interventions. Consequently there has been a growth of 'attachment therapies', most of which are not evidence-based interventions and some of which have been highly contentious (Mercer 2013). We tend to side with authors such as Slade who propose the main function of attachment theory and research is not to generate new therapies but to help us make better use of those we already have (Slade 2008).

That said, many schools of psychotherapy now integrate attachment theory into their clinical practice. Some of these interventions are aimed at improving children's attachment security and/or sensitivity in parents, a few of which are evidence-based (see *The Routledge Handbook of Attachment: Implications and interventions* (Holmes & Farnfield 2014).

Culture

The ABC + D attachment categories appear to be finite; no others have been identified indicating they are based on the primitive evolutionary responses to the threat of danger of fight, flight, freeze (to increase the chance of survival) together with approach (to obtain safety). However, these personality types are distributed in different proportions across cultures and within subcultures with 'the general cultural pressure towards selection of the secure attachment pattern in the majority of children' (Van IJzendoorn & Sagi-Schwartz 2008: 900). For example, social groups who put a premium on individualism, such as the middle class in Germany, the UK and the USA, have a disproportionate number of infants in type A (Grossman *et al.* 1985; Crittenden & Claussen 2000) whereas those who favour the primacy of the group over the individual, such as Italy (although see Cassibba *et al.* 2013), Israel and Japan, produce more in Type C (Van IJzendoorn & Kroonenberg 1988; Oppenheim *et al.* 1988; Miyake *et al.* 1985; Takahishi 1986; Crittenden & Claussen 2000).

As Chisholm notes, human nature is essentially local; that is it emerges in response to specific conditions (Chisholm 1999: 135). However, attachment theory continues to raise objections that it is biased towards Western middle-class models of family functioning (Keller 2013). There is an urgent need to develop systemic models of attachment that move the theory from individuals and dyads to the extended family structures in which the majority of the world's children grow up (De Loache & Gottlieb 2000; Weisner & Gallimore 1977).

Security versus danger

In terms of the evolutionary function of attachment Bowlby emphasised 'man's environment of evolutionary adaptedness': the environment of the first hominids in which social groups of biologically related people organised their behaviour to protect the tribe against predators (Bowlby 1969). His later emphasis on the secure base as a concept of basically a one-to-one relationship was taken up by many attachment scholars with the result that safety and feeling safe (felt security) tended to be seen as the primary goal both of attachment and, by extension, interventions.

For Crittenden what needs explaining is human survival not under conditions of safety but conditions of danger. Her theory is predicated on the ability of endangered people and populations to organise strategies that will protect them from severe and sometimes enduring danger and maximise the chances of passing on their genes (Crittenden 2002).

Fonagy, on the other hand, sees attachment as crucial to the development of social cooperation; the ability to achieve complex tasks in organised groups (see Chapter 2 of this volume). Each of these positions offers different lenses for viewing the contribution that attachment makes to culture. With Crittenden we can see culture as the stories that a people tell about the dangers they faced and what they have learnt about survival (Crittenden & Claussen 2000). For Fonagy, culture is part of what it means to be human: mentalising utilises the higher cortical faculties of humans and gives us the United Nations, the ability to build bridges between people and acts of great leadership. We should further add the higher cortical faculties can also be used for purposes of deception and acts of organised cruelty, as John Gray notes: 'Genocide is as human as art or prayer' (2002: 91).

Note

1 Children and adults are more than the sum of their attachment strategy and so throughout these books we have described people as being *in* Type A, B or C rather than being Type A and so forth.

References

Ainsworth, M.D., Blehar, M.C., Waters, E., and Wall, S. (1978) *Patterns of Attachment: A psychological study of the Strange Situation*, Hillsdale, NJ: Erlbaum.
Ainsworth, M.D. & Bowlby, J. (1991) 'An ethological approach to personality development', *American Psychologist*, 46(4): 333–341.
Bowlby, J. (1953) *Child Care and the Growth of Love*, Baltimore, MD: Pelican Books.
Bowlby, J. (1969) *Attachment Separation and Loss Volume 1: Attachment*, London: The Hogarth Press.
Bowlby, J. (1988) *A Secure Base: Clinical applications of attachment theory*, London: Routledge.
Carr, A. (2009) *What Works with Children, Adolescents and Adults? A review of research on the effectiveness of psychotherapy*, Hove: Routledge.
Cassibba, R., Sette, G., Bakermans-Kranenburg, M.J., & Van IJzendoorn, M.H. (2013) 'Attachment the Italian way: In search of specific patterns of infant and adult attachments in Italian typical and atypical samples', *European Psychologist*, 18(1): 47–58.
Chisholm, J.S. (1999) 'Steps to an evolutionary ecology of mind', in A. Hinton (ed.) *Biocultural Approaches to the Emotions*, Cambridge: Cambridge University Press, pp. 117–150.
Corcoran, J. (2011) *Mental Health Treatment for Children and Adolescents*, New York: Oxford University Press.
Crittenden, P.M. (2002) 'Attachment, information processing, and psychiatric disorder', *World Psychiatry*, 1(2): 72–75.
Crittenden, P.M. & Claussen, A. (eds) (2000) *The Organization of Attachment Relationships: Maturation, culture and context*, New York: Cambridge University Press.
Crittenden, P.M., Farnfield, S., Landini, A., & Grey, B. (2013) 'Assessing attachment for family court decision-making: A forensic protocol for empirically-based evidence regarding attachment', *Journal of Forensic Practice*, 15(4): 237–248.
DeLoache, J. & Gottlieb, A.H. (eds) (2000) *A World of Babies: Imagined childcare guides for seven societies*, Cambridge: Cambridge University Press.

Farnfield, S. (2008) 'A theoretical model for the comprehensive assessment of parenting', *British Journal of Social Work*, 38(6): 1076–1099.

Farnfield, S. & Holmes, P. (eds) (2014) *The Routledge Handbook of Attachment: Assessment*, London and New York: Routledge.

Fonagy, P., Target, M., Cottrell, D., Phillips, J., & Kurtz, Z. (2002) *What Works for Whom? A critical review of treatments for children and adolescents*, New York: The Guilford Press.

Gray, J. (2002) *Straw Dogs: Thoughts on humans and other animals*, London: Granta.

Grossmann, K., Grossmann, K.E., Spangler, G., Suess, G., & Unzner, L. (1985) 'Maternal sensitivity and newborns' orientation responses as related to quality of attachment in Northern Germany', in I. Bretherton & E. Waters (eds) *Growing Points of Attachment Theory and Research, Monographs of the Society for Research in Child Development*, 50(1–2): 233–256.

Hesse, E. (1996) 'Discourse, memory, and the Adult Attachment Interview: A note with emphasis on the emerging Cannot Classify category', *Infant Mental Health Journal*, 17: 4–11.

Hesse, E. & Main, M. (1999) 'Second-generation effects of unresolved trauma in non-maltreating parents: Dissociated, frightened, and threatening parental behaviour', *Psychoanalytic Inquiry*, 19: 481–540.

Holmes, P. & Farnfield, S. (eds) (2014) *The Routledge Handbook of Attachment: Implications and interventions*, London and New York: Routledge.

Keller, H. (2013) 'Attachment and culture', *Journal of Cross Cultural Psychology*, 44(2): 175–194.

Main, M. & Goldwyn, R. (1984) *Adult Attachment Scoring and Classification System*, Unpublished manuscript, University of California at Berkeley.

Main, M. & Solomon, J. (1986) 'Discovery of a new, insecure-disorganised/disorientated attachment pattern', in M. Yogman & T. Brazelton (eds) *Affective Development in Infancy*, Norwood, NJ: Ablex, pp. 95–124.

Main, M., Hesse, E., & Hesse, S. (2011) 'Attachment theory and research: Overview with suggested applications to child custody', *Family Court Review*, Special issue: Special issue on attachment, separation, and divorce: Forging coherent understandings for family law, 49(3): 426–463.

Mercer, J. (2013) 'Holding therapy in Britain: Historical background, recent events and ethical concerns', *Adoption and Fostering*, 37(2): 144–156.

Miyake, K., Chen, S., & Campos, J.J. (1985) 'Infant temperament, mother's mode of interaction, and attachment in Japan: An interim report', I. Bretherton & E. Waters in (eds) *Monographs of the Society for Research in Child Development*, 50(1–2): 276–297.

Moran, G., Bailey, H.N., Gleason, K., DeOliveira, C.A., & Pederson, D.R. (2008) 'Exploring the mind behind unresolved attachment: Lessons from and of attachment-based interventions with infants and their traumatized mothers', in H. Steele & M. Steele (eds) *Clinical Applications of the Adult Attachment Interview*, New York: The Guilford Press, pp. 371–398.

Oppenheim, D., Sagi, A., & Lamb, M.E. (1988) 'Infant-adult attachments on the kibbutz and their relation to socioemotional development 4 years later', *Developmental Psychology*, 24(3): 427–433.

Roth, A. & Fonagy, P. (2006) *What Works for Whom? A critical review of psychotherapy research*, New York: The Guilford Press.

Slade, A. (2008) 'The implications of attachment theory and research for adult psychother-apy: Research and clinical perspectives', in J. Cassidy & P.R. Shaver (eds) *Handbook of Attachment: Theory, research, and clinical applications*, New York: The Guilford Press, pp. 762–782.

Stovall-McClough, K.C., Cloitre, M., & McClough, J.F. (2008) 'Adult attachment and posttraumatic stress disorder in women with histories of childhood abuse', in H. Steele & M. Steele (eds) *Clinical Applications of the Adult Attachment Interview*, New York: The Guilford Press, pp. 320–340.

Takahashi, K. (1986) 'Examining the Strange Situation procedure with Japanese mothers and 12-month old infants', *Developmental Psychology*, 27(2): 265–270.

Van IJzendoorn, M.H. & Kroonenberg, P.M. (1988) 'Cross cultural patterns of attachment: A meta-analysis of the Strange Situation', *Child Development*, 59: 147–156.

Van IJzendoorn, M.H. & Sagi-Schwartz, A. (2008) 'Cross-cultural patterns of attachment: Universal and contextual dimensions', in J. Cassidy & P.R. Shaver (eds) *Handbook of Attachment: Theory, research and clinical applications*, 2nd edition, New York: The Guilford Press, pp. 880–905.

Weisner, T.S. & Gallimore, R. (1977) 'My brother's keeper: Child and sibling caretaking', *Current Anthropology*, 18(2): 169–190.

Weisz, J.R. & Kazdin, A.E. (eds) (2010) *Evidence-Based Psychotherapies for Children and Adolescents*, 2nd edition, New York: The Guilford Press.

Chapter 1

ABC + D of attachment theory

The Strange Situation procedure as the gold standard of attachment assessment

Lenny van Rosmalen, Marinus H. van IJzendoorn and Marian J. Bakermans-Kranenburg

So saying, glorious Hector stretched out his arms to his boy, but back into the bosom of his fair-girdled nurse shrank the child crying, affrighted at the aspect of his dear father, and seized with dread of the bronze and the crest of horse-hair, as he marked it waving dreadfully from the topmost helm. Aloud then laughed his dear father and queenly mother; and forthwith glorious Hector took the helm from his head and laid it all-gleaming upon the ground. But he kissed his dear son, and fondled him in his arms . . .

(Homer, *The Iliad*, Book VI)

Introduction

The Strange Situation procedure (SSP) and its standard coding protocol (Ainsworth *et al.* 1978) have been used in numerous studies on the antecedents and sequelae of infant attachment. In this chapter we present the SSP and its attachment classifications and we discuss some of the work done on the antecedents of differences in attachment security.

Attachment

What is attachment?

Attachment is the emotional bond between a child and his protective caregiver(s). That bond becomes most obvious in times of fear and tension, for instance during illness, separation or other threatening danger. For regulation of these negative emotions a child feels when scared or tense, the young child depends on a wiser or stronger person who makes sure that negative emotions like fear or sadness do not overwhelm the child and block any (exploratory) behaviour. The caregiver acts as a haven of safety, which causes the child to feel supported and allows it to grow. Attachment is seen in some shape or other in all cultures, and appears to be important in parent–offspring relationships of many animal species as well.

The importance of attachment should not be underestimated. The helpless baby depends on protection in order to survive. This protection is normally provided by its biological parents, because they want their offspring to survive. From an evolutionary viewpoint, attachment is important for the parents so they can hand over their genes to the next generation(s). Attachment theory is essentially an evolutionary theory, and John Bowlby (1973, 1988), the British child psychiatrist and founder of the attachment theory, felt strongly indebted to Charles Darwin.

Even though protection would normally be provided by the parents, a child can also get attached to other caregivers who are in regular contact with the child and make it feel secure in times of need. A good example of a network of attachment relationships in which a child can grow up is found in the citation above – the beautiful description of the departure of Hector, given by Homer almost 3,000 years ago in *The Iliad*. It clearly shows that attachment is not a new phenomenon in human history, and that it is not just about the bond between mother and child.

The way Hector says goodbye to his loving wife Andromache shortly after in the same scene illustrates the importance of attachment for adults. Bowlby (1973, 1988) looked upon attachment as a lifelong attribute of people and their relationships. At no point in our lives can we escape the need for closeness to a protecting and loving partner in times of fear and tension. The fact that separation hurts in adulthood makes it clear that we depend on attachment figures to help us face the challenges of life. Hector has to face the battle with the enraged Ajax who can easily take him on. Hector suspects his end is near and wants to see his wife and son once more to pick up the courage to enter the life-or-death battle.

Attachment relationships are extremely important for development. Children who grow up in an orphanage from birth, having to go without the availability of a specific caregiver as an attachment figure, are especially at risk of suffering from delayed growth and delayed motor, cognitive and social-emotional development (Van IJzendoorn 2008). Children who grow up in children's homes often have disturbed neurophysiological emotion regulation, which becomes apparent from the dysregulation of the production of the stress hormone cortisol (Gunnar & Vasquez 2001). Normally a child becomes attached to one or more caregivers, even if these caregivers neglect or maltreat the child. Obviously, the quality of the attachment relationship suffers in such cases, but even under these circumstances feelings of attachment persist (Cyr *et al.* 2010). Attachment is seen as a milestone in the development of a child and a condition for a balanced development of a person (Bowlby 1953). Early experience with attachment relationships is assumed to be a decisive factor for the way children are later able to create bonds with other people, their future partners or their own children, and how they see themselves in relation to the outside world (Bowlby 1988).

The development of attachment

The tendency to become attached is inborn in every human child. It is the result of a millennia-long evolution in which it was favourable for survival and reproduction of humans to get attached to a stronger, protective person during the first year of life. Children are, in fact, born 'prematurely' because they cannot move themselves from one place to another, they cannot feed themselves or keep themselves warm, and depend totally on their social environment for survival. The idea that babies become attached to their mother purely because she provides them with food and fulfils their basic needs cannot stand if we look at ethology. Young geese that have just crawled out of their eggs follow the first moving figure they see, even if that is not their mother but, for instance, the ethologist studying them. Konrad Lorenz has given lively descriptions of this phenomenon (Lorenz 1952).

Human babies, however, do not have an instinct that causes them to become attached to the first living being they encounter. They get attached to the person who takes care of them the most during the first few months of life. In most cases that is the mother, but it could just as well be someone else. Through directing its attachment behaviour (crying, laughing, following) at a specific person, the child makes this individual feel responsible for him or her at times of imminent danger – a very efficient system to ensure survival in environments of evolutionary adapt-edness (Bowlby 1969) that, for millennia, were far from safe.

Four phases of developing attachment

Bowlby (1982) has described four hypothetical phases through which attach-ment would develop during the first few years of life. The first phase, orientation towards people without differentiating between them, starts with the preference of the baby for the human smell, the sound of the human voice, and the rough out-lines of the human face. This phase starts shortly after birth and lasts for the first few months of life. During the second phase, orientation towards specific people in the child's environment makes the baby focus on people it sees regularly and with whom he or she becomes familiar. This phase can be observed in the second half of the first year. The baby develops a preference for one or a few specific peo-ple to whom the child becomes attached during the third phase, the phase of spe-cific attachment (from age 10 months to 3 years). It will want to be around these attachment figures when frightened or stressed. During the fourth phase, the phase of goal-oriented attachment which starts around the third birthday, the child can take the perspective of the attachment figure and take his or her expectations into account with the development of plans, for instance when playing with unfamiliar children in an unfamiliar environment, during the first day of school. Even though the child will want the attachment figure to be around, it will also be prepared to wait until the caregiver is available again. Attachment, in this phase, has devel-oped from a relatively solid behavioural pattern aimed at physical proximity, to a mental representation of a protecting and comforting caregiver who is available to the child when the child needs him or her. The phases are still hypothetical in the sense that the age ranges are educated guesses without a firm empirical foundation of longitudinal research.

No critical period for attachment

It has been said that age 0–6 years is the critical period for becoming attached. There are two reasons why this assumption cannot be right. First of all, it is near impossible for a child not to become attached. Children practically always become attached and have great ability to recover. Even autistic children are attached to their parents, in spite of their social handicaps (Van IJzendoorn *et al.* 2007). Also, children who are being maltreated or neglected are attached, even though this is usually an insecure or disorganised attachment (Cyr *et al.* 2010). The exception to the rule might be children who grow up in crowded orphanages without regular caregivers – a situation that is deviant from an evolutionary point of view.

Second, a cutoff point at age six is not based on empirical research. Bowlby suggested on theoretical grounds that until age five, attachment is open to influences from the environment – good or bad – but that even after that, it is possible for corrective attachment experiences to help the child back on track to a secure attachment. Empirical research into the development of adopted children has proven Bowlby right. Age at adoption is important for development – adoption before the child's first birthday usually results in better development, including attachment quality, than adoption when the child is older. Similarly, children who are placed with foster parents at a later age are more difficult to bring up than children who are placed with foster parents a few months after birth. But this does not mean there is a critical period for human children to get attached, a time frame in which certain skills have to be learned, lest they disappear altogether.

There are *sensitive* periods in which it is easier to learn these skills and after which it will be more difficult to learn or unlearn them, but children possess the ability to make an amazing recovery once they find themselves in a safe and stimulating environment. This becomes evident from research with children who are being adopted from orphanages. The developmental leaps these children take in a relatively short period of time are enormous: from dwarfism to average length, head circumference and weight, and from mental retardation to a level of cognitive functioning that is 15 to 20 IQ points higher than at the time of arrival at the adoptive family. Something similar is possible in the area of attachment. It is true that, sadly, some children are scarred for life, but for the majority of adopted children the cognitive and physical differences between them and biological children are small and the adopted children manage to catch up at surprising speed (Van IJzendoorn & Juffer 2006).

Attachment over the life course

Even though we have established that there is no critical period in which the attachment representation is supposed to take shape, most children, in interaction with their caregivers, develop a mental representation of attachment during the first five years of life. Bowlby (1973) calls this an 'internal working model' of attachment. However, this mental representation of attachment is not solid and unchangeable at age five. It is not an absolute and definitive model but a *working model* that continually keeps processing information from the environment and keeps adjusting itself to the changing circumstances.

The attachment representation that arises during the first few years of life does appear to leave its traces in adulthood. Three longitudinal studies show strong relationships between the quality of attachment in the first year of life and attachment representations during adolescence and early adulthood. Main and Hesse (Hesse 1999), Waters (Waters *et al.* 2000) and Hamilton (Beckwith *et al.* 1999) found continuity in quality of attachment in 70–77 per cent of cases of children in diverse populations. A secure attachment relationship with a parent at age one predicted a secure attachment representation in adolescence, 16 to 18 years later. These are robust data. It is particularly interesting to look more closely at the cases that did change. Waters and Hamilton showed that radical change of situation (for instance, divorce of the parents, or serious illness) could predict changes in attachment representation. Knowing that, it is plausible that intervention or therapy can also produce such effects.

There are studies, however, that show less or no continuity. The most important of these is the Minnesota longitudinal study conducted by Sroufe and colleagues (2005) which could not find any notable continuity of attachment across the first 18 years of life in a high-risk group of children (poor, and with abused or sometimes abusing parents). However, this is less surprising when one realises that this group of deprived children and families had to try to survive in very unstable social circumstances. This could be a group with a majority of children experiencing (radical) change of situation, which in turn may change attachment representation.

Measuring attachment

Even though virtually all children become attached, the quality of their attachment relationship differs. This quality of attachment can be observed in stressful situations where the caregiver is not immediately available to comfort the child. The SSP was designed by Mary Ainsworth (Ainsworth *et al.* 1978) and is a standardised simulation of a stressful situation. It has been in use for decades and is the best-known instrument for measuring infant attachment.

The origins of the Strange Situation procedure

The SSP was not invented overnight. The roots of its development date back to the first half of the twentieth century. Mary Ainsworth wrote her dissertation in 1939 under the guidance of William Blatz, often referred to as the Doctor Spock of Canada (Wright 1996). It is very possible that this is where her interest in what we now call attachment stems from. Blatz lectured on his security theory for years and wrote briefly about it in his books, but only clearly put his complete theory in writing in his last book, *Human Security*, which was published posthumously

(Blatz 1966). According to Blatz, a child starts off having to depend on his parents. If the child feels certain the parent is going to be there for him, no matter what, the dependence is 'secure' and the child feels comfortable to go and explore. The parent acts as a 'secure base'. The exploration will result in development towards a state of 'independent security', although Blatz admits in his later writings that independent security can probably never be reached completely, and that a form of 'mature secure dependency' on friends and/or a partner is possibly the highest achievable goal. In the meantime, some people will remain 'immaturely dependent' or rely on defensive mechanisms in order to deal with feelings of insecurity.

Ainsworth's dissertation was based on Blatz's security theory. She designed an instrument to measure security in (young) adults comprising an extensive questionnaire and an in-depth interview which she kept expanding and improving upon until 1958 (Ainsworth & Ainsworth 1958).

When Ainsworth followed her husband to London in 1950 she started working with Bowlby at the Tavistock Clinic, researching the effects on young children of being separated from their mother. Ainsworth assisted James Robertson with analysing the detailed notes he made while observing young children during situations of separation, for instance in hospitals or in institutions (Bretherton 1992). By doing this she gained a great deal of experience in the analysis of observational data.

In 1953 Ainsworth followed her husband again, this time to Uganda. There, Ainsworth studied normative development and mother–infant interaction. She did this by observing 26 mothers with their child(ren) at their homes for a few hours every two weeks. She also conducted interviews with the mothers (Ainsworth 1967). When studying these mother–child dyads, she saw increasing evidence for Bowlby's theory about attachment being something that is based on interaction rather than on the mother providing food and other basic needs. Ainsworth left 11 years between finalising data collection in Uganda and publishing the book about the study. She commented that

> the full significance of what I observed and recorded in my field reports emerged only gradually, not merely in the process of analyzing my observations, but also in the course of reading, discussions with others interested in mother-infant interaction, and further research into the early development of attachment.
>
> (Ainsworth 1967: ix)

Ainsworth first presented the findings of her Uganda study at the Tavistock Mother–Infant Interaction Study Group in London in 1961. Here we see emerging for the first time specific criteria to determine if the infant had 'formed an attachment to his mother as a special person' (Ainsworth 1963). Ainsworth found that only looking at crying, following and clinging as reactions to (threatening) separation was not enough to establish the strength of attachment. The general opinion up to that point had been that the securely attached child is the one who protests loudly at the departure of his mother, and/or clings to her. Schaffer and Emerson (1964) for instance, stated that intensity of protest of the baby when separated from the parent was indicative of the intensity of attachment.

Ainsworth, however, believed that it was the anxious child who needed close physical contact with his mother, and for whom maintaining interaction from a (small) distance, even part of the time, was not enough (Ainsworth 1964). After examining her field notes exhaustively Ainsworth came up with the following types of attachment behaviour: differential crying, smiling, and vocalisation, visual-motor orientation towards mother, crying when mother leaves, following, 'scrambling' over mother, burying face in mother's lap, exploration from mother as a secure base, clinging, and greeting by lifting arms, clapping hands, or approaching through locomotion.

When the Uganda book finally appeared in 1967, Ainsworth had divided the children into three attachment groups, or classifications: non-attached, secure-attached and insecure-attached. Classifications were based purely on observations in the home. Regarding the judgement of quality of attachment through the behaviour of the child Ainsworth was now confident that a close attachment could develop simultaneously with increasing competence and independence. Again she pointed out that it was the insecure child who would cling to his mother and refuse to leave her (Ainsworth 1967: 447).

In 1963 Ainsworth started the Baltimore Study, in which she and her colleagues observed mother–infant interaction in 26 families during three-weekly home visits of about four hours each. The study was initially intended as a replication of the Uganda study. Data collection went on until 1966. Each infant–mother pair in this study was observed in a final session when the child was 12 months old. This final session, the SSP, was originally designed to assess the child's use of the mother as a secure base, inspired by Blatz, as we saw before, but also by Harlow (1960), who had observed monkeys, and by Arsenian (1943) who had observed preschool children. Both Harlow and Arsenian reported that the baby, once it had developed an attachment to its mother, used her as a secure base or a 'haven of safety' from which it would go out and explore, ready to face external threats without panic (Ainsworth 1964). At the same time, the child's use of the mother as a secure base could be seen as an indicator for attachment since Ainsworth regarded being able to use the mother as a secure base for exploration necessary for a healthy attachment.

The first report on the use of the SSP (Ainsworth and Wittig 1969), describes 14 infants from the Baltimore Study who were divided into three groups, based on their behaviour during the Strange Situation: Group A, containing children that we would now classify as insecure-avoidant; Group B, containing the securely attached children; and Group C, containing the children that we would now classify as insecure-ambivalent. Between the first results of the Baltimore Study and the last results, Ainsworth moved from determining the quality of attachment from the behaviour of the child during the mother's absence, to the behaviour of the child at the moment of reunion. Attachment classification in the Baltimore Study was, however, not just based on the SSP. The results of the extensive home observations were decisive for the final classification system of the SSP (Ainsworth *et al.* 1978).

The Strange Situation procedure today

The SSP as it is used today is exactly the same procedure Ainsworth used in the Baltimore Study. It is a situation that children also experience in day-to-day life, for instance when visiting the doctor or the well-baby clinic, or during the first few visits to a day care centre. During the SSP the child is sequentially confronted with a strange room (a play room), an unknown experimenter, and two short periods of separation from the caregiver (see below). Usually the behaviour of the child is recorded on video and carefully coded afterwards. Special attention is paid to the episodes in which the caregiver is being reunited with the child after the brief separations. During those reunion episodes the behaviour of the child shows how much it trusts the caregiver and how long it takes before the balance between exploration of the environment and focus on the parent or caregiver has been restored. The SSP is used for parents or caregivers and their 12–72-month-old children. The original coding system is used for children from 12 to 20 months of age, whereas for older children adapted coding systems are used, in particular the Cassidy/Marvin system (Cassidy & Marvin 1992) to take into account the broader representational and behavioural repertoire of these children.

The SSP consists of eight episodes of about three minutes each in which the child is being observed.

1   The caregiver and the infant enter the room.
2   The caregiver and the infant are in the room.
3   A stranger enters.
4   The caregiver leaves the room. The stranger and the infant are together in the room.
5   The caregiver returns (first reunion) and the stranger leaves. At the end of this episode the caregiver leaves for the second time.
6   The infant is alone in the room.
7   The stranger comes back.
8   The caregiver returns (second reunion) and the stranger leaves.

Being separated twice from the caregiver in an unknown environment is stressful for children and prompts attachment behaviour. Especially the way in which the child approaches the caregiver at the reunion, and seeks contact, or tries to avoid contact, is angry, or acts in a disorganised way, is of interest. That is why the behaviour of the child during the two reunions is the decisive factor for the attachment classification.

The ABC + D of attachment in children

A, B & C

Securely attached children (classification B, see below) are upset when they are being left alone by their attachment figure in an unknown environment. Many (but by no means all) securely attached children are clearly upset, cry, and look for their caregiver. Their exploration and play come to a standstill. When the caregiver returns, these children will openly show their feelings of distress and will immediately start looking for reassurance and comfort from the attachment figure, but after a short while they will be able to go back to playing and exploring. Their curiosity about the nice toys in the playroom will prevail over their longing for immediate proximity to the caregiver. Securely attached children possess a basic trust – a general sense that the world is predictable and reliable – which is formed over time by a sensitive and comforting caregiver.

Children classified as *insecure-avoidant* (attachment classification A) experience stress during the SSP, as becomes apparent from their accelerated heartbeat, but they will not show this stress to the caregiver. When the caregiver returns, they seem to be engrossed in play and they seem to want to avoid being close to the caregiver. In the meantime, however, the child is actually watching their caregiver in an unobtrusive way, and after a while she/he may look for some contact and closeness, still not showing any negative emotions. It is probable that this is a result of earlier, similar experiences in which the child's negative emotions were rejected by the caregiver. These caregivers are normally capable of dealing with positive emotions of the child, but feel at a loss or even threatened by their child showing feelings of stress or sadness. This, in turn, might be due to their own experiences as a child with a caregiver who ignored or rejected their feelings of stress or sadness.

Children classified as *insecure-ambivalent* (attachment classification C) do the opposite and emphasise their negative emotions, for instance by crying loudly, and they continue to do so when the caregiver returns. They desperately try to get close to the caregiver and want to be picked up and to sit on their lap. But at the same time they seem to want to show the caregiver their disappointment in having been left alone in a strange situation full of unknown threats, even for a short time. They grab hold of the caregiver but at the same time push him or her away, hence the term 'ambivalent'. While the insecure-avoidant children suppress their negative emotions, the insecure-ambivalent children let their tears run freely. Their experience has taught them that they can only get the caregiver's attention by screaming loudly or by making it obvious in other ways that they need to be comforted by a grown-up. The caregiver might have been inconsistently sensitive and available to the child, possibly because of previous experiences and problems during his or her own childhood.

The three main classifications of attachment have been divided into subcategories in order to do justice to the variety of behavioural patterns within each main classification. An 'angry' insecure-ambivalent child shows totally different behaviour from a 'passive' insecure-ambivalent child, but both belong to the same main classification and both have the same background with regards to their upbringing by their caregivers.

A1   Avoids the caregiver in a conspicuous way during the episodes of reunion (for instance by ignoring him or her, by fixing its attention on toys, by turning away or crawling away). Does not attempt to approach the caregiver, or stops halfway. When being picked up by the caregiver makes no attempt to maintain contact. The stranger may be being approached in the same way as the caregiver.

A2   Greets or approaches the caregiver, but this greeting or approach is mixed with a tendency to turn around, or turn away, or to ignore the caregiver. There may be some tendency to maintain contact, but the context of avoidance remains predominant.

B1   Greeting at reunion takes place through positive interaction from a distance rather than approaching and seeking bodily contact. Little attempt to maintain contact when picked up. Little sadness during separation, and maybe some avoidance during reunion.

B2   Inclination to approach and greet caregiver, but hardly any attempts to make bodily contact. Some possible avoidance at first reunion, but no avoidance at the second reunion. No striving to maintain contact when picked up.

B3   Actively seeks bodily contact at reunion and actively tries to make it last. Seeks comfort, which is given by the caregiver until the child is at ease again, and goes back to exploring the environment in the presence of the caregiver. Very little avoidant or resistant behaviour.

B4   Clearly seeks contact, especially during reunions, but contact seeking and maintaining are less explicit and less effective than the contact seeking of B3 children. Derives insufficient security and comfort from the presence of the caregiver to be able to explore independently after a period of separation. May show some resistance towards the caregiver, and can only really be comforted on the caregiver's lap.

C1   Specifically seeks closeness and contact during reunions, mixed with distinctly resistant, angry behaviour. Experiences a lot of distress during periods of separation. Will often not go back to playing independently.

C2   Is extremely passive, with very little exploration in any episode, and little contact seeking or maintaining. Cries to show the need to be held. Resistance is not as strong as with the C1 children, but remains upset all through the reunion period, even if in bodily contact with the caregiver.

The various main classifications (ABC + D) have been studied rather thoroughly and sufficient psychometric validation has been conducted to be sure of their status as descriptors of child–parent attachment relationships. The sub-classifications, however, have received very little empirical attention as yet, because it is difficult to get sufficient numbers of children classified in each of the categories for the purpose of validation. Also, it appears to be difficult to establish sufficient chance-corrected intercoder reliability on the sub-classifications in relatively normal, non-clinical populations. This problem is in no way unique for the SSP sub-classifications but is inherent to any coding system with too many categories. The SSP subcategories are helpful when coding complex behaviour patterns but do not (yet) have the status of individual classifications of attachment with predictable and specific determinants and effects.

Children who are securely attached, but also children who have an insecure-avoidant attachment or insecure-ambivalent attachment, display an organised strategy to maintain interaction with the attachment figure. Insecurely attached children use resistant or avoidant behaviour to realise as much closeness to the potentially protecting caregiver as possible, even though their attachment relationship does not fulfil all their needs.

ABC + D

However, as well as a secure, insecure-avoidant or insecure-ambivalent classification, children's behaviour can be classified as *disorganised* (D) as discovered by Main and Solomon (1990). The essence of disorganised attachment is that the child is at times scared of the attachment figure, even though the attachment figure is, at the same time, their only source of protection and safety. This is an insoluble paradox that causes the child to behave in a disorganised way (for instance when the caregiver returns, the child might come to a complete standstill for 30 seconds or so, as if frozen, see below for more indicators). Disorganised attachment is not permanently visible and sometimes only becomes apparent during short episodes in the SSP.

Disorganised attachment always goes hand in hand with an 'organised' type of secure or insecure attachment, which is considered the basic attachment classification of the child. There are indications that especially insecure-avoidant or insecure-ambivalent attachment types combined with disorganised behaviour causes psychological and behavioural problems (Schuengel *et al.* 1999).

Indicators of disorganised behaviour in the SSP in children of 12–18 months, when the caregiver is present are the following (Main & Solomon 1990):

- simultaneous display of contradictory behaviour (for instance, the child approaches the caregiver with its back towards him/her);
- sequential display of contradictory behaviour (for instance, the child approaches the caregiver but just before reaching him/her, it turns around);
- undirected, misdirected, incomplete, or interrupted movements or facial expressions, stereotypies, asymmetrical movements, mistimed movements, anomalous postures;
- freezing, stilling, and slowed movements and expressions;
- direct signs of apprehension towards the caregiver;
- disoriented behaviour, especially at the return of the caregiver.

Determinants of differences in attachment

The bulk of studies looking at attachment in non-risk populations shows that about two-thirds of children are securely attached, one-fifth have an insecure-avoidant attachment classification and about one-tenth an insecure-ambivalent attachment classification. On top of that, about 15 per cent of children are classified as dis-organised. What causes these differences? Each child has an inborn inclination to become attached but not every child becomes securely attached. Is this due to genetic make-up, or is parenting the deciding factor? And is a child attached in the same way to all his caregivers: mother, father, and other caregiving adults like caregivers at the day care centre?

The effects of parenting

One of the bolder statements in attachment theory is that parenting is crucial, especially the way in which caregivers are sensitive in interacting with the child. Ainsworth (Ainsworth *et al.* 1978) described sensitivity as the ability to notice attachment signals of the child in time to interpret them correctly and to react to them promptly and adequately.

Research shows that sensitive caregivers do indeed more often have securely attached children. In a large meta-analysis, De Wolff and Van IJzendoorn (1997) found an effect size of about $r = .24$, or half a standard deviation. That is a robust effect and it justifies the conclusion that sensitivity of caregivers determines, at least in part, the quality of the attachment relationship with the child.

The fact that parenting is extremely important to the quality of attachment also becomes obvious when we look at the large number of properly designed intervention studies (with random allocation to the intervention group and con-trol group). These interventions aim at changing the behaviour of the caregivers, and if, as a result of this change, the attachment quality of the children changes as well, the causal relationship between sensitivity and attachment has experi-mentally been proven. In a large meta-analysis looking at all interventions aimed at improving sensitivity and attachment, Bakermans-Kranenburg and colleagues (2003) showed that in this respect attachment theory stands up to scientific scru-tiny. When parents or other caregivers become more sensitive, chances for their children to be securely attached increase. Sensitivity of the caregiver is therefore a determinant of the quality of attachment relationship with the child. Neverthe-less, a 'transmission gap' between parental attachment representation and child attachment has been documented to exist (Van IJzendoorn 1995). Security of attachment in the parent leads to higher levels of sensitivity to the child's signals which, in its turn, leads to a more secure relationship between the child and the parent. Parental sensitivity thus mediates the association between parental and child attachment. But the mediation is incomplete, and only part of the inter-generational transmission of attachment seems to go through sensitive parent-ing. Other factors might play a role, such as other dimensions of parenting (for example, support of exploratory behaviour) or genetic similarities between parent and child (Van IJzendoorn 1995).

The effects of genes

Other studies have looked at genetic effects on attachment. Studying just one child in a family cannot answer the question which of the two is the determining factor: genes or environment (Harris 1998). To be able to unravel the influence of genetic determinants and determinants of parenting, you need two children per family, preferably twins, who are either genetically identical (monozygotic) or who share on average half of their genes (dizygotic). A twin study conducted in Leiden (Bokhorst *et al.* 2003) showed no effect of genetic differences on the type of attachment these children had with their father or mother. Shared environment and unique environment, however, were important, which is what attachment theory predicts.

The fact that attachment is not dependent on the child's genes also becomes clear from research into attachment networks. Most children do not grow up with just one caregiver. Sarah Hrdy (2009) shows that from an evolutionary viewpoint it would have been impossible for single mothers to bring up their children without help from family or group members. Even just the amount of food necessary for a newborn baby to grow into a relatively independent teenager is so extremely large that one single adult could never get this together. Evolution has shaped the biological mother to share the upbringing with others, and the child has been shaped to accept other caregivers as attachment figures that can provide food and protection when the biological mother is absent. This is also the case if the mother has passed away. The risk of dying in the 'original environment of evolutionary adaptedness' (Bowlby 1969) was obviously much higher than in today's industrialised world.

The attachment network

Children can become attached to any caregiver in their environment who makes the effort to spend time with them on a regular basis. In our modern world, too, a child builds up an attachment network with mother, father, caregiver at day care, grandparents and other caregivers, and every one of those attachment relationships is a unique result of interactions with the child. Goossens and Van IJzendoorn (1990) found in a first study into the network of attachment relationships with father, mother and caregiver at day care that a child can become attached in every possible way to each person from the network, depending on the quality of the interactions with that person. A secure attachment to mother is no guarantee of a secure attachment to father or caregiver at day care. This shows that attachment does not depend on a biological tie with the attachment figure or on provision of food or physical care. Sensitive interactions cause a child to become securely attached. As a child develops, the separate attachment relationships he has built up with the different caregivers melt into one integrated cognitive representation of attachment, which becomes apparent through the Adult Attachment Interview (Hesse 2008). When and how this merging takes place is as yet unclear, but it is an intriguing subject for longitudinal research.

Attachment and child maltreatment

Disorganised attachment

At the moment, attachment is one of the key concepts in intervention programmes for deprived, neglected and/or maltreated children (for reviews see Bakermans-Kranenburg *et al.* 2003, 2005; Berlin *et al.* 2005; Oppenheim & Goldsmith 2007). The focus is, in particular, on disorganised attachment (D classification), the most anxious type of attachment. Disorganised attachment seems to be caused mainly by frightening or frightened and extreme insensitive behaviour of parents (Hesse & Main 2006; Lyons-Ruth *et al.* 1999; Main & Hesse 1990; Schuengel *et al.* 1999).

As mentioned earlier, disorganised children are caught in an irresolvable situation: their attachment figure and source of comfort and safety is, at the same time, threatening and a source of fright (Hesse & Main 2006). Recent studies with children who were not neglected or maltreated, support this hypothesis. They show that abnormal behaviour of the parent, for instance when the parent suffers from temporary dissociation, assumes an attack position, speaks or shouts in a booming voice, handles the child roughly, or shows extremely introvert behaviour as in a still-face procedure, evokes disorganised attachment (for a meta-analytic review see Madigan *et al.* 2006).

Neglect and maltreatment are extremely frightening for a child. In families where there is neglect and maltreatment, relationships between parent and child are dysfunctional. These parents set boundaries in a notably inadequate way: they more often use threats, punishments, force and power to get the child to cooperate (Chilamkurti & Milner, 1993; Loeber *et al.* 1994). Mothers who maltreat their children show more rejecting and controlling behaviour towards their child, while neglecting mothers are mainly inconsistent in their reactions and cannot set boundaries that fit with the age of the child (Bousha & Twentyman 1984; Crittenden 1981). Both these hostile and helpless behavioural patterns have been observed by Lyons-Ruth and colleagues (1999) in mothers of disorganised children. These parents are not sensitive to feelings of fright in their child and, therefore, are not able to regulate these feelings or form a buffer for the child, while at the same time they evoke fear which activates the attachment system of their child. This, in turn, results in 'fright without solution', so often seen in maltreated or neglected children. This fright without solution is probably the most important process through which these children develop a disorganised attachment.

Different ways to disorganised attachment

From the meta-analysis of Cyr and her colleagues (2010) looking at the influence of maltreatment and other risk factors for attachment, it appears that children with at least five parental social-emotional risk factors (low income, single mother, adolescent mother, low education, ethnic minority, and/or substance abuse) have just as much chance of disorganised attachment as do children who have suffered neglect or maltreatment. Of course, it is possible that in families with an accumulation of risks a lot of unproven or undiscovered cases of maltreatment exist. Another explanation could be that a different kind of parental behaviour, as yet unidentified but of which the effects are as bad as those of maltreatment, is the determining factor in the relationship between social economic risks and disorganised attachment in the child.

Research into frightened and frightening behaviour of parents (Hesse & Main 2000, 2006) might shed light on the behavioural mechanisms that cause risk factors in the family to influence the development of disorganised attachment. Up to now we know that disorganised attachment comes into existence when the child is afraid of the parent. This fear hinders the development of an organised attachment strategy or causes the (temporary) disappearance of an existing strategy to use the parent as a safe haven at times of stress. Hesse and Main (2006) suggest that frightening behaviour of parents can stem from unintegrated memories and emotions that are linked to traumatic experiences, such as loss or maltreatment. Parents who are surrounded by risks are more likely to have suffered loss or other traumatic experiences than parents in low-risk environments (Lynch & Cicchetti 1998; Oravecz *et al.* 2008). The child possibly reminds the parent of old traumas, which can cause dissociation – the parent tries to (unconsciously) detach him or herself from those same environments. This increases the risk of frightening or frightened behaviour of the parent (for instance talking in a strangely high-pitched voice, freezing of all movement, acting as if the child is in control) which puts the child into the irresolvable situation of seeing its parent simultaneously as a safe haven and a threat, resulting in disorganised attachment.

Schuengel and colleagues (1999) provided empirical support for this association. When direct maltreatment or neglect are absent, it seems possible that frightening behaviour of the parent can be a key mechanism through which parents prompt disorganised attachment.

Apart from these speculative explanations there are two other conceivable pathways to disorganised attachment. In the first place, the attachment system of the child could be chronically hyper-activated if the parent withdraws from interaction with the child due to overwhelming personal or social-economical problems and daily pursuits. It is possible that children in high-risk families are dealing with a type of neglect that is inevitable in chaotic environments. Solomon and George (1999) expanded on the idea of 'fright without solution' and proposed that parents who continuously fail to protect the child or fulfil its needs for attachment in stressful situations, will bring the child into an extreme and continuous state of fear. Eventually the child will come to the frightening conclusion that the caregiver does not offer a safe haven when the child needs protection, and that the caregiver will not fulfil its needs for proximity and protection (Madigan *et al.* 2006).

Along the same lines Lyons-Ruth and colleagues (1999) suggest that disorganised attachment does not only originate from frightening or frightened behaviour of the parent, but also from extreme insensitive behaviour of the caregiver. In their model, a lack of response (for instance, withdrawal from interaction), or extreme insensitive reactions, such as aggression towards the child, harsh discipline, lack of supervision in dangerous situations or ever-recurring miscalculations in affective communication, can be just as frightening to the child as can behaviour of the parent that directly prompts fear. In a sample of families at risk, including a number of maltreated children, it was found that both frightening behaviour and extremely insensitive behaviour were more characteristic for mothers of a child with a disorganised attachment than for mothers of a child with an insecure organised attachment (Lyons-Ruth *et al.* 1999; Lyons-Ruth & Jacobvitz 2008).

A second alternative pathway to disorganised attachment could be the increased chance children of families with multiple risks have of experiencing domestic violence (Cicchetti & Lynch 1993). Children who witness domestic violence, including violence by one parent towards the other, have a higher risk of having a disorganised attachment. Zeanah and colleagues (1999) expect that witnessing parental violence will frighten a young child and make him or her worry about the wellbeing of the mother and her ability to protect both herself and the child against the violence.

In short, it looks as if there are a number of non-exclusive ways that can lead to disorganised attachment: maltreatment of the child by the caregiver, growing up in a family surrounded by a combination of risks, unresolved trauma in a caregiver, or extremely insensitive behaviour of the caregiver.

Conclusion

Early experience with attachment relationships is assumed to be a decisive factor for the way children are later able to create bonds with other people, their future partners or their own children. The tendency to become attached is inborn, and even children who are being maltreated or neglected become attached, although this is usually an insecure or disorganised attachment. No effect of genetic differences has been found, but the effect of parenting appears to be strong, especially the way in which caregivers are sensitive in interaction with the child. The attachment representation that arises during the first few years of life does appear to leave its traces in adulthood, but studies show that the environment can change the attachment representation. Attachment is presently one of the key concepts in intervention programmes for deprived, neglected and/or maltreated children. Quality of attachment can be measured with the SSP, originally designed by Mary Ainsworth to measure the infant's use of its mother as a secure base, and subsequently further developed into an instrument used to determine the attachment classification of young children.

The SSP – far from strange to attachment researchers – has for decades been regarded as the gold standard for measuring attachment, and will most probably continue to allow us to classify attachment quality of infants for decades to come.

References

Ainsworth, M.D.S. (1963). The development of infant–mother interaction among the Ganda. In B.M. Foss (ed.), *Determinants of infant behavior II* (pp. 67–104). New York: Wiley.

Ainsworth, M.D. (1964). Patterns of attachment behavior shown by the infant in interaction with his mother. *Merrill-Palmer Quarterly, 10*, 51–58.

Ainsworth, M.D.S. (1967). *Infancy in Uganda: Infant care and the growth of love.* Baltimore, MD: The Johns Hopkins University Press.

Ainsworth, M.D.S., & Ainsworth, L.H. (1958). *Measuring security in personal adjustment.* Toronto: University of Toronto Press.

Ainsworth, M.D.S., & Wittig, B.A. (1969). Attachment and the exploratory behaviour of one-year-olds in a strange situation. In B.M. Foss (ed.), *Determinants of infant behaviour IV* (pp. 113–136). London: Methuen.

Ainsworth, M.D.S., Blehar, M.C., Waters, E., & Wall, S. (1978). *Patterns of attachment: A psychological study of the Strange Situation.* Hillsdale, NJ: Lawrence Erlbaum.

Arsenian, J.M. (1943). Young children in an insecure situation. *Journal of Abnormal and Social Psychology, 38*, 225–249.

Bakermans-Kranenburg, M.J., Van IJzendoorn, M.H., & Juffer, F. (2003). Less is more: Meta-analysis of sensitivity and attachment interventions in early childhood. *Psychological Bulletin, 129*, 195–215.

Bakermans-Kranenburg, M.J., Van IJzendoorn, M.H., & Juffer, F. (2005). Disorganized infant attachment and preventive interventions: A review and meta-analysis. *Infant Mental Health Journal, 26*, 191–216.

Beckwith, L., Cohen, S.E., & Hamilton, C.E. (1999). Maternal sensitivity during infancy and subsequent life events relate to attachment representation at early adulthood. *Developmental Psychology, 35*, 693–700.

Berlin, L.J., Ziv, Y., Amaya-Jackson, L., & Greenberg, M.T. (2005). *Enhancing early attachments: Theory, research, intervention and policy.* New York: The Guilford Press.

Blatz, W.E. (1966). *Human security, some reflections.* London: University of London Press Ltd.

Bokhorst, C.L., Bakermans-Kranenburg, M.J., Fearon, R.M.P., Van IJzendoorn, M.H., Fonagy, P., & Schuengel, C. (2003). The importance of shared environment in mother-infant attachment security: A behavioral genetic study. *Child Development, 74*(6), 1769–1782.

Bousha, D.M., & Twentyman, C.T. (1984). Mother–child interactional style in abuse, neglect, and control groups. *Journal of Abnormal Psychology, 93*, 106–114.

Bowlby, J. (1953). *Child care and the growth of love.* Baltimore, MD: Penguin Books.

Bowlby, J. (1969). *Attachment and loss. Vol. 1: Attachment.* New York: Basic Books and London: Pimlico.

Bowlby, J. (1973). *Attachment and loss. Vol. 2: Separation: Anxiety and anger*. New York: Basic Books.

Bowlby, J. (1982). *Attachment and loss. Vol. 1: Attachment* (2nd ed.). New York: Basic Books.

Bowlby, J. (1988). *A secure base: Clinical applications of attachment theory*. London: Routledge.

Bretherton, I. (1992). The origins of attachment theory: John Bowlby and Mary Ainsworth. *Developmental Psychology, 28*, 759–775.

Cassidy, J., & Marvin, R.S. with the MacArthur Working Group. (1992). *Attachment organization in preschool children: Procedures and coding manual*. Unpublished manuscript, University of Virginia.

Chilamkurti, C., & Milner, J.S. (1993). Perceptions and evaluations of child transgressions and disciplinary techniques in high- and low-risk mothers and their children. *Child Development, 64*, 1801–1814.

Cicchetti, D., & Lynch, M. (1993). Toward an ecological transactional model of community violence and child maltreatment: Consequences for children's development. *Psychiatry – Interpersonal and Biological Processes, 56*, 96–118.

Crittenden, P.M. (1981). Abusing, neglecting, problematic and adequate dyads: Differentiating by patterns of interaction. *Merrill-Palmer Quarterly, 27*, 201–218.

Cyr, C., Euser, E.M., Bakermans-Kranenburg, M.J., & Van IJzendoorn, M.H. (2010). Attachment security and disorganization in maltreating and high-risk families: A series of meta-analyses. *Development & Psychopathology, 22*, 87–108.

De Wolff, M.S., & Van IJzendoorn, M.H. (1997). Sensitivity and attachment: A meta-analysis on parental antecedents of infant attachment. *Child Development, 68*, 571–591.

Goossens, F.A., & Van IJzendoorn, M.H. (1990). Quality of infants' attachment to professional caregivers: Relation to infant–parent attachment and day-care characteristics. *Child Development, 61*, 832–837.

Gunnar, M.R., & Vasquez, D.M. (2001). Low cortisol and a flattening of expected daytime rhythm: Indices of risk in human development. *Development and Psychopathology, 13*, 515–538.

Harlow, H.F. (1960). Primary affectional patterns in primates. *American Journal for Orthopsychiatry, 30*, 676–684.

Harris, J.R. (1998). *The nurture assumption: Why children turn out the way they do. Parents matter less than you think and peers matter more*. New York: Free Press.

Hesse, E. (1999). The Adult Attachment Interview: Historical and current perspectives. In J. Cassidy & P.R. Shaver (eds), *Handbook of attachment: Theory, research, and clinical implications* (pp. 395–433). New York: The Guilford Press.

Hesse, E. (2008). The Adult Attachment Interview: Protocol, method of analysis, and empirical studies. In J. Cassidy & P.R. Shaver (eds), *Handbook of attachment: Theory, research, and clinical applications* (pp. 552–598). New York: The Guilford Press.

Hesse, E., & Main, M. (2000). Disorganized infant, child, and adult attachment: Collapse in behavioral and attentional strategies. *Journal of American Psychoanalytic Association, 48*(4), 1097–1127.

Hesse, E., & Main, M. (2006). Frightened, threatening, and dissociative (FR) parental behavior as related to infant D attachment in low-risk samples: Description, discussion, and interpretations. *Development and Psychopathology, 18*, 309–343.

Homer. *The Iliad*. Translated by A.T. Murray (1924) Loeb Classical Library Volumes. Cambridge, MA: Harvard University Press and London: William Heinemann Ltd.

Hrdy, S.B. (2009). *Mothers and others: The evolutionary origins of mutual understanding.* Cambridge, MA and London: Harvard University Press.

Loeber, R., Felton, D., & Reid, J.B. (1994). A social learning approach to the reduction of coercive processes in child abusive families: A molecular analysis. *Advances in Behavior Research and Therapy, 6,* 29–45.

Lorenz, K.Z. (1952). *King Solomon's ring* (M.K. Wilson, trans). New York: Crowell.

Lynch, M., & Cicchetti, D. (1998). An ecological-transactional analysis of children and contexts: The longitudinal interplay among child maltreatment, community violence, and children's symptomatology. *Development and Psychopathology, 10,* 235–257.

Lyons-Ruth, K., & Jacobvitz, D. (2008). Attachment disorganization: Genetic factors, parenting contexts, and developmental transformation from infancy to adulthood. In J. Cassidy & P.R. Shaver (eds), *Handbook of attachment: Theory, research and clinical applications* (pp. 666–687). New York: The Guilford Press.

Lyons-Ruth, K., Bronfman, E., & Parsons, E. (1999). Maternal frightened, frightening, or atypical behavior and disorganized infant attachment patterns. In J. Vondra & D. Barnett (eds), *Atypical patterns of infant attachment: Theory, research, and current directions. Monographs of the Society for Research in Child Development, 64* (3, Serial No. 258).

Madigan, S., Bakermans-Kranenburg, M.J., Van IJzendoorn, M.H., Moran, G., Pederson, D.R., & Benoit, D. (2006). Unresolved states of mind, anomalous parental behavior, and disorganized attachment: A review and meta-analysis of a transmission gap. *Attachment & Human Development, 8,* 89–111.

Main, M., & Hesse, E. (1990). Parents' unresolved traumatic experiences are related to infant disorganized attachment status: Is frightened and/or frightening parental behavior the linking mechanism? In M.T. Greenberg, D. Cicchetti, & E.M. Cummings (eds), *Attachment in the preschool years: Theory, research, and intervention. The John D. and Catherine T. MacArthur Foundation series on mental health and development* (pp. 161–182). Chicago, IL: The University of Chicago Press.

Main, M., & Solomon, J. (1990). Procedures for identifying infants as disorganized/disoriented during the Ainsworth Strange Situation. In M.T. Greenberg, D. Cicchetti, & E.M. Cummings (eds), *Attachment in the preschool years: Theory, research, and intervention* (pp. 121–182). Chicago, IL: The University of Chicago Press.

Oppenheim, D., & Goldsmith, D.F. (2007). *Attachment theory in clinical work with children: Bridging the gap between research and practice.* New York: The Guilford Press.

Oravecz, L.M., Koblinsky, S.A., & Randolph, S.M. (2008). Community violence, interpartner conflict, parenting, and social support as predictors of the social competence of African American preschool children. *Journal of Black Psychology, 34*(2), 192–216.

Schaffer, H.R., & Emerson, P.E. (1964). Patterns of response to physical contact in early human development. *Journal of Child Psychology and Psychiatry, 5,* 1–13.

Schuengel, C., Bakermans-Kranenburg, M.J., & Van IJzendoorn, M.H. (1999). Frightening maternal behavior linking unresolved loss and disorganized infant attachment. *Journal of Consulting and Clinical Psychology, 67,* 54–63.

Solomon, J., & George, C. (1999). The place of disorganization in attachment theory: Linking classic observations with contemporary findings. In J. Solomon & C. George (eds), *Attachment disorganization* (pp. 3–32). New York: The Guilford Press.

Sroufe, L.A., Egeland, B., Carlson, E.A., & Collins, W.A. (2005). *The development of the person. The Minnesota study of risk and adaptation from birth to adulthood.* New York: Guilford Press.

Van IJzendoorn, M.H. (1995). Adult attachment representations, parental responsiveness, and infant attachment: A meta-analysis on the predictive validity of the Adult Attachment Interview. *Psychological Bulletin, 117*, 387.

Van IJzendoorn, M.H. (2008). *Opvoeding over de grens: Gehechtheid, trauma en veerkracht.* Amsterdam: Boom.

Van IJzendoorn, M.H., & Juffer, F. (2006). The Emanuel Miller Memorial Lecture 2006: Adoption as intervention. Meta-analytic evidence for massive catch-up and plasticity in physical, socio-emotional, and cognitive development. *Journal of Child Psychology and Psychiatry, 47*, 1228–1245.

Van IJzendoorn, M.H., Rutgers, A.H., Bakermans-Kranenburg, M.J., Swinkels, S.H.N., van Daalen, E., Dietz, C. *et al.* (2007). Parental sensitivity and attachment in children with autism spectrum disorders: Comparison with children with mental retardation, language delay and non clinical children. *Child Development, 78*, 597–608.

Waters, E., Hamilton, C.E., & Weinfield, N.S. (2000). The stability of attachment security from infancy to adolescence and early adulthood: General introduction. *Child Development, 71*, 678–683.

Wright, M.J. (1996). William Emet Blatz: A Canadian pioneer. In G.A. Kimble, C.A. Boneau, & M. Wertheimer (eds), *Portraits of pioneers in psychology* (Vol. 2, pp. 199–211). Mahwah, NJ: Erlbaum and Washington, DC: American Psychological Association.

Zeanah, C.H., Danis, B., Hirshberg, L., Benoit, D., Miller, D., & Heller, S.S. (1999). Disorganized attachment associated with partner violence: A research note. *Infant Mental Health Journal, 20*, 77–86.

Chapter 2

Why are we interested in attachments?

Peter Fonagy, Nicolas Lorenzini,
Chloe Campbell and Patrick Luyten

Introduction

Attachment theory describes the ways in which individuals handle their most intimate relationships with their parents, children and life-partners: their attachment figures. When people are at their most vulnerable, frightened or unwell, they will, in different ways, seek comfort and help. This seeking out of help, and the different styles used to obtain help, constitute the attachment process. Attachment, at an evolutionary level, is a basic adaptation for survival – it is the mechanism by which babies elicit essential care. As we understand more, however, about the interface of brain development and early psychosocial experience it becomes clear that the evolutionary role of the attachment relationship goes far beyond giving physical protection to the human infant.

From birth, the interactions of an infant with their primary carers will establish a base for personality development and will mould subsequent close relationships, expectations of social acceptance, and attitudes to rejection. A secure base is formed when the attachment figure (usually the mother) provides stability and safety in moments of stress, which allows the infant to explore his/her surroundings. In this way, the child constructs mental models of him/herself and of others in social interactions ('internal working models'). These working models are formed into their own distinctive shape by the kinds of the interactions he/she experiences from his/her primary attachment figures (Bowlby 1973).

These early attachment experiences are the tools that the mind uses to forge its capacity for affect and stress regulation, attentional control, mentalisation, and self-agency (Fonagy *et al.* 2010). In other words, the major long-term selective advantage conferred by attachment is the opportunity to develop the sophisticated human social intelligence that physical and emotional nearness to concerned adults affords. Attachment ensures that the brain processes serving social cognition are appropriately organised and prepared to equip the individual for the collaborative and cooperative existence with others for which the brain was designed (Fonagy 2003a).

The brain is experience-expectant (Siegel 1999); thus, processes as fundamental as gene expression or changes in neuron receptor densities can be influenced by the infant's environment (e.g. Meaney & Szyf 2005). In other words, we are interested in attachments because not only are they normative and necessary for human (and mammalian) survival, they are increasingly understood as providing both the neurological and the psychological framework for the development of personality.

Attachment research has been based on the Strange Situation procedure (SSP) for infants (developed by Mary Ainsworth) and its corollary for assessing adults, the Adult Attachment Interview (AAI) (first developed by Mary Main and her colleagues). These assessment tools are described in detail in the *Routledge Handbook of Attachment: Assessment* (Farnfield & Holmes 2014).

In the SSP infants are briefly separated from their caregivers and left with a stranger in an unfamiliar setting. The way they respond falls into three distinct patterns of behaviour: secure (63% of children in various community samples); anxious/resistant or ambivalent (16%); and avoidant (21%). In adults, attachment style is respectively classified as secure/autonomous (58% of the non-clinical population), avoidant/dismissing (23%), and anxious/preoccupied (19%) (Main *et al.* 1985; Bakermans-Kranenburg & Van IJzendoorn 2009). More recent research has revealed a fourth pattern, disorganised attachment (Main & Solomon 1986; Levy *et al.* 2011).

A *securely attached* infant during the SSP readily explores his/her new surroundings in the primary caregiver's presence, shows anxiety in the stranger's presence, is distressed by the caregiver's brief absence, rapidly seeks contact with the caregiver upon reunion, and is reassured by renewed contact, rapidly reassuming exploration. Likewise, an adult categorised as secure/autonomous during the AAI coherently integrates attachment memories into a meaningful narrative and shows appreciation for attachment relationships.

An *anxious/avoidant* infant appears less upset at separation, might not seek contact with the caregiver on his/her return, and might not prefer the caregiver to the stranger. In adults, *avoidant/dismissing* AAI narratives will lack coherence; patients will be unable to recall specific memories in support of general arguments and will idealise or devalue their early relationships (Fonagy *et al.* 2010). These behaviours appear as the result of a hyper-deactivation of the attachment system characterised by inhibition of proximity-seeking and a determination to handle stress alone, which implies a clear attempt to inhibit negative emotions through a non-interpersonal way of regulating them (Barone *et al.* 2011).

An *anxious/resistant* infant shows limited exploration and play, seems highly distressed by the separation, and does not easily settle after reunion. Correspondingly, an *anxious/preoccupied* adult's AAI narratives will show confusion, anger, or fear in relation to early attachment figures (Fonagy *et al.* 2010). This corresponds to the hyper-activation of proximity-seeking and protection-seeking strategies, to a (chronic) hypersensitivity to signs of possible rejection of abandonment, and to an intensification of undesirable emotions (Barone *et al.* 2011).

A *disoriented/disorganised* infant will show undirected or bizarre behaviour such as freezing, hand clapping or head banging. The infant might try to escape the situation. Comparably, an *unresolved/disorganised* adult's narratives about bereavements or childhood traumas will contain semantic and/or syntactic confusions. This corresponds to the breakdown of strategies to cope with stress, which leads to partial or even pervasive emotion dysregulation.

The relationship between styles of attachment and personality development

Bowlby proposed that internal working models of the self and others developed in infancy provide prototypes for all later relationships. And, indeed, recent attachment research has shown that these styles of attachment behaviour do remain strikingly consistent across life (Bakermans-Kranenburg & Van IJzendoorn 2009): there is a 68–75 per cent correspondence between attachment classification in infancy and in adulthood (Fonagy et al. 2010). Individual differences in attachment classification have been studied in relation to an exceptionally wide range of later outcomes, spanning cognitive capacities such as verbal IQ, interpersonal capacities and psychopathology.

The most important predictor of attachment style change during life is negative early life events, such as loss of a parent, parental divorce, life-threatening illness of a parent or child, parental psychiatric disorder, physical maltreatment, or sexual abuse (Johnson et al. 1999; Waters et al. 2000).

The stable nature of attachment styles accounts for the development of enduring strategies to regulate emotion and social contact. For example, the increased control of the secure child permits him/her to move toward the ownership of inner experience, and toward an understanding of self and others as intentional beings whose behaviour is organised by mental states, thoughts, feelings, beliefs and desires. Consistent with this, prospective longitudinal research has demonstrated that children with a history of secure attachment are independently rated as more resilient, self-reliant, socially oriented, and empathic to distress, with deeper relationships and higher self-esteem. Securely attached individuals trust their attachment figures and perceive little environmental threat; as a result, they can respond appropriately to environmental challenges and are able to process emotions in a fluid and non-defensive way (Nolte et al. 2011).

Dismissing individuals may have a higher threshold for experiencing negative emotions or perceiving attachment needs, exhibiting what Bowlby called 'compulsive self-reliance' (Bowlby 1980: 365). Preoccupied individuals, who are wary following a history of inconsistent support from caregivers, are likely to have a lower threshold for perceiving environmental threat and, therefore, stress. This is likely to contribute to frequent activation of the attachment system, with the concomitant distress and anger such activation can cause. Hence, they are likely to manifest compulsive care-seeking and over-dependency.

Unresolved/disorganised individuals – the adult analogue of disorganised/disoriented infants – frequently have parents who are themselves abusive or unresolved regarding their own losses or abuse experiences (Lyons-Ruth & Block 1996; Botbol 2010; Fonagy & Target 2005; Slade et al. 2005).

Evidence linking attachment in infancy with more general personality character-istics is stronger in some studies than in others. Findings from the Minnesota Study cohort show a prediction from infantile attachment insecurity to adult measures of psychiatric morbidity, with many potential confounding factors controlled for, linking attachment insecurity and adversity to indications of personality disorder (PD) (Carlson *et al.* 2009). A 'dose–response' relationship between psychological disturbance and insecurity is suggested by the observation of Kochanska and Kim (2013), who found that children who are insecure with both parents tend to report more overall problems, and to be rated by teachers as having more externalising (such as overt anger) problems than those who are secure with at least one parent.

However, in contrast to Bowlby's prediction, the avoidant and resistant classifi-cations tend not to be strongly related to later measures of maladaptation although there is also some evidence to suggest a connection between avoidance and inter-nalising conditions such as depression and anxiety (Groh *et al.* 2012).

It is the disorganised/disoriented infant category which appears to have the strongest predictive significance for later psychological disturbance (Fearon *et al.* 2010).

Evidence is accumulating that long-term physical health may be influenced by early attachment through a person's immune response as well as the now well-accepted links to future psychopathology or mental health resiliency. For exam-ple, the prevalence of obesity in adolescence was found to be more than twice as high among youth with poor-quality early relationships than those with better relationships (Anderson *et al.* 2012). At this point it is important to recall that the classification of attachment is a summary variable that incorporates various quali-ties of mother/infant relationship. In this study low maternal sensitivity was more strongly associated with later obesity than insecure attachment. A 32-year study reported insecurity at 12–18 months to be associated with increased risk of inflam-matory illnesses in adulthood (Puig *et al.* 2012).

It is easy to alight on the negative outcomes of insecure attachment and for-get about the evolutionary functions, the biological nature of the mechanisms underpinning it, which are ultimately oriented toward optimising the chances of reproduction (Hamilton 1964). The findings of Belsky, Routs and Fearon (2010), who followed 373 women enrolled in the National Institute of Child Health and Human Development Study of Early Child Care and Youth Development Study, is poignant. Annual physical examinations from the ages of 9.5 years to 15.5 years revealed that individuals who had been insecure infants initiated and completed pubertal development earlier and had an earlier age of menarche compared with individuals who had been secure infants, even after accounting for age of men-arche in the infants' mothers.

Insecure attachment may indicate environmental adversity. Early procreation might be an adaptive strategy to deal with the reduced likelihood of survival in a combative challenging environment. This kind of observation raises questions about the biological mechanisms responsible for the attachment effects and these are considered below.

Attachment, biology and social cognition

The neurobiology of attachment is now fairly well understood (as will be dis-cussed further by Graham Music in Chapter 7). Attachment has evolved to change the internal (stress/fear response mediated by noradrenaline through the amygdala and insula, and cortisol via the hypothalamic–pituitary–adrenal [HPA] axis) and external conditions associated with threats to the survival of the organism. Dis-tress triggers an attachment signal from the infant, who seeks to counter threat and avoid harm by evoking proximity, and a matching regulating, protective response from a caretaker disposed to reciprocate, form emotional bonds, mentalise, and teach (i.e. contingent, attuned, marked mirroring from the caretaker).

Mother–infant, infant–mother, and romantic-partner attachment have a shared neurobiological basis (that is there is a reciprocal response in each individual). This is linked to the mesocorticolimbic dopaminergic reward circuit, which also plays a key role in mediating the process of physical (as well as emotional) addic-tion: attachment can be thought of as an 'addictive disorder' (Insel 2003).

Two major neural systems have been shown to play a critical role in attach-ment behaviours: the dopaminergic reward-processing system and the oxytocin-ergic system (Fonagy *et al.* 2011). The role of the dopaminergic reward system in attachment behaviour is understood as an evolutionary mechanism to motivate reproductive mating, maternal care and, ultimately, offspring survival. It leads individuals to seek close relations with other humans and produces satisfaction when they are attained.

Broadly speaking, we may envisage three types of association between aspects of social cognition and attachment. These are created by (a) attachment relation-ships based upon intense romantic and maternal love, (b) attachment relationships based upon threat/fear, and (c) secure and predictable attachment relationships. Although any given attachment relationship can have features of each of these three possibilities, they are important to distinguish, as the relationship between attachment activation and mentalising can differ considerably depending on which feature is activated within an attachment relationship. The three cognitive processes connected with attachment are:

1   Mediated by dopaminergic structures of the reward system in the presence of oxytocin and vasopressin, the love-related activation of the attachment system can inhibit the neural systems that underpin the generation of negative affect.
2   The threat-related activation of the attachment system (e.g. triggered by per-ceived threat, loss, or harm) might also evoke intense arousal and overwhelm-ing negative affect, bringing about an activation of posterior cortical and sub-cortical areas and switching off frontal cortical activity including mentalisa-tion (Arnsten 1998; Arnsten *et al.* 1999; Mayes 2000).
3   Meanwhile, a secure and predictable attachment relationship might be most effective in *pre-empting* threat, which possibly reduces the need for frequent activation of the attachment system.

It is perhaps worth noting that Bowlby assumed fear, in particular fear of the loss of the attachment figure, to be the primary reason for activation of the attachment system (Bowlby 1959, 1969, 1973). An unpredictable, insecure caregiver–infant relationship is likely to result in frequent activation of the attachment system accompanied by the deactivation of neural structures underpinning aspects of social cognition. Evidence also suggests that the level of attachment anxiety is positively correlated with activation in emotion-related areas of the brain (e.g. the anterior temporal pole, which is activated when we are sad) and inversely correlated with activation in a region associated with emotion regulation (the orbitofrontal cortex) (Gillath *et al.* 2005). These findings suggested that anxiously attached people might under-recruit brain regions normally used to downregulate negative emotions.

Adult attachment experiences and mentalisation

Bowlby's theory of attachment was famously met with a barrage of almost unanimous criticism from the usually divided world of psychoanalysis; this intellectual standoff was compounded when Bowlby himself responded to this denunciation with an equally bullish stance. But in the past 10 to 15 years, there has been a conspicuous and highly creative rapprochement: a slew of new work has appeared that integrates psychodynamic clinical work with attachment theory and research. This interest in attachment has consolidated so exponentially because the theory provides such a convincing overarching framework for understanding and elaborating the processes by which the human mind is able to explore the subtleties of subjectivity; of who we are and how we interact with other people.

Attachment theory cannot and does not aspire to specify the full richness of the subjective contents that preoccupy the ordinary mind, let alone the mind in distress. Few attachment theorists would claim that Bowlby's theory, even with its recent elaborations, can provide a full account of human motivation and experience, which is the declared aim of a psychoanalytic psychology. Nevertheless, it is also evident that the gulf between the two is narrowing rapidly.

A relatively new concept, mentalisation-based theory and treatment, further integrates psychoanalytic thinking with attachment theory and research. Mentalisation, which is considered in more detail by Luyten and Fonagy in Chapter 6, is the impulse to understand and imagine both our own and other people's thoughts; it is one of humanity's most pervasive and powerful characteristics. The first minds that small children are presented with, to wonder about and interpret, are of course those of their most intimate family. This family – primarily the major attachment figures – provides the earliest formative lessons in other people's thinking, and also, through these people's reactions, for learning about how our thoughts are perceived: who we are imagined to be by others. The mentalisation model specifically concerns itself with the parent's understanding and reflection on the infant's internal world, and claims a vital relationship between attachment processes and the growth of the child's capacity to understand interpersonal behaviour in terms of mental states (Fonagy *et al.* 2002).

Understanding the relationship between attachment and mentalising

Many studies support the suggestion that secure children are better than insecure children at mentalisation (measured as passing theory of mind tasks earlier) (see, e.g., de Rosnay & Harris 2002). Children with secure attachment relationships assessed by the Separation Anxiety Test do better than children with disorganised attachment on a test of emotion understanding (Fonagy *et al.* 1997a). The first of these findings, reported from the London Parent–Child Project (Fonagy *et al.* 1997b), found that 82 per cent of children who were secure with the mother in the SSP passed Harris' Belief-Desire-Reasoning Task at 5.5 years, compared with 50 per cent of those who were avoidant and 33 per cent of the small number who were preoccupied. Findings along these lines are not always consistent (see, e.g., Meins *et al.* 2002), but it generally seems that secure attachment and mentalisation are subject to similar social influences. Two decades of research have confirmed parenting as the key determinant of attachment security. Can certain aspects of parenting account for the overlap between mentalisation and attachment security?

Researchers describe the mother's capacity to take a psychological perspective on her child using different terms, including maternal mind-mindedness, insightfulness and reflective function (RF). These overlapping attributes appear to be associated with both secure attachment and mentalisation (Sharp *et al.* 2006). Meins *et al.* (2001), Oppenheim and Koren-Karie (2002), and Slade (Slade *et al.* 2005) have sought to link parental mentalisation with the development of affect regulation and secure attachment by analysing interactional narratives between parents and children. Although Meins assessed parents' quality of narrative about their children in real time (while the parents were playing with their children) while Oppenheim's group did this in a more 'offline' manner (parents narrating a videotaped interaction), both concluded that maternal mentalising was a more powerful predictor of attachment security than, say, global sensitivity. Meins and colleagues found that mind-related comments by mothers at six months predicted attachment security at 12 months (Meins *et al.* 2001), mentalising capacity at 45 and 48 months (Meins *et al.* 2002), and performance in a stream of consciousness task at 55 months (Meins *et al.* 2003). Oppenheim and Koren-Karie (2002) found that a secure mother–child relationship was predicted by high levels of mentalisation about the child's behaviour.

Slade and colleagues (2005) also observed a strong association between infant attachment and the quality of the parent's mentalising about the child. Rather than using an episode of observed interaction, Slade *et al.* used an autobiographical memory-based interview about the child, the Parent Development Interview (PDI). High scorers on the PDI's mentalising scale are aware of the characteristics of their infant's mental functioning, and they grasp the complex interplay between their own mental states and the child's putative inner experience. They are likely to have secure relationships with infants whom they describe in a mentalising way. Low mentalising mothers were more likely to show atypical maternal behaviour on the AMBIANCE (Atypical Maternal Behaviour Instrument for Assessment and Classification) system (Bronfman *et al.* 1999), which relates not only to infant attachment disorganisation but also to unresolved (disorganised) attachment status in the mother's AAI (Grienenberger *et al.* 2005).

Taken together, these results suggest that a mentalising style of parenting might well facilitate the development of mentalisation. Mindful parenting probably enhances both attachment security and mentalisation in a child. These findings are of significance when considering social or therapeutic interventions (see *The Routledge Handbook of Attachment: Implications and Interventions* (Holmes & Farnfield 2014)).

The process of acquiring mentalisation is so ordinary and normal that it might be more correct to consider secure attachment as removing obstacles to it, rather than actively and directly facilitating its development. Coherent family discourse characteristic of secure attachment (Hill *et al.* 2003) helps to generate explanatory schemas by means of which the behaviour of others can be understood and predicted. It is fair to say that, under normal circumstances, conversations with children which include frequent accurate elaboration of psychological themes could be the 'royal road' to understanding minds (Harris 2005). Main's (2000) groundbreaking work has linked attachment to this kind of communication with words. The key to understanding the interaction of attachment with the development of mentalisation might be to look at instances where normally available catalysts for mentalisation are absent.

Mentalisation and maltreatment

Maltreatment disorganises the attachment system (see Cicchetti & Valentino 2006 for a comprehensive review). There is also evidence to suggest that it may disrupt mentalisation. Young maltreated children manifest certain characteristics that could suggest problems with mentalisation:

1   they engage in less symbolic and dyadic play (Alessandri 1991);
2   they sometimes fail to show empathy when witnessing distress in other children (Klimes-Dougan & Kistner1990);
3   they have poor affect regulation (Maughan & Cicchetti 2002);
4   they make fewer references to their internal states (Shipman & Zeman 1999);
5   they struggle to understand emotional expressions, particularly facial ones (During & McMahon 1991), even when verbal IQ is controlled for (Camras *et al.* 1990).

Maltreated children tend to misattribute anger (Camras *et al.* 1996) and show elevated event-related potentials to angry faces (Cicchetti & Curtis 2005). The evidence for significant developmental delay in the emotional understanding of maltreated young children is consistent (Pears & Fisher 2005), if slightly reduced, when IQ and socioeconomic status are controlled for (Smith & Walden 1999). Understanding sad and angry emotions at age six predicts social competence and social isolation at eight (Rogosch *et al*. 1995).

In addition to problems of emotional understanding, there have also been reports of delayed theory of mind understanding in maltreated children (Cicchetti *et al*. 2003; Pears & Fisher 2005). The capacity to parse complex and emotionally charged representations of the parent and of the self might even deteriorate with development (Toth *et al*. 2000).

Considered in relation to attachment, mentalisation deficits associated with childhood maltreatment may be a form of decoupling, inhibition, or even a phobic reaction to mentalising.

1   Adversity may undermine cognitive development in general (Cicchetti *et al*. 2000; Crandell & Hobson 1999).
2   Mentalisation problems may reflect arousal problems associated with exposure to chronic stress (see Cicchetti & Walker 2001).
3   The child may avoid mentalisation to avoid perceiving the abuser's frankly hostile and malevolent thoughts and feelings about him/her (e.g. Fonagy 1991).

These are all potential problems that will have a significant negative impact on a child's psychological, emotional, social and educational development.

Maltreatment can contribute to an acquired partial 'mind-blindness' by compromising open reflective communication between parent and child. Maltreatment may undermine the benefit derived from learning about the links between internal states and actions in attachment relationships (e.g. the child might be told that he or she 'deserves', 'wants', or even 'enjoys' the abuse). This is more likely to be destructive if the maltreatment is perpetrated by a family member. Even when this is not the case, parents' ignorance of maltreatment taking place outside the home may invalidate the child's communications with the parents about his/her feelings. The child finds that reflective discourse does not correspond to these feelings, a consistent misunderstanding that could reduce the child's ability to understand/ mentalise verbal explanations of other people's actions. In such circumstances, the child is likely to struggle to detect mental states behind actions, and will tend to see these actions as inevitable rather than intended. This formulation implies that treatments should aim to engage maltreated children in causally coherent psychological discourse.

The speculations above clearly imply that the foundations of subjective selfhood will be less robustly established in individuals who have experienced early neglect. Such individuals will find it harder to learn about how subjective experiences inevitably vary between people. In some longitudinal investigations, low parental affection or nurturing in early childhood appears more strongly associated with elevated risk for borderline, antisocial, paranoid, and schizotypal PDs diagnosed in early adulthood than even physical or sexual abuse in adolescence

(Johnson et al. 2006). A number of studies have pointed to the importance of neglect, low parental involvement, and emotional maltreatment rather than the presence of abuse as the critical predictor of severe PD (e.g. Johnson et al. 2001). Studies of family context of childhood trauma in borderline personality disorder (BPD) tend to see the unstable, non-nurturing family environment as the key social mediator of abuse (Bradley et al. 2005), while under-involvement is the best predictor of suicide (Johnson et al. 2002) and personality dysfunction (Zweig-Frank & Paris 1991).

We have argued that insecure and unpredictable attachment relationships between parent and infant may create an adverse social environment that limits the infant's opportunity to acquire 'mind-reading'. But why should evolution allow for such variation if mentalising is such a valuable adaptive capacity? In social environments where resources are limited, non-mentalising might be adaptive. The parent's lack of mirroring behaviour might serve as a signal for limited resources, warning the child that he/she will need to use physical force (even interpersonal violence) to survive. Violence is incompatible with mentalisation (Fonagy 2003b, 2003c). If violence rather than collaboration is required to survive, and violence is possible only when we avoid contemplating the mental state of the victim, then the child's lack of mentalising capacity could increase his/her chances of survival. By contrast, in resource-rich environments, adult carer-teachers are in a better position to facilitate the child's access to subjectivity. If parent–child interaction lacks marking, contingency, and other ostensive cues, mentalisation will be less firmly established and more readily abandoned under emotional stress. The child may then manifest early aggression and conduct problems (Lyons-Ruth 1996). From the point of view of appropriate intervention, it is probably more helpful to view this kind of aggression as an understandable adaptation rather than demonising it as an incomprehensible genetic aberration, even if these behaviours are primed in some individuals by a very sizeable genetic component (e.g. Silberg et al. 2007).

Attachment and the development of personality disorders

One of the areas where attachment is being particularly applied is in our understanding and treatment of PDs (Aaronson et al. 2006; Adshead & Sarkar 2012; Bakermans-Kranenburg & Van IJzendoorn 2009; Brennan et al. 1998).

PDs are defined as enduring behaviours that have an intrapersonal component (dysregulation of arousal, impulse and affect), an interpersonal component (dysfunctional relationship patterns), and a social component (which creates conflicts with others and with social institutions) (Adshead & Sarkar 2012) and has significant implications for an adult's capacity for managing in society and as a parent. Attachment theory accounts for these four characteristics of PDs (Westen et al. 2006) and provides an ideal standpoint from which to understand these disorders.

Good-quality interactions with early caregivers are the critical element in the development of secure attachment. In turn, secure emotional attachment is crucial for the development of a healthy personality (Braun & Bock 2011). It is thus unsurprising that there is a high prevalence of childhood trauma in both insecurely attached individuals and patients with PDs (Bakermans-Kranenburg & Van IJzendoorn 2009; Buchheim *et al.* 2008; Gabbard 2005; Lyons-Ruth *et al.* 2005; Riggs *et al.* 2007; Teicher *et al.* 2002). Further childhood trauma is strongly correlated with an incoherent/disorganised adult attachment style more than just to the general category of attachment insecurity (Barone 2003; Westen *et al.* 2006).

Among individuals with PDs, rates of childhood trauma are high (73% report abuse, of which 34% is sexual abuse, and 82% report neglect). Compared with healthy adults, PD patients are four times as likely to have suffered early trauma (Johnson *et al.* 1999). Childhood physical abuse increases the risk for adult antisocial, borderline, dependent, depressive, passive-aggressive, and schizoid PDs (McGauley *et al.* 2011). Infantile neglect is associated with risks for antisocial, avoidant, borderline, narcissistic and passive-aggressive PDs (Battle *et al.* 2004; Bennett 2005; Johnson *et al.* 1999).

BPD is more consistently associated with childhood abuse and neglect than other PD diagnoses (Baird *et al.* 2005; Battle *et al.* 2004; Buchheim *et al.* 2008; Fonagy & Bateman 2008; Fonagy *et al.* 2003; Johnson *et al.* 1999; Teicher *et al.* 2002). Obsessive-compulsive PD has been associated with sexual abuse by non-caretakers (Battle *et al.* 2004). However, not all people who have suffered childhood trauma develop adult psychopathology. The effects of trauma are mediated by attachment (Riggs *et al.* 2007) and by biological dispositions. For example, female victims of maltreatment and sexual abuse in adolescence or adulthood are at greater risk of developing posttraumatic symptoms if they have an anxious attachment style (Sandberg *et al.* 2010). Likewise, female victims of childhood trauma are more likely to develop somatisation symptoms if they are fearfully attached (Waldinger *et al.* 2006). If traumatic events provoke an activation of the attachment system, then individuals who tend to respond to these experiences through the inhibition of mentalising function and emotional regulation are less likely to resolve these events, and more likely to manifest personality pathology later in life (Bateman & Fonagy 2012).

An environment in which a child experiences insecure and unpredictable attachment relations might be expected to disrupt the acquisition of robust mentalisation or 'mind-reading'. However, within the contexts of deprivation and risk, mentalisation could hold the key to breaking the cycle of abuse and deprivation for that child growing up, and for the children he/she later has. BPD is characterised by the holding of schematic, extreme views and the display of powerful emotions and impulsive behaviour. According to our theory, this can be seen as a failure, or breakdown, of mentalising, brought about by overpowering emotional arousal, the activation of attachment needs, or by a strong impulse to deflect attention away from threat or hostility as a consequence of severe maltreatment. There are, therefore, significant clinical implications of this mentalisation-based approach to BPD; helping to improve the capacity to mentalise, particularly in relation to traumatic experiences, enables the individual to resist difficulties in affect regulation and the pull back toward modes of primitive mental functioning.

Conclusions

Secure attachment is the firm expectation of distress being met with comfort and reassurance. But beyond this, because secure attachment facilitates the emergence of psychic structures linked to emotion, the entire representational system is likely to be more stable and coherent with a history of generally secure attachment experiences. The way we experience thoughts, including attachment-related thoughts and the cognitive structures that underpin these, may be seen as linked to physical aspects of early infantile experience. Attachment immediately takes centre stage once we recognise the physical origins of thought. We now see insecure patterns of attachment as adaptations that maximise the chances of survival of the infant to reproductive maturity despite adverse conditions for child-rearing. Continuing to cry when comforted may bring vital resources when individual attention is a rare commodity.

Bowlby was right that it is not hunger and nurturance that provide the evolutionary key. The drive for the process of bonding is the experience of the infant's body (his/her movements) as allowing him/her to control the caregiver's responses (Watson 2001). This is primarily a physical, sensory-motor experience. In this sense attachment theory may be closer in spirit to the emerging neuroscience approach of embodied cognition than it is to traditional cognitive psychology.

Missing out on early attachment experience (as was the case for the Romanian orphans) creates a long-term vulnerability from which the child might never recover – the capacity for mentalisation is never fully established, leaving the child vulnerable to later trauma and unable to cope fully with attachment relationships (e.g. Rutter & O'Connor 2004). More importantly, by activating attachment, trauma will often decouple the capacity for mentalisation. This, of course, is further exacerbated when the trauma is attachment trauma. The capacity for mentalisation in the context of attachment is likely to be in certain respects independent of the capacity to mentalise about interpersonal experiences outside the attachment context (Fonagy & Target 1997).

Changes in cognitive science call for at least a partial review of some attachment ideas, seeing the brain as more continuous with the mind and seeing the mind as ever reflecting its bodily origin. We are increasingly aware that the brain is the organ of the mind and disorders of the mind are also disorders of the brain. We see that attachment relationships have a unique brain representation, and empathy or sensitivity depend on the effective functioning of specific brain centres. Considerable evidence is accumulating that disorders of the capacity to form relationships with one's infants or in adulthood can be characterised meaningfully at the level of brain activation. Attachment turns out to be more firmly embedded in the interface of bodily and environmental contexts than was the cognitive science of the 1970s. Cognitive neuroscience, psychoanalysis, and new attachment theory can come together in the foregrounding of feeling and the confluence of thought, bodily states and action. Attachment has been selected by evolution as the principal 'training ground' for the acquisition of mentalisation. It is the evolutionary instrument for humanity's most defining feature: the capacity for a rich social understanding that makes use of a wide range of intentional states, and which can seek to fathom both our self and others.

References

Aaronson, C. J., Bender, D. S., Skodol, A. E., & Gunderson, J. G. (2006). Comparison of attachment styles in borderline personality disorder and obsessive-compulsive personality disorder. *Psychiatric Quarterly, 77*, 69–80.

Adshead, G., & Sarkar, J. (2012). The nature of personality disorder. *Advances in Psychiatric Treatment, 18*, 162–172.

Alessandri, S. M. (1991). Play and social behaviours in maltreated preschoolers. *Development and Psychopathology, 3*, 191–206.

Anderson, S. E., Gooze, R. A., Lemeshow, S., & Whitaker, R. C. (2012). Quality of early maternal–child relationship and risk of adolescent obesity. *Pediatrics, 129*, 132–140.

Arnsten, A. F. T. (1998). The biology of being frazzled. *Science, 280*, 1711–1712.

Arnsten, A. F. T., Mathew, R., Ubriani, R., Taylor, J. R., & Li, B.-M. (1999). Alpha-1 noradrenergic receptor stimulation impairs prefrontal cortical cognitive function. *Biological Psychiatry, 45*, 26–31.

Baird, A. A., Veague, H. B., & Rabbitt, C. E. (2005). Developmental precipitants of borderline personality disorder. *Development and Psychopathology, 17*, 1031–1049.

Bakermans-Kranenburg, M. J., & Van IJzendoorn, M. H. (2009). The first 10,000 Adult Attachment Interviews: Distributions of adult attachment representations in clinical and non-clinical groups. *Attachment and Human Development, 11*, 223–263.

Barone, L. (2003). Developmental protective and risk factors in borderline personality disorder: A study using the Adult Attachment Interview. *Attachment and Human Development, 5*, 64–77.

Barone, L., Fossati, A., & Guiducci, V. (2011). Attachment mental states and inferred pathways of development in borderline personality disorder: A study using the Adult Attachment Interview. *Attachment and Human Development, 13*, 451–469.

Bateman, A. W., & Fonagy, P. (eds) (2012). *Handbook of Mentalizing in Mental Health Practice*. Washington, DC: American Psychiatric Publishing.

Battle, C. L., Shea, M. T., Johnson, D. M., Yen, S., Zlotnick, C., Zanarini, M. C. et al. (2004). Childhood maltreatment associated with adult personality disorders: Findings from the Collaborative Longitudinal Personality Disorders Study. *Journal of Personality Disorders, 18*, 193–211.

Belsky, J., Routs, R., & Fearon, P. (2010). Infant attachment security and the timing of puberty: Testing an evolutionary hypothesis. *Psychological Studies, 21*, 1195–1201.

Bennett, C. S. (2005). Attachment theory and research applied to the conceptualization and treatment of pathological narcissism. *Clinical Social Work Journal, 34*, 45–60.

Botbol, M. (2010). Towards an integrative neuroscientific and psychodynamic approach to the transmission of attachment. *Journal of Physiology (Paris), 104*, 263–271.

Bowlby, J. (1959). Separation anxiety. *International Journal of Psycho-Analysis, 41*, 1–25.

Bowlby, J. (1969). *Attachment and Loss, Vol. 1: Attachment.* London: Hogarth Press and Institute of Psycho-Analysis.

Bowlby, J. (1973). *Attachment and Loss, Vol. 2: Separation: Anxiety and Anger.* London: Hogarth Press and Institute of Psycho-Analysis.

Bowlby, J. (1980). *Attachment and Loss, Vol. 3: Loss: Sadness and Depression.* London: Hogarth Press and Institute of Psycho-Analysis.

Bradley, R., Jenei, J., & Westen, D. (2005). Etiology of borderline personality disorder: Disentangling the contributions of intercorrelated antecedents. *Journal of Nervous and Mental Disease, 193,* 24–31.

Braun, K., & Bock, J. (2011). The experience-dependent maturation of prefronto-limbic circuits and the origin of developmental psychopathology: Implications for the pathogenesis and therapy of behavioural disorders. *Developmental Medicine and Child Neurology, 53 (Suppl. 4),* 14–18.

Brennan, K. A., Clark, C. L., & Shaver, P. R. (1998). Self-report measurement of adult attachment: An integrative overview. In J. A. Simpson & W. S. Rholes (eds), *Attachment Theory and Close Relationships* (pp. 46–76). New York: Guilford Press.

Bronfman, E., Parsons, E., & Lyons-Ruth, K. (1999). *Atypical Maternal Behavior Instrument for Assessment and Classification (AMBIANCE): Manual for coding disrupted affective communication, version 2. Unpublished manuscript.* Cambridge, MA: Harvard Medical School.

Buchheim, A., Erk, S., George, C., Kachele, H., Kircher, T., Martius, P., *et al.* (2008). Neural correlates of attachment trauma in borderline personality disorder: A functional magnetic resonance imaging study. *Psychiatry Research, 163,* 223–235.

Camras, L. A., Ribordy, S., Hill, J., Martino, S., Sachs, V., Spaccarelli, S., & Stefani, R. (1990). Maternal facial behavior and the recognition and production of emotional expression by maltreated and nonmaltreated children. *Developmental Psychology, 26,* 304–312.

Camras, L. A., Sachs-Alter, E., & Ribordy, S. C. (1996). Emotion understanding in maltreated children: Recognition of facial expressions and integration with other emotion cues. In M. D. Lewis & M. Sullivan (eds), *Emotional Development in Atypical Children* (pp. 203–225). Mahwah, NJ: Erlbaum.

Carlson, E. A., Egeland, B., & Sroufe, L. A. (2009). A prospective investigation of the development of borderline personality symptoms. *Development and Psychopathology, 21,* 1311–1334.

Cicchetti, D., & Curtis, W. J. (2005). An event-related potential study of the processing of affective facial expressions in young children who experienced maltreatment during the first year of life. *Development and Psychopathology, 17,* 641–677.

Cicchetti, D., & Valentino, K. (2006). An ecological-transactional perspective on child maltreatment: Failure of the average expectable environment and its influence on child development. In D. Cicchetti & D. J. Cohen (eds), *Developmental Psychopathology* (2nd ed., Vol. 3, pp. 129–201). New York: John Wiley & Sons.

Cicchetti, D., & Walker, E. F. (2001). Editorial: Stress and development: Biological and psychological consequences. *Development and Psychopathology, 13,* 413–418.

Cicchetti, D., Rogosch, F. A., & Toth, S. L. (2000). The efficacy of toddler–parent psychotherapy for fostering cognitive development in offspring of depressed mothers. *Journal of Abnormal Child Psychology, 28,* 135–148.

Cicchetti, D., Rogosch, F. A., Maughan, A., Toth, S. L., & Bruce, J. (2003). False belief understanding in maltreated children. *Development and Psychopathology, 15,* 1067–1091.

Crandell, L. E., & Hobson, R. P. (1999). Individual differences in young children's IQ: A social-developmental perspective. *Journal of Child Psychology and Psychiatry, 40*, 455–464.

de Rosnay, M., & Harris, P. L. (2002). Individual differences in children's understanding of emotion: The roles of attachment and language. *Attachment and Human Development, 4*, 39–54.

During, S., & McMahon, R. (1991). Recognition of emotional facial expressions by abusive mothers and their children. *Journal of Clinical and Consulting Psychology, 20*, 132–139.

Farnfield, S., & Holmes, P. (eds) (2014) *The Routledge Handbook of Attachment: Assessment.* London and New York: Routledge.

Fearon, P., Bakermans-Kranenburg, M. J., Van IJzendoorn, M. H., Lapsley, A. M., & Roisman, G. I. (2010). The significance of insecure attachment and disorganization in the development of children's externalizing behavior: A meta-analytic study. *Child Development, 81*, 435–456.

Fonagy, P. (1991). Thinking about thinking: Some clinical and theoretical considerations in the treatment of a borderline patient. *International Journal of Psycho-Analysis, 72*, 1–18.

Fonagy, P. (2003a). The development of psychopathology from infancy to adulthood: The mysterious unfolding of disturbance in time. *Infant Mental Health Journal, 24*, 212–239.

Fonagy, P. (2003b). The developmental roots of violence in the failure of mentalization. In F. Pfäfflin & G. Adshead (eds), *A Matter of Security: The application of attachment theory to forensic psychiatry and psychotherapy* (pp. 13–56). London: Jessica Kingsley.

Fonagy, P. (2003c). Towards a developmental understanding of violence. *British Journal of Psychiatry, 183*, 190–192.

Fonagy, P., & Bateman, A. (2008). The development of borderline personality disorder: A mentalizing model. *Journal of Personality Disorders, 22*, 4–21.

Fonagy, P., & Target, M. (1997). Attachment and reflective function: Their role in self-organization. *Development and Psychopathology, 9*, 679–700.

Fonagy, P., & Target, M. (2005). Bridging the transmission gap: An end to an important mystery of attachment research? *Attachment and Human Development, 7*, 333–343.

Fonagy, P., Redfern, S., & Charman, T. (1997a). The relationship between belief-desire reasoning and a projective measure of attachment security (SAT). *British Journal of Developmental Psychology, 15*, 51–61.

Fonagy, P., Steele, H., Steele, M., & Holder, J. (1997b). Attachment and theory of mind: Overlapping constructs? *Association for Child Psychology and Psychiatry Occasional Papers, 14*, 31–40.

Fonagy, P., Gergely, G., Jurist, E., & Target, M. (2002). *Affect Regulation, Mentalization and the Development of the Self.* New York: Other Press.

Fonagy, P., Target, M., Gergely, G., Allen, J. G., & Bateman, A. (2003). The developmental roots of borderline personality disorder in early attachment relationships: A theory and some evidence. *Psychoanalytic Inquiry, 23*, 412–459.

Fonagy, P., Luyten, P., Bateman, A., Gergely, G., Strathearn, L., Target, M., & Allison, E. (2010). Attachment and personality pathology. In J. F. Clarkin, P. Fonagy & G. O. Gabbard (eds), *Psychodynamic Psychotherapy for Personality Disorders: A clinical handbook* (1st ed., pp. 37–88). Washington, DC: American Psychiatric Publishing.

Fonagy, P., Luyten, P., & Strathearn, L. (2011). Borderline personality disorder, mentalization, and the neurobiology of attachment. *Infant Mental Health Journal, 32*, 47–69.

Gabbard, G. O. (2005). Mind, brain, and personality disorders. *American Journal of Psychiatry, 162*, 648–655.

Gillath, O., Bunge, S. A., Shaver, P. R., Wendelken, C., & Mikulincer, M. (2005). Attachment-style differences in the ability to suppress negative thoughts: Exploring the neural correlates. *Neuroimage, 28*, 835–847.

Grienenberger, J., Kelly, K., & Slade, A. (2005). Maternal reflective functioning, mother–infant affective communication, and infant attachment: Exploring the link between mental states and observed caregiving behaviour in the intergenerational transmission of attachment. *Attachment and Human Development, 7*, 299–311.

Groh, A., Roisman, G., Van IJzendoorn, M., Bakermans-Kranenburg, M., & Fearon, R. (2012). The significance of insecure and disorganized attachment for children's internalizing symptoms: A meta-analytic study. *Child Development, 83*, 591–610.

Hamilton, W. D. (1964). The genetic evolution of social behaviour. *Journal of Theoretical Biology, 7*, 1–52.

Harris, P. (2005). Conversation, pretence and theory of mind. In J. Astington & J. Baird (eds), *Why Language Matters for Theory of Mind* (pp. 70–83). New York: Oxford University Press.

Hill, J., Fonagy, P., Safier, E., & Sargent, J. (2003). The ecology of attachment in the family. *Family Process, 42*, 205–221.

Holmes, P., & Farnfield, S. (eds) (2014). *The Routledge Handbook of Attachment: Implications and interventions*. London and New York: Routledge.

Insel, T. R. (2003). Is social attachment an addictive disorder? *Physiology & Behavior, 79*, 351–357.

Johnson, J. G., Cohen, P., Brown, J., Smailes, E. M., & Bernstein, D. P. (1999). Childhood maltreatment increases risk for personality disorders during early adulthood. *Archives of General Psychiatry, 56*, 600–605.

Johnson, J. G., Cohen, P., Smailes, E., Skodol, A., Brown, J., & Oldham, J. (2001). Childhood verbal abuse and risk for personality disorders during adolescence and early adulthood. *Comprehensive Psychiatry, 42*, 16–23.

Johnson, J. G., Cohen, P., Gould, M. S., Kasen, S., Brown, J., & Brook, J. S. (2002). Childhood adversities, interpersonal difficulties, and risk for suicide attempts during late adolescence and early adulthood. *Archives of General Psychiatry, 59*, 741–749.

Johnson, J. G., Cohen, P., Kasen, S., Ehrensaft, M. K., & Crawford, T. N. (2006). Associations of parental personality disorders and axis I disorders with childrearing behavior. *Psychiatry, 69*, 336–350.

Klimes-Dougan, B., & Kistner, J. (1990). Physically abused preschoolers' responses to peers' distress. *Developmental Psychology, 25*, 516–524.

Kochanska, G., & Kim, S. (2013). Early attachment organization with both parents and future behavior problems: From infancy to middle childhood. *Child Development, 84*, 283–296.

Levy, K. N., Ellison, W. D., Scott, L. N., & Bernecker, S. L. (2011). Attachment style. *Journal of Clinical Psychology, 67*, 193–203.

Lyons-Ruth, K. (1996). Attachment relationships among children with aggressive behavior problems: The role of disorganized early attachment patterns. *Journal of Consulting and Clinical Psychology, 64*, 32–40.

Lyons-Ruth, K., & Block, D. (1996). The disturbed caregiving system: Relations among childhood trauma, maternal caregiving and infant affect and attachment. *Infant Mental Health Journal, 17*, 257–275.

Lyons-Ruth, K., Yellin, C., Melnick, S., & Atwood, G. (2005). Expanding the concept of unresolved mental states: Hostile/helpless states of mind on the Adult Attachment Interview are associated with disrupted mother-infant communication and infant disorganization. *Development and Psychopathology, 17*, 1–23.

Main, M. (2000). The organized categories of infant, child and adult attachment: Flexible vs. inflexible attention under attachment-related stress. *Journal of the American Psychoanalytic Association, 48*, 1055–1096.

Main, M., & Solomon, J. (1986). Discovery of an insecure-disorganized/disoriented attachment pattern. In T. B. Brazelton & M. W. Yogman (eds), *Affective Development in Infancy*. Norwood, NJ: Ablex.

Main, M., Kaplan, N., & Cassidy, J. (1985). Security in infancy, childhood, and adulthood: A move to the level of representation. *Monographs of the Society for Research in Child Development, 50*, 66–104.

Maughan, A., & Cicchetti, D. (2002). Impact of child maltreatment and interadult violence on children's emotion regulation abilities and socioemotional adjustment. *Child Development, 73*, 1525–1542.

Mayes, L. C. (2000). A developmental perspective on the regulation of arousal states. *Seminars in Perinatology, 24*, 267–279.

McGauley, G., Yakeley, J., Williams, A., & Bateman, A. (2011). Attachment, mentalization and antisocial personality disorder: The possible contribution of mentalization-based treatment. *European Journal of Psychotherapy and Counselling, 13*, 371–393.

Meaney, M. J., & Szyf, M. (2005). Environmental programming of stress responses through DNA methylation: Life at the interface between a dynamic environment and a fixed genome. *Dialogues in Clinical Neuroscience, 7*, 103–123.

Meins, E., Fernyhough, C., Fradley, E., & Tuckey, M. (2001). Rethinking maternal sensitivity: Mothers' comments on infants' mental processes predict security of attachment at 12 months. *Journal of Child Psychology and Psychiatry, 42*, 637–648.

Meins, E., Fernyhough, C., Wainwright, R., Das Gupta, M., Fradley, E., & Tuckey, M. (2002). Maternal mind-mindedness and attachment security as predictors of theory of mind understanding. *Child Development, 73*, 1715–1726.

Meins, E., Fernyhough, C., Wainwright, R., Clark-Carter, D., Das Gupta, M., Fradley, E., & Tuckey, M. (2003). Pathways to understanding mind: Construct validity and predictive validity of maternal mind-mindedness. *Child Development, 74*, 1194–1211.

Nolte, T., Guiney, J., Fonagy, P., Mayes, L. C., & Luyten, P. (2011). Interpersonal stress regulation and the development of anxiety disorders: An attachment-based developmental framework. *Frontiers in Behavioral Neuroscience, 5*, 55.

Oppenheim, D., & Koren-Karie, N. (2002). Mothers' insightfulness regarding their children's internal worlds: The capacity underlying secure child-mother relationships. *Infant Mental Health Journal, 23*, 593–605.

Pears, K. C., & Fisher, P. A. (2005). Emotion understanding and theory of mind among maltreated children in foster care. *Development and Psychopathology, 17*, 47–65.

Puig, J., Englund, M. M., Simpson, J. A., & Collins, W. A. (2012). Predicting adult physical illness from infant attachment: A prospective longitudinal study. *Health Psychology, 32*, 409–417.

Riggs, S. A., Sahl, G., Greenwald, E., Atkison, H., Paulson, A., & Ross, C. A. (2007). Family environment and adult attachment as predictors of psychopathology and personality dysfunction among inpatient abuse survivors. *Violence and Victims, 22*, 577–600.

Rogosch, F. A., Cicchetti, D., & Aber, J. L. (1995). The role of child maltreatment in early deviations in cognitive and affective processing abilities and later peer relationship problems. *Development and Psychopathology, 7*, 591–609.

Rutter, M., & O'Connor, T. G. (2004). Are there biological programming effects for psychological development? Findings from a study of Romanian adoptees. *Developmental Psychology, 40*, 81–94.

Sandberg, D. A., Suess, E. A., & Heaton, J. L. (2010). Attachment anxiety as a mediator of the relationship between interpersonal trauma and posttraumatic symptomatology among college women. *Journal of Interpersonal Violence, 25*, 33–49.

Sharp, C., Fonagy, P., & Goodyer, I. M. (2006). Imagining your child's mind: Psychosocial adjustment and mothers' ability to predict their children's attributional response styles. *British Journal of Developmental Psychology, 24*, 197–214.

Shipman, K. L., & Zeman, J. (1999). Emotional understanding: A comparison of physically maltreating and nonmaltreating mother–child dyads. *Journal of Clinical Child Psychology, 28*, 407–417.

Siegel, D. J. (1999). *The Developing Mind: Toward a neurobiology of interpersonal experience*. New York: The Guilford Press.

Silberg, J. L., Rutter, M., Tracy, K., Maes, H. H., & Eaves, L. (2007). Etiological heterogeneity in the development of antisocial behavior: The Virginia Twin Study of Adolescent Behavioral Development and the Young Adult Follow-Up. *Psychological Medicine, 37*, 1193–1202.

Slade, A., Grienenberger, J., Bernbach, E., Levy, D., & Locker, A. (2005). Maternal reflective functioning, attachment, and the transmission gap: A preliminary study. *Attachment and Human Development, 7*, 283–298.

Smith, M., & Walden, T. (1999). Understanding feelings and coping with emotional situations: A comparison of maltreated and nonmaltreated preschoolers. *Social Development, 8*, 93–116.

Teicher, M. H., Andersen, S. L., Polcari, A., Anderson, C. M., & Navalta, C. P. (2002). Developmental neurobiology of childhood stress and trauma. *Psychiatric Clinics of North America, 25*, 397–426, vii–viii.

Toth, S. L., Cicchetti, D., Macfie, J., Maughan, A., & Vanmeenen, K. (2000). Narrative representations of caregivers and self in maltreated pre-schoolers. *Attachment and Human Development, 2*, 271–305.

Waldinger, R. J., Schulz, M. S., Barsky, A. J., & Ahern, D. K. (2006). Mapping the road from childhood trauma to adult somatization: The role of attachment. *Psychosomatic Medicine, 68*, 129–135.

Waters, E., Merrick, S. K., Treboux, D., Crowell, J., & Albersheim, L. (2000). Attachment security from infancy to early adulthood: A 20 year longitudinal study. *Child Development, 71*, 684–689.

Watson, J. S. (2001). Contingency perception and misperception in infancy: Some potential implications for attachment. *Bulletin of the Menninger Clinic, 65*, 296–320.

Westen, D., Nakash, O., Thomas, C., & Bradley, R. (2006). Clinical assessment of attachment patterns and personality disorder in adolescents and adults. *Journal of Consulting and Clinical Psychology, 74*, 1065–1085.

Zweig-Frank, H., & Paris, J. (1991). Parents' emotional neglect and overprotection according to the recollections of patients with borderline personality disorder. *American Journal of Psychiatry, 148*, 648–651.

Chapter 3

The Dynamic-Maturational Model (DMM) of attachment

Steve Farnfield and Martin Stokowy

Introduction

This chapter gives an introduction to Patricia Crittenden's Dynamic-Maturational Model (DMM) of attachment in terms of its theoretical underpinnings and array of strategies. The DMM represents a significant split from the mainstream of attachment theory, a split which, like many family disagreements, has generated considerable emotional heat at times while the origins of the arguments are difficult to locate.

The intellectual debate tends to coalesce around the concept of 'disorganisation'. Put simply Mary Ainsworth's pioneering work on the Strange Situation procedure (SSP) identified three types of infant attachment behaviour which Ainsworth and Bowlby decided to call A, B and C until they had a better idea of what they meant (Karen 1998) (see also Van Rosmalen *et al.* Chapter 1 and Fonagy *et al.* Chapter 2 in this book). However, there were a number of video tapes that did not fit the ABC categories, some of which involved infants who had been maltreated. In 1982 Mary Ainsworth discussed these anomalies with two of her students, Mary Main and Patricia Crittenden. Their debate focused on the discrepancy between the observed behaviour (about which they mostly agreed) and the meaning of this behaviour, on which they deeply disagreed (Crittenden, personal communication). This was a crucial meeting which set off two branches of research and theorising.

On one side, Main and Solomon conceptualised the discrepant infant behaviour in terms of collapses or interruptions to organised behaviour when under stress (an approach-avoidance conflict when faced with a frightened or frightening attachment figure) which they termed 'disorganized and/or disorientated' together with a best fitting Type A, B, C category (Main & Solomon 1986, 1990; Main 1995; see also Shemmings in Chapter 5).

For her part, Crittenden interpreted most of the same behaviours in terms of alternating use of the A and C strategies or A/C together with precursors of what she later called in the DMM A3-4 and C3-4 patterns. The DMM further subdivides the A and C types into subgroups as we describe below (Crittenden 1985, 1995). The alternating Type A/C was also proposed by Radke-Yarrow and colleagues (Radke-Yarrow *et al.* 1985).

This analysis of the atypical infant responses to the SSP established two pathways of theory and research which we refer to as ABC + D and the DMM; the second of which is the subject of this chapter.

Back to Darwin: the environment of evolutionary adaptedness

Bowlby was fascinated by both Darwin's scientific theories and by Darwin as a man and published a biography of him (Bowlby 1991). Attachment has been described as a middle level evolutionary theory (Simpson & Belsky 2008) in that it can use empirical research to test aspects of a universal or grand theory (Darwin's evolutionary theory) (Merton 1949). The function of attachment is to protect the self and one's progeny long enough for our genes to be passed on through succeeding generations. In order to understand how this process developed Bowlby argued it is necessary to establish a model of the environment of evolutionary adaptedness (EEA) in which our ancestors lived for two million years (Bowlby 1969).

Adaptation to different environmental conditions requires not one but a variety of responses for both self-protection and reproduction and survival of the species. Bowlby and Ainsworth wanted to explain the conditions under which the insecure A and C infant patterns might be functional. However, despite Bowlby's emphasis on the threats posed by climate and predators there was a tendency among early attachment theorists to privilege secure attachment over the insecure patterns (Simpson & Belsky 2008). The result was that balanced or secure Type B became something of a 'natural' or desired state, while the A and C variants were seen as pathological.

Crittenden goes back to the evolutionary roots of the theory by emphasising danger, not safety, as the dominant feature of the EEA. By extension she argues that no single attachment strategy[1] has primacy over others, so that humans will have evolved a variety of responses to danger in order to maximise survival and reproductive fitness (passing on our genes). In doing so Crittenden ties together survival, which was the focus of much of the early work on infant attachment, with mate selection, sexual behaviour and reproduction (Crittenden 2002, 2008).

Just as survival is enhanced by the availability of a range of self-protective strategies, so reproductive success is increased by various forms of mate selection and caregiving (parenting). To give an example, when conditions are safe people can defer reproduction and have fewer children on whom they can devote more attention. Conversely harsh environments, such as those involving poverty or conflict, are conducive to earlier reproduction and having more children for whom parental resources are spread more thinly (Simpson & Belsky 2008; Barkow et al. 1992).

Taken together, staying alive and reproducing constitute the basic biological imperatives of any species. For humans, these result in three related, but sometimes competing, motivations: protecting the self, finding a sexual partner, and protecting one's progeny until they reach reproductive maturity (Crittenden 2008: 11).

Thus Crittenden defines attachment as having three equally important aspects:

1   a unique, enduring, and affectively charged relationship (e.g., with one's mother, with one's spouse);
2   a strategy for protecting oneself (of which there are three basic strategies, Types A, B, and C, as identified by Ainsworth, and many sub-strategies, as described by the DMM);
3   The pattern of information processing that underlies the strategies.

(Crittenden 2008: 12)

Dispositional representations

Information processing was introduced into attachment theory by Bolwby (1980) and provides the motor for DMM theory. We give a brief introduction in the next section before presenting the array of DMM strategies, after which we return to information processing, in terms of memory systems, in more detail.

The human brain is conceptualised by Crittenden as an organ devoted to receiving signals from the body together with stimulae from the environment in order to generate meaning regarding danger and sexual opportunity. The word 'mind' can be construed as referring to the mental representations of this information which occur at both conscious and unconscious levels (Crittenden 1994). These mental representations are continually reworked according to the intensity of the stimulae and the perceived levels of threat in the environment.

Current work in cognitive neuroscience, which was unavailable to Bowlby, indicates that representation is an active process with more than one representation being generated for every interaction with attachment figures and, indeed, all other situations. For example, that most cited of attachment figures, your mother, does not exist as a complete person in a single site of your brain but all over it in many Dispositional Representations (Damasio 1994). Damasio uses the term 'Dispositional Representations' to indicate the wide range of possibilities that come to mind every time you think about 'your mother'. These possible mothers are the product of all the interactions you have had with her over time, including the thoughts you have had about her when she was not even there.[2] When you think about 'mother' she will be reconstructed in a variety of ways: her voice, odour, face, caress and so on. And every time you think about her the mothers in your mind are reworked. Hence memories are not so much pictures in the head but the traces in the brain made by the last time your mother came to mind (Damasio 2000).

To match this complexity of representation, Crittenden has replaced Bowlby's use of the 'internal working model' with the term 'Dispositional Representations' (DRs) (Crittenden 2006). A DR of attachment is a disposition to act that connects the child or person to the context in a particular way, together with an expected outcome of their action (Crittenden, personal communication). DRs are physiological or bodily states. They lie dormant and implicit but many of them can be made explicit at any time and simultaneously. In developmental terms, Damasio sees layers of DRs beginning with genetically given dispositions, those acquired in the interaction of genes and the environment (Bowlby's first three phases of attachment, see Marvin & Britner 2008) and, living in the shadow of these layers, dispositions that are formed and constantly reworked by autobiographical or episodic memory (phase 4 and the rest of your life) (Damasio 2000). The mother in your brain exists in different sites and Type B mental integration (associated with the highest level of mentalisation see Allen 2013) depends on interconnections between these sites (see Damasio 2000: 223).

Seen like this, the approach/flight response of 'disorganised' infants is the result of a conflict between the genetic disposition to attach (approach and seek safety) and the learning that has taken place following abuse or rejection that approach to a 'secure base' might not bring safety. The availability of a conscious autobiographical or episodic memory (see below) would offer the possibility of a more organised response which, in many cases, is what happens; i.e. with development disorganised infants develop an organised, albeit insecure, attachment strategy (Main & Cassidy 1988; Solomon & George 2011).

Rather than an aberration, multiple, and possibly mutually conflicting, dispositions actually appear to be the norm. What matters is the ability to organise them in the mind which, in turn, means the various dispositions of mother are brought together and integrated in convergence zones in the brain; a position very similar to the one predicted by Bowlby (1973). This can only be done under conditions of moderate arousal (i.e. safety).

Transformations of information: cognition and affect

Transformation of sensory information produces meaning in the mind. In line with Bowlby's 'defensive exclusion', insecure attachment strategies can be defined in terms of how the mind distorts or omits information which, if it were psychologically available for processing, would increase anxiety to unbearable levels (Bowlby 1980). Conversely, secure Type B attachment involves a relatively low level of distortion or omission associated with greater periods of safety, which allow reflection, and lower levels of anxiety.

In the DMM the simplest forms of transformation of information are organised according to cognition and affect, i.e. two of the three traditional dimensions of mental functioning (Le Doux 2002). The third is motivation, which in the DMM refers to protection of the self from danger and, in adulthood, sex and reproduction together with protection of our offspring.

Crittenden's use of the term cognition is restricted to learned behaviour based on temporal order. In the DMM-based analysis of the Adult Attachment Interview (AAI) speech patterns (discourse analysis), cognitive statements typically take a when/then or if/then form. For example, 'When my gran was at home I knew my father wouldn't touch me'. Cognition provides information about the relationship between events or causality. Crittenden refers to this as the 'when' in a sequence of one's behaviour there might be danger or sexual opportunity.

In Crittenden's theory affect refers to the intensity of feelings when under stress, with particular emphasis on three physical states: the *desire* for comfort and nurture which motivates approach; *anger* (fight); and *fear* of hurt or abandonment (flight or freezing). Affective information is tied to the context; a sudden noise or eerie silence; the smell of alcohol or feeling someone is behind you – all signal changes in the environment and indicate 'where' in relation to the self there might be danger or sexual opportunity (Crittenden & Landini 2011).

Both sources of information are prone to error. We can think or feel we are safe when we are actually in danger and vice versa. Crittenden lists seven transformations of cognitive and affective information:

- Truly predictive.
- Erroneous information.
- Distorted information such as idealising (Type A) or excessively blaming (Type C) an attachment figure.
- Omitted information. For example disregarding one's desire for comfort in Type A or the complexity of causal relations in Type C.
- False information such as smiles that cover anger: Type A+ false positive affect (below) or deception in Type C+ regarding the true intention of an aggressor.
- Denied information such as denial of negative affect in Type A or one's own part in causing a dangerous event in Type C.
- Delusional information. For example idealisation of an attachment figure who was actually abusive (Type A7 below) or delusional representations of the self as all-powerful and others as evil (Type C7-8).

Strategies: the Dynamic-Maturational Model of attachment

The DMM strategies are clustered in five developmental stages: infancy; preschool; school age; adolescence and adulthood. These stages offer the possibility of deepening the strategic use of existing strategies or reorganising to a new strategy that comes 'on stream' with increasing age and social, emotional and cognitive maturation. These possible developments are noted by the higher number added to the A and C attachment strategies (e.g. C4 or A5). In DMM notation a plus sign is used as a shorthand to convey DMM strategies A3-8 (i.e. A+) and C3-8 (C+).

Infancy

Figure 3.1 depicts the Ainsworth ABC infant strategies which are observable in the SSP at 11 to 15 months (Ainsworth *et al.* 1978; Ainsworth & Wittig 1969) together with the DMM extensions (see above). Coding of A1-2, B1-4 and C1-2 strategies produces similar results whichever system of analysis (ABC + D or DMM) is used. Crittenden added B5.

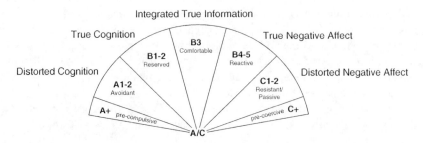

Figure 3.1 Infant attachment strategies (Dr Patricia Crittenden: with permission)

Infants in Type B have integrated cognitive and affective information – 'I feel cold, I cry, my mother comes, she does useful things, I feel better.' Needless to say this is done at a procedural not conscious level but affective signals from the child predictably elicit positive outcomes.

Infants in Type A1-2 have attachment figures who reject unnecessary displays of attachment seeking behaviour. These infants learn to control the display of negative affect (anger/desire for comfort) forbidden by their parents, thus taking something of their parent's perspective on what is 'good' or 'bad' about their own behaviour. Although all infants do this, those in Type A1-2 overemphasise the need to inhibit the feelings adults in their life dislike. Their carers tend to be protective but not comforting and so for the children cognition is a better predictor of how to act than affect which can lead to trouble.

The proportion of infants in normative samples whose behaviour is rated Type C in the SSP is about 6–7 per cent (Cassibba *et al.* 2013) but shows a rise in the preschool years (NICHD 2001) with, what in the UK is called the 'terrible twos' for whom expressed affect is all powerful. Not all cultures identify toddlers as difficult, suggesting perhaps that the Type A in British society has found displays of affect difficult to manage!

Crittenden argues that the organisation of coercive (Type C) behaviour depends on the growing ability of toddlers to understand the impact of their behaviour on their attachment figures; i.e. emergent mentalising (the capacity to understand the minds of other people) can be used cooperatively to solve problems, as in Type B, or to regulate the behaviour of others (Type C) (Crittenden 2000).

The attachment figures of children in Type C1-2 tend to be comforting and responsive at least some of the time (they are inconsistently emotionally available to the child), typically attending to behaviour they express not to want while ignoring positive behaviour. In order to maintain parental attention their children learn to exaggerate the display of strong or negative affect: Type C1 (threateningly angry strategies to obtain attention and comfort) and C2 (disarmingly and demandingly desirous of comfort). Infants in Type C rely on affective logic rather than cognitive information.

The criteria for D (Disorganised and/or disorientated; Main & Solomon 1990) overlap with the DMM subclassifications; that is A/C, pre-compulsive and pre-coercive.

The infant ABC strategies do not necessarily mature into higher DMM subscripts. That is, a child may start in Type B and remain secure for the rest of her life, likewise children in Types A1-2 and C1-2. Although the strategic range of their attachment behaviour will expand with age and experience the self-protective function of the ABC strategies remains the same; i.e. people in A inhibit negative affect, those in C exaggerate one or more negative affects and those in Type B use these strategies in an even-handed and integrated way.

Preschool and school age

The preschool and school years are combined in Figure 3.2.

Types A and C

A3 and 4

One of Crittenden's major contributions to understanding development under less than optimal conditions is compulsivity in the Type A+ strategies. Whereas infants in Type A1-2 learn to inhibit unnecessary displays of forbidden negative affect, maturation in the preschool years enables more threatened children to increase the strategy by displays of false positive affect (e.g. smiling when feeling rejected) which function to elicit adult approval. Compulsive behaviour means the child or adult feels compelled to act in certain ways in order to maximise the possibility of safety. This concept has strong antecedents in the literature including Winnicott's

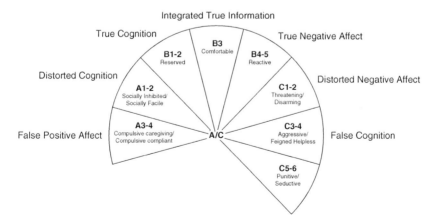

Figure 3.2 Strategies in the preschool and school years (Dr Patricia Crittenden: with permission)

observations on a 'false self' (Winnicott 1960) and Ferenczi's on the child as a little psychiatrist who learns to read the behaviour of mad and abusive adults thus taking on the perspective of her aggressors (Ferenczi 1933).

Pre-schoolers in Type A3 (compulsive caregiving) inhibit the desire for comfort and nurture while displaying a false brightness that functions to maintain the psychological availability of carers who are, typically, withdrawn and sometimes depressed and thus consistently emotionally absent for the child. Some of these children are predicted to go on to become health and social care professionals while those in Type A1-2 may enter professions that stress the importance of cognition and the inhibition of overtly expressed emotion, such as academics or lawyers.

Those in Type A4 (compulsive compliance) inhibit anger and conform to the demands of controlling, sometimes frankly abusive parents (Crittenden 1992b; Crittenden & Landini 2011: 158ff.).

Subtypes of these strategies are Type A3- (compulsive attention to a psychologically needy but not abusive or withdrawn parent) and Type A4- compulsive performance in which parental approval, and hence affirmation of the self, is achieved at the expense of becoming the child parents want (excelling academically or in sports, for example).

C3 and 4

The term coy behaviour was first used by Hinde (1982). The crucial (intrinsic biological) features of coy behaviour are: exposure of neck, belly, and genitals, smiling with covered teeth, looking out of the corner of the eyes, a 'broken ankle' stance, and the no weapons or praying hands. All these behaviours signal that the child is no threat and adorable. Used on its own coy behaviour enables a 'cute kid' to elicit positive attention from adults and, when used in conjunction with threatening or even aggressive behaviour, disarms adult authority and aggression. With practice this strategy can involve deception; Johnny in Type C3 is not as aggressive as he looks (inside he is anxious and vulnerable) and Hattie in Type C4 is not so cute and vulnerable as she appears (inside she is angry). Both children may alternate angry-disarming strategies according to adult responses, thus maintaining attention on themselves for considerable periods of time. This is particularly useful in circumstances where children are not only confronted with temporarily unavailable attachment figures, but are threatened by them or deceived regarding dangerous situations (Crittenden & Landini 2011: 197).

The similarity of (childlike) coy behaviour with (adult) sexual behaviour is of considerable importance as the sexual abuse of children frequently includes adult misinterpretation of childlike coy behaviour as sexual signals (Crittenden 2008: 26ff.).

C5 and 6

In the school years the DMM sees an extension on the C side with the C5-6 obsessive strategies (Crittenden 1994). These strategies develop when the relatively simple bluff of the C3-4 strategies no longer elicits parental attention and caregiving. Due to their maturing cognitive abilities, school-aged children are now much better able to deceive adults than they were in the preschool period. Their attachment figures are either unavailable or overprotective, may threaten or deceive the children. In particular, the family system is frequently organised around adult behaviours that involve the child without explaining the motives behind it (Marvin 2003; Dallos 2014); for example, Johnny is not daddy's child but everyone pretends he is while sometimes acting as if he is not. Johnny does not understand why and how things happen and tends to over-attribute the cause of problems to himself (note the massive problem Johnny has with source memory – see modifiers below).

A5 and 6

While caregiving conducive to Type C+ is enmeshed and triangulated the child in Type A+ finds no easy way of eliciting care (Marvin 2003; Dallos 2014). While children in Type C+ sometimes act as if they feel invisible and not held in the minds of their parents those in Type A+ act as if they would like to be invisible because they have a pervasive sense of shame.

Adolescence and adulthood

Figure 3.3 shows the A5-6 strategies available in adolescence together with the full range of DMM adult patterns.

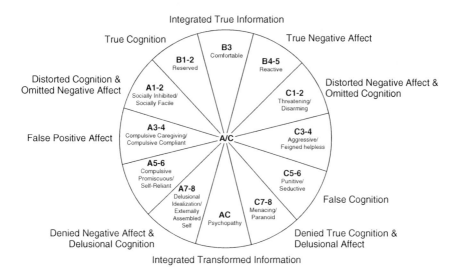

Figure 3.3 Adolescent and adult strategies (Dr Patricia Crittenden: with permission)

In adolescence, 'the onset of sexual desire and behaviour', writes Crittenden, 'changes . . . everything!' (Crittenden 2008: 55). With sexual maturity children in Type A+ face a contradictory imperative: sex requires a partner but intimacy in Type A promotes anxiety. Possible solutions to this are Type A5 compulsive promiscuity (sexual and/or social) and Type A6 compulsive self-reliance. In some cases these develop out of the failure of the Type A3-4 strategies to yield protection in the school years.

Attachment is often described as a theory of affect regulation. Crittenden highlights the difference between mid-range states of arousal, such as anger, desire for comfort, boredom, and the extremes such as rage, terror, depression. People in extremis 'live on the edge'; they experience and exhibit extreme emotional states which can alarm, frighten or sometimes seduce other people, including professionals, as well as jam other people's thought processes.

Arousal in Type A+ may swing from intensely low, depressed states, to outbursts of forbidden affects (see modifiers below) involving rage and or sexual aggression. The absence of an authentic self can lead to acts of self-harming which are designed not to worry and elicit the attention of others (as in Type C6) but as a last ditch effort to locate a self that can feel something, so that the intrusion of pain 'becomes the only and last resort to feeling alive' (Sahhar 2014).

Of particular interest is the confusion of anxious arousal, associated with self-protection, with sexual arousal. This is important for understanding situations where this confusion leads, for example, to child sexual abuse; intra-family incest where the perpetrator seeks comfort but misreads the child's behavioural signals and his own bodily signals. Note this approach to incest, as an adult comfort disorder, is counter to the dominant model of perpetrator power and grooming.

The crossover between sex and danger is of equal importance with regard to high states of sexual arousal which switch from aggression to submission (sado-masochistic sex), sexual terror and pain to possible death (Crittenden 2008). These are features of work with people in extremis and the DMM offers a way of thinking about them without resorting to moral judgements.

A7-8 and C7-8

Psychopathology in adulthood is seen in DMM terms as attempts at self-protection or finding a reproductive partner which are maladaptive. That is, strategies which were functional and self-protective when first developed in childhood have become dysfunctional because the environment and/or the self have changed (Crittenden 2002). In particular, strategies forged under dangerous circumstances may result in isolation or conflict when the context becomes safer.

Those people in Types A7-8 and C7-8 run high risks of psychopathology. Type A7 approximates to the Stockholm syndrome, whereby attachment figures who were life threateningly dangerous during childhood are now construed as protective and loving. This is also a likely outcome of abuse in an adult relationship (domestic violence). The Type A8 pattern reflects a loss of self-representation in the context of (normally very early) absent attachment figures, as in multiple out-of-home placements. Individuals using this pattern refer to the external world, in particular the opinions of doctors, therapists, social workers and official records and reports as a means of establishing their identity (Crittenden & Landini 2011).

Whereas anger/revenge and seductive vulnerability in the C5-6 strategies are focused, in C7-8, anger and or fear become pervasive to the point where comfort and safety are no longer deemed possible and overtures of nurture and concern from other people may be misread as concealed threats. Type C7 exaggerates anger menacingly, often in pre-emptive attacks, whereas Type C8 exaggerates fear to the point of paranoia. The C7-8 defences are likely forged in home environments where the child was deceived in order to be abused or where parental signals of love and nurture resulted in pain, rejection and humiliation. People in Type C7-8 are thus likely to be deeply suspicious of overtures of compassion and nurture from well meaning professionals in what the AAI terms Type naive B.

Survival under high levels of threat also heightens the risk of inflicting injury on the self and others. People in Type C5-8 are capable of becoming so consumed with revenge, for example, that they take risks with their own safety and those of their progeny. Risks in Type A+ include greater vulnerability to depression than the B and C strategies. This is due to the inhibition of forbidden negative affect together with over-attributing responsibility to the self for relationship problems. Intrusions of (forbidden) negative affect (INAs, see below) can result in explosions of rage or sexual violence with obvious consequences to the victim. Likewise the dismissal of other people's feelings in the C5-8 patterns enables sadistic, planned rather than spontaneous, attacks on other people.

One of the important aspects of this part of DMM theory is its relation to the work by Fonagy and colleagues on mentalising; the ability to differentiate between one's own mental states and those of other people (Allen 2013; and see Chapter 6). The capacity to mentalise adequately represents the optimum form of information processing in humans and so has a desired state rather similar to the primacy sometimes given to secure attachment. However, Crittenden emphasises that under some dangerous circumstances distortions of mentalising have more self-protective value than true mentalising. It can also be used to harm others. For example, intelligent psychopathy in the DMM – the integration of false, denied and delusional information – could result in accurate reading of other people's mental states in order to harm or exploit them (Crittenden & Landini 2011).

Lack of resolution of loss and trauma and modifiers

The DMM adult patterns together with most forms of lack of resolution and the modifiers were theorised by Crittenden from the coding of thousands of AAIs (Crittenden & Landini 2011: 336). This has been followed by a small but growing number of empirical studies using the DMM-AAI with clinical (e.g. Zachrisson & Kulbotten 2006; Ringer & Crittenden 2007; Crittenden & Newman 2010;

Farnfield in press) and normative populations (Strathearn *et al.* 2009; Shah *et al.* 2010; Hautamäki *et al.* 2010).

As noted above, the DMM A+ and C+ strategies are functional within the context under which they were developed. As a rough generalisation people in the top third (A1-2, B1-5 and C1-2) are expected to show few major psychosocial problems, those in the middle segments (A3-6 and C3-6) to run increasingly greater risks of such problems and those in the bottom part of the model (A7-8 and C7-8) are expected to experience major problems with a significant proportion showing up in clinical in-patient populations and prison. Likewise the further we go down the DMM model the greater the expected increase in unresolved loss and trauma.

Lack of resolution

Crittenden likens the impact of unresolved loss and trauma to land mines: we are proceeding using an established strategy when suddenly – boom! Bad things flood in from the past and our strategic Type A or C behaviour breaks down. In line with the psychiatric clusters of posttraumatic symptoms, lack of resolution follows a dismissed (Type A) or preoccupied (Type C) form; frequently the two are combined in an alternating fashion. Unresolved loss (typically death of an attachment figure or sibling) also involves the dismissal and/or preoccupation with the impact of the death on the self.

In the DMM-AAI Crittenden identifies 14 different forms of lack of resolution: dismissed forms (dismissed, displaced, blocked and denied), preoccupying forms (preoccupied, vicarious, imagined, suggested, hinted and anticipated) and others (delusional repair, delusional revenge, disorganised, depressed) (Crittenden & Landini 2011).

Modifiers

Whereas the ʻland minesʼ associated with the lack of resolution may temporarily disrupt strategies, ʻmodifiers are like a full-fledged, unlimited (by time or space) war. Nothing is safe or comfortable and the individual has no self-protective strategyʼ (Crittenden & Landini 2011: 254–5). Hence modifiers can result in a major disruption to psychosocial functioning by rendering attachment behaviour non-strategic for, sometimes, long periods of time.

Depression

Depression was identified as a modifier during the development of the Preschool Assessment of Attachment (PAA), the DMM equivalent of the Cassidy Marvin system (Cassidy *et al.* 1987–92), both of which use the SSP. The other modifiers are coded for in the child systems but originate from work on the DMM-AAI. Depression is not a proxy psychiatric diagnosis but refers to an awareness by the subject that their strategy (A, B or C) does not function strategically. Signifying behaviours of depression, such as flat affect, hopelessness, together with negative beliefs about the self and the future are also relevant depending on which procedure (child or adult) is being coded.

Intrusions of forbidden negative affect

Intrusions of forbidden negative affect (INAs) refer to explosive intrusions of rage or sexual behaviour in a Type A3-8 strategy. Essentially, inhibition breaks down and the person loses control of the self. Unlike people in Type C who are adept at using displays of emotion strategically, those in Type A+ have no such control, with the result that they may commit serious acts of violence followed by deep remorse and, sometimes, the inability to remember what they did (Crittenden & Landini 2011).

Disorientation

Disorientation means the speaker, in a DMM-AAI, has problems with source memory leading to confusion regarding the contents of one's own mind. Johnny gives too much self-relevance to information that had more complex sources but which even in adulthood remain hidden to him. Disorientation always modifies a Type A/C pattern in which the speaker seems to flip from A to C and back again without finding that either strategy (other people's perspective in A and self-perspective in C) organises their behaviour in a self-protective fashion. Disorientation was also a feature of a significant number of DMM-AAIs with prospective adoptive parents who appeared confused regarding fertility, i.e. whether they wanted to pass on their own genes or those of the child they might adopt (Farnfield 2012).

Expressed somatic symptoms

Expressed somatic symptoms are non-verbal behaviours that, in the AAI, interfere with the interpersonal process of the interview. These include behaviours such as tics, repeated coughing without a cold, jigging parts of the body and even falling asleep. Crittenden and Landini note that 'it is thought that [expressed somatic symptoms] represent conflict between what is known or suspected and what one is permitted to know or to say' (2011: 270).

Reorganisation

Finally reorganisation modifies strategic functioning because it involves integrating previously distorted information to achieve a more balanced Type B strategy.

Memory systems

The clinical attraction of the DMM lies in its potential to help formulate interventions that meet the needs of specific individuals. As Crittenden notes, the only information we have is about the past but the information we actually need is that which will predict dangers in the future (Crittenden 2002: 72). Thus current behaviour is biased towards responses influenced by past experience.

A central feature of the DMM is Crittenden's expansion of Bowlby's use of memory systems in the processing of information about safety, danger and repro-duction. An understanding of an individual's use of different memory systems, through for example an analysis of an AAI transcript, allows for an understanding of the strategies they use for their self-protection.

The DMM employs six types of representation or memory systems (see Fig-ure 3.4) which are organised in four different ways: cognitive or affective and implicit or explicit (unconscious and conscious) (Schacter & Tulving 1994; Crit-tenden 2008). All but one, connotative language, will be familiar to cognitive psychologists.

Implicit memory systems

Implicit memory starts to function in infancy and before the development of language.

Procedural memory is cognitively based and describes 'knowing how' to do things, like riding a bicycle or playing piano, without having to think about what we are doing. In terms of attachment, procedural memory is assessed by the infant

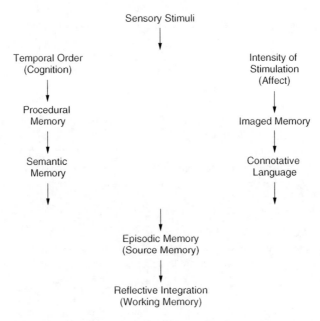

Figure 3.4 Transformation of information: the organisation of memory systems (Dr Patricia Crittenden: with permission)

SSP, i.e. what the infant has learned regarding the likely response of his mother when he feels and shows distress.

Imaged memory is organised around sensory inputs and consists of the impressions from all five senses that accompany our experiences. Images of touch, taste and smell are particularly powerful.

Explicit memory systems

Explicit memory systems (associated with memories that can be actively recalled) develop later.

Semantic memory develops, with language, from the second year of life and can be thought of as procedural memory in a verbal form. It includes family scripts as to how to behave and, in the preschool years, involves children adopting parental observations about their own behaviour. For example, 'good girl, you put away your toys' can form the basis of a rule, namely: 'Mummy approves of girls who tidy their toys.'

Connotative language has been introduced by Crittenden as the verbal counterpart of imaged memory. Language may arouse the self, and others, with rhyme or alliteration ('you pot bellied bastard piss off!') or function in a dry, analytic way to control or down-regulate affective states ('one doesn't usually get annoyed about such things but there's a time and place').

Episodic memory

Unlike semantic memory, which functions to abstract common information across multiple experiences, episodic *memory* most approximates to the common meaning of memory; a story about a time when something happened (Bowlby 1980). It develops from the third year of life and consists of the integration of cognitive and affective information about past events. Episodic memory 'is a transient construction that contains not only reactivation of neural networks that were active during the event itself, but also networks that represent the state of the self in the present' (Crittenden & Landini 2011: 61) Hence, we continue to work on our 'episodes' long after the actual event.

An important subset of episodic memory is source memory. In the preschool years attachment figures are crucial in helping children to scaffold memories and organise their experience. Although pre-schoolers are not totally reliant on adults to generate information, in the school years children are able to distinguish between what they 'know' from what their parents tell them: 'Mum says he's just a friend but I know they sleep together.' That is, they are able to identify both what they know or think and the source of the information. In adults this also includes awareness that a childhood 'memory' 'could be something I saw or maybe I remember it because my mother was always talking about it'.

In the DMM-AAI the disorientated modifier, which is outlined above, refers to interviews in which the speaker is confused regarding source memory.

Working memory

Rather than a memory system, working memory refers to the process by which information from the other systems is available for inspection. Le Doux calls it a work space (Le Doux 2002). Working memory is an active process in which past and present information can be integrated to create new DRs but, as noted above, this takes time which is not available when we are anxious or under threat or, indeed, sexually aroused.

Implications

Self-protective strategies are largely a matter of perception, i.e. whether they work is less important than believing they work. It is as if people (all of us) get stuck in their 'default' mode in which they, and indeed entire societies, do things which, from the vantage of an outsider, appear to be manifestly bad for them but which, to the people involved, appear to be the only courses of action available to them. Thus, over time, it is not safety that relieves anxiety so much as enacting the strategy we believe will make us safer.

Like all models of behaviour the A+ and C+ strategies are not 'real' but cardboard cut-outs that approximate to reality. Nor are they describing freakish behaviour. What they do describe are exaggerations of typical behaviour. People in Type A+ and C+ overemphasise one or more sources of information at the expense of others. We can also argue that Type B3 does not exist except as the true integration of A and C strategies.

Working with memory systems is very useful in pinpointing what services should be offered and how services might be calibrated for a particular person. To take two simple examples: therapies based on cognitive restructuring, such as cognitative behavioural therapy (CBT), might be effective with people in Type C+ who 'live' in imaged and episodic memory but omit semantic memory from processing. On the other hand, cognitive therapies may be actually harmful for people in Type A who dismiss the impact of imaged and episodic memory and distort semantic memory with regard to over-identifying the self as a cause of current problems (Crittenden 1992a; Main 1995). These people might benefit from a therapeutic process that works with emotions and allows them to start to trust their feelings more (Baim & Morrison 2011).

However, therapies such as CBT or dialectical behaviour therapy (DBT), which includes cognitive behavioural techniques for affect regulation and reality testing together with mindful awareness (Linehan & Dimeff 2001), may assist those who are in Type C and over-reliant on affect-based strategies. Further, the process of therapy can be deepened if we are able to identify and work with the memory system prominent in the moment. Attunement with the client is a feature of all therapeutic modalities, or in Allen's terms, 'plain old therapy' (Allen 2013).

Attachment trauma and posttraumatic stress disorder

The majority of traumas met with in general professional practice are attachment based; they stem from child abuse in which the trauma was either caused by attachment figures or carers who manifestly failed to protect the child when protection was, in fact, possible, i.e. neglect. Allen (2013) views attachment trauma as both what happens in attachment relationships and the impact that trauma has on the ability to mentalise and form secure attachment relationships in the future. All child abuse is fundamentally emotional abuse, in Allen's terms involving a pervasive failure by abusive carers to mentalise (see Luyten & Fonagy in Chapter 6) and thus neglect is central to attachment trauma.

Rather than, in Winnicott's terms, finding a self while alone in the mentalising presence of a parent (Winnicott 1971), abused children suffer alone and without anyone to help them make sense of what is happening to them. Trust has been betrayed and the child grows up unable to trust anyone, including therapists (Allen 2013).

One of the challenges for attachment research is to reliably distinguish insecure attachment from posttraumatic stress disorder (PTSD) and, crucially, the effect that each has on the other. Our experience with the DMM is that the model is like the map of a solar system which works pretty well in explaining the orbit of observable planets (A3-8 and C3-8) and can give a satisfactory account of some of their atypical movements (trauma and loss together with modifiers). However, inevitably, in the outer circles of the model involving people with very complex histories we encounter forces about whose meaning we can only speculate (traumatic black holes maybe).

Although the initial work on disorganisation by Main and colleagues established a link between child maltreatment and disorganisation on the infant SSP (Main & Solomon 1986) and between unresolved status on the parent's AAI and disorganisation in their infant (Main & Hesse 1990), attachment scholars were cautious in tying disorganisation in children and unresolved loss/trauma in adults to PTSD.

More recently, a growing number of studies have found strong associations between diagnosed PTSD and unresolved status on the AAI (Dozier *et al.* 2008; Moran *et al.* 2008; Harari *et al.* 2009), and Joubert, Webster and Hackett (2012) have drawn similar conclusions using the Adult Attachment Projective (George *et al.* 1999).

A DMM-AAI study also found that adults with PTSD (n = 22 compared with 22 mixed non-PTSD diagnosis and 22 non-treatment controls) had the highest proportion with unresolved childhood traumas. The majority of the AAIs were assessed as Type C5-6; the subjects were strategic except when faced with current situations which activated DRs associated with unresolved loss and trauma in childhood. However, a minority of the PTSD AAIs were rated Type A+, many with the depressed modifier, that rendered their A+ strategy non-strategic (Crittenden & Heller, reported in Crittenden & Landini 2011).

Attachment trauma now appears to be a feature not just of PTSD but also some other psychiatric diagnoses, in particular borderline personality disorder (Allen 2013; Luyten & Fonagy Chapter 6).

But not all threats to the self result in PTSD and in both models insecure attachment is viewed as affording some protection against the psychological effects of attachment trauma. In particular, when using the ABC + D model many infants assessed as disorganised on the SSP have been found to reorganise to an insecure pattern by the age of six years; notably controlling punitive or controlling caregiving (Main & Cassidy 1988; Solomon & George 2011; Moss et al. 2011) which appear to match the DMM C3 and A3 strategies.

The DMM A3-6 and C3-6 patterns, in particular, denote organised strategies that function in times of enduring danger either at a familial, interpersonal, or societal level over long periods of time (Terr's Type 2 (Terr 1991)) so that coding of unresolved loss or trauma, particularly if it follows the attachment strategy (i.e. dismissing in Type A and preoccupied in Type C), may be redundant.

However, not all the infants assessed as disorganised on the Main and Solomon SSP reorganise to controlling punitive or controlling caregiving. A significant minority appear to still be disorganised at six years (Moss et al. 2011) and some of these will show up as older children (MacDonald et al. 2008) and adults in the Main and Goldwyn AAI as 'disorganised'; the cannot classify and unresolved categories (Sroufe et al. 2005; Main et al. 2005). This strengthens the argument for treating the information processing (determined by using the AAI) in attachment trauma as related but different from that in organised but insecure attachment.

If the DMM-modifiers represent non-strategic behaviour they invite comparison with ABC + D categories such as 'disorganised' or 'cannot classify'. A fruitful area of enquiry would be to map the DMM constructs against studies which have identified significant 'lapses in the monitoring or reasoning of discourse' using the Main and Goldwyn AAI and which are clustered under the cannot classify (CC) category (Hesse 1996; Hesse & Main 1999). It is also possible that, as with the beginning of the ABC + D and DMM debate over the SSP, the two models are likely looking at the same phenomena (severe disruptions to everyday psychosocial functioning caused by early trauma) but possibly giving them different meanings. For example, Hesse (1996) has criteria for CC based on evidence of Dismissed and Preoccupied strategies in the same interview which are likely A/C in the DMM.

Assessments

There are DMM assessments for each developmental period: The Infant and Toddler CARE-Index which is a carer–child play-based procedure designed to screen for risks in relationships (Crittenden 1979–2010, 1992–2005); the Preschool Assessment of Attachment (PAA) which uses the same procedure as the Ainsworth SSP (Crittenden 1988–2005); the School-Aged Assessment (SAA) which uses picture prompts and a system of discourse analysis drawn from the DMM-AAI to analyse children's stories (Crittenden 1995–2012) and the DMM-AAI that also has a version for adolescents (Crittenden & Landini 2011). (For an overview of all these procedures see Farnfield *et al.* (2010) and Farnfield & Holmes (2014).)

Concluding comments

Although obvious, it is worth stating that people do not seek professional help because they feel too safe. On the contrary, the majority of people with whom health and social care professionals are working have suffered abuse and/or neglect in their childhood with, increasingly, a percentage who have been exposed to wars and political persecution in their countries of origin. Specifically the DMM offers:

- a range of identifiable self-protective strategies that can act as templates for thinking about current behaviour;
- a developmental approach that invites investigation into how past experience has shaped behaviour which is maladaptive in the present;
- a focus on information processing which leads to a functional formulation (Kozlowska *et al.* 2012, 2013) and assists in the selection of treatment.

Remarkably the DMM is the product of its sole creator who has worked alone for decades, outside of the universities and, until recently, DMM studies were without any formal academic base. This has allowed for creativity but also restricted testability of the ideas. Although the infant CARE-Index and PAA procedures are well validated, the empirical evidence for the range of strategies in the school years and adulthood is not extensive (see Farnfield *et al.* 2010 for review).

Crittenden clearly proposes that the DMM is a theory in its own right; that is, a testable set of constructs that have greater explanatory power regarding the identified range of maladaptive behaviours than is provided by the mainstream ABC + D model. The compass of the DMM is actually restricted to two crucial aspects of life:

1   self-protection and survival, sometimes under conditions of great danger to the self and our families;
2   sex and reproduction.

Thus the DMM privileges certain aspects of attachment studies at the expense of others, in particular exploration. If the world is a stage then the DMM wheel of strategies describes the parts of many of the players who appear in the clinics, courts and consulting rooms of everyday practice.

The DMM offers an explanation of human suffering that is rooted less in pathology and more in the limited options that are available to all of us if we are to survive danger.

Tolstoy observed that 'All happy families are alike; each unhappy family is unhappy in its own way'. Crittenden is fond of turning this line on its head: to be a person in your own right, you need to be safe. Misery is uniformly constricting.

Our thanks to Robbie Duschinsky who read and commented on earlier drafts of this chapter.

Notes

1 In keeping with evolutionary theory a strategy is 'designed by natural selection to increase inclusive fitness' (Simpson & Belsky 2008: 138). 'Inclusive fitness' refers to passing on our genes including those of indirect descendants such as nephews and nieces, which also explains caregiving by people who are themselves childless. Strategies operate outside consciousness.
2 This offers intriguing avenues back into the psychoanalytic roots of attachment with regard to the place of defensive processes such as fantasy and splitting.

References

Ainsworth, M.D., Blehar, M.C., Waters, E., & Wall, S. (1978) *Patterns of Attachment: A psychological study of the Strange Situation*, Hillsdale, NJ: Erlbaum.

Ainsworth, M.D.S. & Wittig, D. (1969) 'Attachment and exploratory behaviour of one-year-olds in a Strange Situation'. In B.M. Foss (ed.), *Determinants of Infant Behavior, Vol. 4*. London: Methuen.

Allen, J.G. (2013) *Restoring Mentalizing in Attachment Relationships: Treating trauma with plain old therapy*, Washington, DC: American Psychiatric Publishing.

Baim, C. & Morrison, T. (2011) *Attachment-Based Practice with Adults: A new practice model and interactive resource for assessment, intervention and supervision*, Brighton, UK: Pavilion.

Barkow, J.H., Cosmides, L. & Tooby, J. (1992) *The Adapted Mind: Evolutionary psychology and the generation of culture*, New York: Oxford University Press.

Bowlby, J. (1969) *Attachment. Attachment and Loss (vol. 1)*, New York: Basic Books.

Bowlby, J. (1973) *Separation. Attachment and Loss (vol. 2)*, New York: Basic Books.

Bowlby, J. (1980) *Loss, sadness and depression. Attachment and Loss (vol. 3)*, New York: Basic Books.

Bowlby, J. (1991) *Charles Darwin: A new life*, New York: Norton & Co.

Cassibba, R., Sette, G., Bakermans-Kranenburg, M.J. & Van IJzendoorn, M.H. (2013) 'Attachment the Italian way: In search of specific patterns of infant and adult attachments in Italian typical and atypical samples', *European Psychologist*, 18(1), 47–58.

Cassidy, J., Marvin, R.S. & the Working Group of the John D. and Catherine T. MacArthur Foundation on the Transition from Infancy to Early Childhood (1987/1990/1991/1992) *Attachment organization in three- and four-year olds: Coding guidelines*. Unpublished manuscript, University of Virginia, Charlottesville.

Crittenden, P.M. (1979–2010) *CARE-Index. Infants. Coding manual*. Unpublished manuscript, Miami, FL, USA.

Crittenden, P.M. (1985) 'Social networks, quality of childrearing, and child development', *Child Development*, 56, 1299–1313.

Crittenden, P.M. (1988–2005) *The Preschool Assessment of Attachment: Coding manual*. Unpublished manuscript, Miami, FL, USA.

Crittenden, P.M. (1992–2005) *CARE-Index. Toddlers. Coding manual*. Unpublished manuscript, Miami, FL, USA.

Crittenden, P.M. (1992a) 'Treatment of anxious attachment in infancy and the preschool years', *Development and Psychopathology*, 4, 575–602.

Crittenden, P.M. (1992b) 'Children's strategies for coping with adverse home environments', *International Journal of Child Abuse and Neglect*, 16, 329–343.

Crittenden, P.M. (1994) 'Peering into the black box: An exploratory treatise on the development of self in young children'. In D. Cicchetti & S.L. Toth (eds), *Disorders and Dysfunctions of the Self* (pp. 79–148), Rochester, NY: University of Rochester Press.

Crittenden, P.M. (1995) 'Attachment and psychopathology'. In S. Goldberg, R. Muir & J. Kerr (eds), *Attachment Theory: Social, developmental and clinical perspectives* (pp. 367–406). New York: The Analytic Press.

Crittenden, P.M. (1995–2012) *School-aged Assessment of Attachment. Coding manual using the dynamic-maturational method*. Unpublished manuscript. Miami, FL, USA.

Crittenden, P.M. (2000) 'A dynamic-maturational approach to continuity and change in pattern of attachment'. In P.M. Crittenden & A.H. Claussen (eds), *The Organization of Attachment Relationships: Maturation, culture, and context* (pp. 343–357). New York: Cambridge University Press.

Crittenden, P.M. (2002) 'Attachment, information processing, and psychiatric disorder', *World Psychiatry*, 1(2), 72–75.

Crittenden, P.M. (2006) 'A Dynamic-Maturational Model of Attachment', *Australian and New Zealand Journal of Family Therapy*, 27(2), 105–115.

Crittenden, P.M. (2008) *Raising Parents: Attachment, parenting and child safety*, Cullompton, UK: Willan.

Crittenden, P.M. & Landini, A. (2011) *The Adult Attachment Interview: Assessing psychological and interpersonal strategies*, New York: W.W. Norton & Co.

Crittenden, P.M. & Newman, L. (2010) 'Comparing models of borderline personality disorder: Mothers' experience, self-protective strategies, and Dispositional Representations', *Clinical Child Psychology and Psychiatry*, 15(3), 433–451.

Dallos, R. (2014) 'Assessing attachment in families: Beyond the dyads'. In S. Farnfield & P. Holmes (eds), *The Routledge Handbook of Attachment: Assessment*. London and New York: Routledge.

Damasio, A. (1994) *Decartes' Error: Emotion, reason, and the human brain*, New York: Avon.

Damasio, A. (2000) *The Feeling of What Happens: Body and emotion in the making of consciousness*, London: Vintage.

Dozier, M., Stovall-McClough, K.C. & Albus, K.E. (2008) 'Attachment and psychopathology in adulthood'. In J. Cassidy & P.R. Shaver (eds), *Handbook of Attachment: Theory, research, and clinical applications* (pp. 718–744). New York: The Guilford Press.

Farnfield, S. (In press) 'Assessing attachment in the school years: The application of the Dynamic-Maturational Model of attachment to the coding of a child attachment interview with community and looked after children', *Clinical Child Psychology & Psychiatry*.

Farnfield, S. (2012) 'Bindung und Anpassung bei Ersatzeltern'. In M. Stokowy & N. Sahhar (eds), *Bindung und Gefahr: Das Dynamische Reifungsmodell von Bindung und Anpassung* (pp. 163–186). Giessen: Psychosozial-Verlag.

Farnfield, S. & Holmes, P. (eds) (2014) *The Routledge Handbook of Attachment: Assessment*, London and New York: Routledge.

Farnfield, S., Hautamäki, A., Norbech, P. & Sahhar, N. (2010) 'DMM assessments of attachment and adaptation: Procedures, validity and utility', *Clinical Child Psychology and Psychiatry*, 15(3), 313–328.

Ferenczi, S. (1988/1933) 'Confusion of tongues between adults and the child', *Contemporary Psychoanalysis*, 24(2), 206.

George, C., West, M. & Pettem, O. (1999) 'The Adult Attachment Projective: Disorganization of adult attachment at the level of representation'. In J. Solomon & C. George (eds), *Attachment Disorganization* (pp. 318–346). New York: The Guilford Press.

Harari, D., Bakermans-Kranenburg, M.J., de Kloetb, C.S., Geuzed, E., Vermettend, E., Westenberge, H.G.M. & Van IJzendoorn, M.H. (2009) 'Attachment representations in Dutch veterans with and without deployment-related PTSD', *Attachment & Human Development*, 11(6), 515–536.

Hautamäki, A., Hautamäki, L., Neuvonen, L. & Maliniemi-Piispanen, S. (2010) 'Transmission of attachment across three generations', *European Journal of Developmental Psychology*, 7(5), 618–634.

Hesse, E. (1996) 'Discourse, memory, and the Adult Attachment Interview: A note with emphasis on the emerging cannot classify category', *Infant Mental Health Journal*, 17, 4–11.

Hesse, E. & Main, M. (1999) 'Second-generation effects of unresolved trauma in non-maltreating parents: Dissociated, frightened, and threatening parental behaviour', *Psychoanalytic Inquiry*, 19, 481–540.

Hinde, R. (1982) *Ethology: Its nature and relations with other sciences*, New York: Oxford University Press.

Joubert, D., Webster, L. & Hackett, R.K. (2012) 'Unresolved attachment status and trauma-related symptomatology in maltreated adolescents: An examination of cognitive mediators', *Child Psychiatry and Human Development*, 43, 471–483.

Karen, R. (1998) *Becoming Attached: First relationships and how they shape our capacity to love*, New York: Oxford University Press.

Kozlowska, K., English, M., Savage, B. & Chudleigh, C. (2012) 'Multimodal rehabilitation: A mind–body, family-based intervention for children and adolescents impaired by medically unexplained symptoms. Part 1: The program', *The American Journal of Family Therapy*, 40(5), 399–419.

Kozlowska, K., English, M., Savage, B., Chudleigh, C., Davies, F., Paull *et al.* (2013) 'Multimodal rehabilitation: A mind-body, family-based intervention for children and adolescents impaired by medically unexplained symptoms. Part 2: Case studies and outcomes', *The American Journal of Family Therapy*, 40(5), 212–231.

Le Doux, J. (2002) *Synaptic Self: How our brains become who we are*, London: Macmillan.

Linehan, M.M. & Dimeff, L. (2001) 'Dialectical behaviour therapy in a nutshell', *The California Psychologist*, 34, 10–13.

MacDonald, H.Z., Beeghly, M., Grant-Knight, W., Augustyn, M., Woods, R.W., Cabral, H *et al.* (2008) 'Longitudinal association between infant disorganized attachment and childhood posttraumatic stress symptoms', *Development and Psychopathology*, 20(2), 493–508.

Main, M. (1995) 'Recent studies in attachment: Overview, with selected implications for clinical work'. In S. Goldberg, R. Muir & J. Kerr (eds), *Attachment Theory: Social, developmental, and clinical perspectives* (pp. 407–474). Hillsdale, NJ: The Analytic Press.

Main, M. & Cassidy, J. (1988) 'Categories of response to reunion with the parent at age six: Predictability from infant attachment classifications and stable across a one-month period', *Developmental Psychology*, 24, 415–426.

Main, M. & Hesse, E. (1990) 'Parents' unresolved traumatic experiences are related to infant disorganized attachment status'. In M.T. Greenberg, D. Cicchetti & E.M. Cummings (eds), *Attachment in the Preschool Years: Theory, research, and intervention* (pp. 161–182). Chicago: University of Chicago Press.

Main, M. & Solomon, J. (1986) 'Discovery of a new, insecure-disorganized/disorientated attachment pattern'. In M. Yogman & T. Brazelton (eds), *Affective Development in Infancy* (pp. 95–124). Norwood, NJ: Ablex.

Main, M. & Solomon, J. (1990) 'Procedures for identifying infants as disorganized/disorientated during the Ainsworth Strange Situation'. In M.T. Greenberg, D. Cicchetti & E.M. Cummings (eds), *Attachment in the Preschool Years* (pp. 121–160). Chicago: University of Chicago Press.

Main, M., Hesse, E. & Kaplan, N. (2005) 'Predictability of attachment behaviour and representational processes at 1, 6, and 19 years of age: The Berkeley Longitudinal Study'. In Grossman, K.E., Grossman, K. & Waters, E. (eds), *Attachment for Infancy to Adulthood: The major longitudinal studies* (pp. 245–304). New York: The Guilford Press.

Marvin, R.S. (2003) 'Implications of attachment research for the field of family therapy'. In P. Erdman & T. Caffery (eds), *Attachment and Family Systems: Conceptual, empirical, and therapeutic relatedness* (pp. 3–30). Hove, UK: Brunner-Routledge.

Marvin, R. & Britner, P. (2008) 'Normative development: The ontogeny of attachment'. In J. Cassidy & P.R. Shaver (eds), *Handbook of Attachment: Theory, research and clinical implications*, 2nd edition (pp. 269–294). New York: The Guilford Press.

Merton, R.K. (1949) 'On sociological theories of the middle range'. Reprinted in C. Calhoun, J. Gerteis, J. Moody, S. Pfaff & V. Indermohan (eds) (2012) *Classical Sociological Theory*, 3rd edition (pp. 523–530). Chichester: John Wiley & Sons Ltd.

Moran, G., Bailey, H.N., Gleason, K., DeOliveira, C.A. & Pederson, D.R. (2008) 'Exploring the mind behind unresolved attachment: Lessons from and of attachment-based interventions with infants and their traumatized mothers'. In H. Steele & M. Steele (eds), *Clinical Applications of the Adult Attachment Interview* (pp. 371–398). New York: The Guilford Press.

Moss, E., Bureau, J., St-Laurent, D. & Tarabulsy, G.M. (2011) 'Understanding disorganized attachment at preschool and school age: Examining divergent pathways of disorganized and controlling children'. In J. Solomon & C. George (eds), *Disorganized Attachment & Caregiving* (pp. 52–79). New York: The Guilford Press.

NICHD Early Child Care Research Network, Public Information & Communication Branch (2001) 'Child-care and family predictors of preschool attachment and stability from infancy', *Developmental Psychology*, 37(6), 847–862.

Radke-Yarrow, M., Cummings, E.M., Kuczynski, L. & Chapman, M. (1985) 'Patterns of attachment in two and three-year-olds in normal families and families with parental depression', *Child Development*, 56, 884–893.

Ringer, F. & Crittenden, P.M. (2007) 'Eating disorders and attachment: The effects of hidden processes on eating disorders', *European Eating Disorders Review*, 15, 119–130.

Sahhar, N. (2014) 'An expanded approach to the Adult Attachment Interview: the DMM-AAI'. In S. Farnfield & P. Holmes (eds), *The Routledge Handbook of Attachment: Assessment*. London and New York: Routledge.

Schacter, D.L. & Tulving, E. (1994) 'What are the memory systems of 1994?' In D.L. Schacter & E. Tulving (eds), *Memory Systems* (pp. 1–38). Cambridge, MA: Bradford.

Shah, P.E., Fonagy, P. & Strathearn, L. (2010) 'Is attachment transmitted across generations? The plot thickens', *Clinical Child Psychology and Psychiatry*, 15(3), 329–346.

Simpson, J.A. & Belsky, J. (2008) 'Attachment theory within a modern evolutionary framework'. In J. Cassidy & P.R. Shaver (eds), *Handbook of Attachment: Theory, research and clinical implications*, 2nd edition (pp. 131–157). New York: The Guilford Press.

Solomon, J. & George, C. (eds) (2011) *Disorganized Attachment & Caregiving*, New York: The Guilford Press.

Sroufe, L.A., Egeland, B., Carlson, E.A. & Collins, W.A. (2005) *The Development of the Person: The Minnesota study of risk and adaptation from birth to adulthood*, New York: Guilford Publications.

Strathearn, L., Fonagy, P., Amico, J.A. & Montague, P.R. (2009) 'Adult attachment predicts mother's brain and oxytocin response to infant cues', *Neuropsychopharmacology*, 34(13), 2655–2666.

Terr, L. (1991) 'Childhood trauma: An outline and overview', *American Journal of Psychiatry*, 148, 10–20.

Winnicott, D.W. (1960) 'Ego distortion in terms of true and false self'. In *The Maturational Processes and the Facilitating Environment*. New York (1965): International Universities Press.

Winnicott, D.W. (1971) *Playing and Reality*, London: Tavistock.

Zachrisson, H.D. & Kulbotten, G.R. (2006) 'Attachment in anorexia nervosa: An exploration of associations with eating disorder psychopathology and psychiatric symptoms', *Eating and Weight Disorders*, 11, 163–170.

Chapter 4

Similarities and differences between the ABC + D model and the DMM classification systems for attachment

A practitioner's guide

Prachi E. Shah and Lane Strathearn

Introduction

Infant–mother attachment, as initially conceptualised by John Bowlby (Bowlby 1969), describes the quality of the relationship between a caregiver and the infant. Bowlby conceptualised infancy as a period of helplessness and vulnerability, in which the child is dependent on the caregiver to meet his physical and emotional needs. His seminal work in attachment theory was grounded on the evolutionary basis that a child's attachment behaviours serve to bring him into closer proximity to his attachment figure, for the purpose of obtaining comfort, safety, security and protection, when feeling distressed or threatened. Mary Ainsworth expanded Bowlby's theoretical work by developing a classification system to describe the individual differences in patterns of infant attachment behaviour (Ainsworth *et al.* 1978). Her data from the first year of life indicated that infant patterns of attachment were tied to the quality of maternal 'sensitive responsiveness' to infant distress during the first year of life.

Ainsworth's ABC classification system

Ainsworth's classification system was based on infant and mother behaviour during the Strange Situation procedure (SSP), an observational assessment involving a series of introductions, separations and reunions, designed to activate the infant's attachment system.

The quality of the infant's interactive behaviour with respect to the caregiver, after two episodes of separation and reunion, were coded on 7-point Likert scales for the presence of the following behaviours: proximity and contact seeking, contact maintaining, resistance, avoidance, search behaviours, and distance interaction. She later clustered these patterns of dyadic interaction into three categories: Type A ('avoidant') characterised by avoidance of proximity or interaction with the caregiver in the reunion episodes; Type B ('secure') characterised by the infant actively seeking proximity or contact with his mother, with little demonstration of resistance or avoidance with the mother, and contact with the mother effectively terminating distress; and Type C ('ambivalent') with the infant demonstrating

Table 4.1 Summary of episodes of the Strange Situation procedure (Ainsworth et al. 1978: 37)

Episode	Persons present	Duration	Brief description of action
1	Mother, baby, & observer	30 sec.	Observer introduces mother and baby to experiment room then leaves.
2	Mother & baby	3 min.	Mother is a nonparticipant while baby explores; if necessary, play is stimulated after 2 minutes.
3	Stranger, mother, & baby	3 min.	Stranger enters. First minute: stranger is silent. Second minute: stranger converses with mother. Third minute: stranger approaches baby. After 3 minutes mother leaves unobtrusively.
4	Stranger & baby	3 min. or less	First separation episode: Stranger's behaviour is geared to that of the baby.
5	Mother & baby	3 min. or more	First reunion episode: Mother greets and/or comforts baby, then tries to settle him again in play. Mother leaves again, saying 'bye-bye'.
6	Baby alone	3 min. or less	Second separation episode.
7	Stranger & baby	3 min. or less	Continuation of second separation. Stranger enters and gears her behaviour to that of baby.
8	Mother & baby	3 min. or more	Second reunion episode: Mother enters, greets baby then picks him up. Meanwhile stranger leaves unobtrusively.

both *resistance to* and *initiation of* contact and interaction with the caregiver during the reunion episodes (Ainsworth *et al.* 1978).

Type A: avoidant

Infant behaviour was labelled as (A) avoidant if they demonstrated conspicuous avoidance of proximity or interaction with the mother in the reunion episodes, characterised by the infant ignoring the mother upon her return, with limited initiation to seek proximity, interact, or maintain contact with the mother. If picked up, the infant demonstrated little resistance to being picked up and, similarly, demonstrated little tendency to cling to the caregiver. Infants in Type A were characterised by the apparent lack of distress during the separation, which, if present, was thought to be related to the infant being left alone, rather than the caregiver's departure (Ainsworth *et al.* 1978). It was theorised that infants who manifest avoidant attachment had experienced a history of rejecting caregiving, in which the infants' signals to their caregivers were rebuffed. It is believed that the repeated experience of having bids for contact rejected results in the infant developing the compensatory defence mechanism of avoidance, wherein he learns to *minimise* his bids when distressed, in the hope of maintaining proximity to the caregiver, and minimising her rejection and departure from the infant (Ainsworth 1979).

Type B: secure

Infants were considered securely attached if they demonstrated an interest in seeking proximity or initiating and maintaining contact with the caregiver during the reunion episodes. According to Ainsworth, the hallmark of the securely attached infant was that contact with the caregiver was effective in terminating any distress, and the infant was readily able to return to exploration or interactive play with the parent. The securely attached infant neither resisted contact or interaction with the caregiver, nor demonstrated avoidance (i.e. rejection, ignoring or 'snubbing') of the caregiver in the reunion. If the infant was not distressed in the separation, the reunion was characterised by an affective connection between the infant and caregiver at the time of reunion (e.g. the infant acknowledged the mother upon return by looking or smiling) (Ainsworth *et al.* 1978). It is believed that infants who were securely attached experienced a history of contingent caregiving, in which their caregivers were consistently responsive to their signals during the first year of life. This history of consistent, sensitive responsiveness at times of infant distress is theorised to be the foundation upon which the infant develops an internalised representation that his caregiver is accessible, and will be responsive to him when he is in need. This consistent responsiveness of the caregiver to the infant's signals when distressed is thought to be the foundation for infant security (Ainsworth 1979).

Type C: ambivalent (resistant & passive)

Infants were placed in Type C (Ambivalent) if they demonstrated ambivalence to reunion with the caregiver, characterised by resistant behaviour to both contact and interaction, in combination with contact and proximity-seeking behaviour. The 'ambivalent' infant was observed to demonstrate paradoxical behaviour in reunion episodes: while the infant did not 'ignore' the mother during the reunion episodes (as did infants in Type A (avoidant), the Type C infant demonstrated behaviour that was maladaptive to reunion, characterised by anger, or conversely, increased passivity (Ainsworth *et al.* 1978). For the infants who were classified in

Type C, it is notable that although the parent's departure caused the infant extreme distress, return of the parent was not soothing or reassuring. It is theorised that ambivalent (Type C) attachment had its origins in a history of inconsistent maternal care characterised by 'uncertain maternal availability'. The infant in Type C had a mother who was neither 'consistently responsive' (as is seen with an infant in Type B), nor 'consistently rejecting' (as is seen with Type A infants). Rather, the infant in Type C had the difficult paradox of not knowing whether his caregiver would be responsive or unavailable. Consequently, the infant's 'ambivalent' pattern of behaviour emerged: because the infant was uncertain about the mother's responsiveness, he remained close with increased attachment behaviours, but because of her history of inconsistency, the infant demonstrated increased monitoring of the caregiver, with decreased exploratory behaviour.

The expansion of Ainsworth's classifications

In early work with Ainsworth's classification system, a percentage of infants were unable to be classified in the original ABC classification system. Sroufe and Waters published one of the first references to the difficulty of classifying infants, in which they identified the behaviour of 10 per cent (7 out of 70) of their white, middle-class sample that could not be readily classified into one of Ainsworth's three categories (Sroufe & Waters 1977). Additional work in the 1980s by Main and Weston further identified infants who were 'unclassifiable' in the Ainsworth System (Main & Weston 1981), who demonstrated 'secure behaviour' to both the parent and stranger in reunion episodes, in combination with extreme avoidance and extreme distress throughout the SSP. These 'unclassifiable' behaviours were identified in both low-risk and high-risk samples which were characterised by 'odd' and 'conflicted' behaviours in the SSP that appeared to lack an *organised* strategy to deal with the circumstances. Additional work by Mary Main (Main & Hesse 1990) identified 13 per cent of infants in their low-risk Berkeley, California sample to be unclassifiable in the SSP according to Ainsworth's original method, with what appeared to be an over-assignment of infants to Type B, secure attachment.

To resolve this problem, two of Ainsworth's students, Mary Main and Patricia Crittenden, expanded Ainsworth's classificatory system by developing new categories and coding guidelines. The similarities and differences between the two models: ABC + D (Main) and the Dynamic-Maturational Model of Attachment and Adaptation, the DMM (Crittenden), are highlighted in this chapter.

Infant 'disorganised' and adult patterns of attachment: the work of Mary Main

Addition of the D (disorganised) infant category

Mary Main expanded Ainsworth's original classificatory system with her addition of a fourth category called 'disorganised' attachment in infancy (Type D)

(Main & Solomon 1990) as well as 'unresolved' and 'cannot classify' categories in adulthood (Hesse 1996; Main 2000). Main theorised that disorganised infant attachment had its origins in maladaptive early caregiving experiences, characterised by threatening parental behaviour toward the infant, or by frightened parental behaviour in response to the infant. Main proposed that having a frightened or frightening mother made it impossible for the infant to organise a *coherent* pattern of attachment, and the result was an *incoherent* or *disorganised* strategy (cf. Main 1995, 1996). Disorganisation was initially described in a normative sample of 12-month-old infants who demonstrated conflicted or anomalous behaviour during reunions in the SSP (Main & Solomon 1990).

For Main, the infant's anomalous behaviour reflected the lack of a strategy to manage fear associated with the caregiver's frightening behaviour: the infant's fear could not be deactivated by a shift in attention, that is, Ainsworth's A (avoidant) pattern, nor could it be ameliorated through approaching the caregiver, that is, Ainsworth's B (secure) and C (ambivalent) patterns. Furthermore, Main theorised that the caregiver's frightening behaviour was connected with a history of unresolved loss or trauma and was, in fact, a maladaptive response to a history of traumatic memories (Main & Hesse 1990).

In addition, following Bowlby (1980), Main proposed that each individual had one enduring 'inner working model' (IWM) of attachment. When individuals were not able to form a single model, or they oscillated among models, it was treated as disorganisation. This approach, which is focused on continuity and disorganisation, is described as the 'ABC + D' classification. Anomalous infant behaviours meeting the criteria for '*disorganisation*' included:

- sequential or simultaneous display of contradictory behaviours;
- misdirected, incomplete or interrupted movements and expressions;
- stereotypies, asymmetrical movements and anomalous postures;
- freezing, stilling, or slowed movements;
- evidence of apprehension toward the parent;
- evidence of disorientation, disorganisation or confusion (Hesse & Main 2000).

Disorganised behaviour was thought to arise when the infant was markedly frightened by his attachment figure, as was characterised by infants with a history of maltreatment (Carlson 1998; Hesse & Main 2000; Lyons-Ruth 1996). The maltreated infant was thought to experience an irresolvable paradox in which his primary attachment figure, who should be his source of protection and safety in the face of danger, was simultaneously the source of threat to the infant, and the origin of his fear (Lyons-Ruth 1999). In addition, caregivers who demonstrated frightened behaviour in the presence of the infant, manifested by the caregiver reacting to the infant as if the *infant* were the source of threat and danger, contributed to the development of infant disorganisation. The caregiver who demonstrated fright in the presence of the infant (as was seen with traumatised parents) sent a signal to the infant, that the caregiver who should be available to protect the infant in the face of danger was, rather, repelled and frightened by the infant, and was unavailable to be a source of safety and protection. The infant is then thought to perceive that he is the reason for the caregiver's distance, and is left without an organised strategy to compensate for the caregiver's unavailability, resulting in a disorganised pattern of attachment (Main & Hesse 1990).

Development of the Adult Attachment Interview: expansion of infant attachment to include adult representations

Concurrent with the identification of infants who could not be classified in Ainsworth's ABC classification system (Main & Weston 1981), Main expanded her work in attachment to include a focus on parents' representational processes, and response to memories. Along with Carol George and colleagues at the University of California at Berkeley, she helped develop the Adult Attachment Interview (AAI) to ascertain caregivers' 'states of mind' with respect to attachment (George et al. 1985, 1996). The coding system for the AAI (George et al. 1985) was constructed to maximise the correspondence between AAI classifications and infants' pre-existing SSP classifications based on Main's beliefs in (1) the 'transmission' of attachment from mother to infant and (2) continuity of attachment across the lifespan (George et al. 1985; Main 2000; Main et al. 1985). The coding schema of the AAI was developed through identification of commonalities in the interview responses of mothers whose infants shared the same attachment classification. Blind coding of AAI interviews using the newly developed Main and Goldwyn method (M&G-AAI) revealed matching of SSP coding of security versus insecurity in 75 per cent of cases (Main et al. 1985).

The AAI was predicated on the adult's current mental representation of childhood experiences, and was formulated based on two assumptions:

> (a) autobiographical memory is the ongoing reconstruction of one's own past in light of new experiences, and (b) idealization of the past, particularly negative childhood experiences, can be traced by studying the form and content of the autobiographical narrative separately.
>
> (Van IJzendoorn 1995)

The AAI was developed as a semi-structured interview, designed to probe for general descriptions and specific memories of relationships with parents. In the AAI, the interviewee is asked to provide attachment-related memories from childhood, and to evaluate memories from their current perspective (George et al. 1985). The coding of the AAI transcripts is not based on the participant's description of their childhood experiences but, rather, on the coherence of the narrative which probes the effects of the early experiences on current functioning (Van IJzendoorn 1995). The coding of the AAI was formulated to evaluate participants' coherence in their use of language (Main & Goldwyn 1995). The coding system of the AAI includes three major adult classification systems, which correspond to three distinct types of narratives related to early attachment experiences. Interviews are rated as *autonomous* or secure (F) if the presentation and interpretation of attachment-related experiences (whether positive or negative) is succinct, clear, coherent and relevant. Interviews are classified as *dismissing* (D) when the narrative is discordant, characterised by describing parents in highly positive terms, with a lack of supporting examples, or the presence of contradictory statements later in the interview, with narratives typically minimising attachment-related experiences (Main 2010). Interviews are classified as *preoccupied* (E) when their narratives demonstrated a confused, angry or passive preoccupation with attachment figures. These interviews are characterised by excessive attention to attachment-related memories, combined with an incoherent (e.g. rambling) discourse. Finally, interviews may be classified as *unresolved/disorganised* (cannot classify, CC) when the narratives are characterised by a lack of resolution of trauma, manifest by lapses in the discourse when discussing traumatic events. Interviews classified as unresolved/disorganised also receive the additional underlying classification of autonomous, dismissing or preoccupied (Hesse 1996).

The AAI was developed to correlate parents' mental representations of attachment-related experiences with the pattern of their infants' behaviours in the SSP. As such, there are notable similarities in the ABC + D classification system between infant and adult patterns of attachment classification: *secure* (B) patterns of infant behaviour are similar to *autonomous* (F) patterns of adult representations, *avoidant* (A) patterns of infant attachment are similar to *dismissing* (D) patterns of adult attachment, *resistant* (C) patterns of infant attachment mirror *preoccupied* (E) patterns of adult attachment, and the disorganisation characteristic of 'D' infants is similar to the unresolved/disorganised adults (CC) in the AAI. Thus, the patterns of attachment characterised as ABC + D in infancy correspond to the DEF + CC patterns of attachment in adulthood.

Reformulation of attachment classification into the Dynamic-Maturational Model: the work of Patricia Crittenden

Concurrent with Main's development of the continuity-and-disorganisation expansion of Ainsworth's work, Patricia Crittenden expanded Ainsworth's original classificatory system based on patterns of information processing and memory systems. She believed that, with maturation of the brain, more sophisticated strategies could develop in a dynamic interaction with ongoing experience. These strategies were described in a series of papers (e.g. Crittenden 1981, 1985, 2008; Crittenden & Ainsworth 1989) and were incorporated into what has become known as the Dynamic-Maturational Model (DMM) of Attachment and Adaptation. This included a new coding method for the SSP, and modified questions in the Adult Attachment Interview (DMM-AAI) including additional questions on trauma and integration.

In Crittenden's model, patterns of attachment were considered to be 'self-protective strategies' that varied *dimensionally* (rather than *categorically*) in terms of the relative use of *cognitive*-contingent information or *affect*-arousing information to organise behaviour. She theorised that sensory stimulation is transformed into temporally ordered 'cognitive' information, and intensity-based arousal or 'affective' information. Type A attachment organisation was characterised by a cognitive bias in information processing, whereas Type C attachment was associated with an affective bias. Type B organisation was thought to be a balanced integration of both sources of cognitive and affective information.

For example, Crittenden proposed that Type A individuals tend to dismiss their own feelings, intentions and perspectives, and rely more upon rules and learned temporal relations in predicting future outcomes. They behave as if following the rule: 'Do the right thing – from the perspective of other people, without regard to your own feelings or desires' (Crittenden & Landini 2011). She suggested that Type C individuals, in contrast, organise their behaviour around affective information, such as fear, anger or desire for comfort. They tend to be preoccupied by their own feelings and perspectives, while omitting or distorting temporally ordered or cognitive information. They function as if under the dictum: 'Stay true to your feelings, and do not delay, negotiate or compromise' (Crittenden & Landini 2011). Individuals with Type B or balanced patterns of attachment are able to integrate temporally ordered information regarding causal effect and more affect-based information, such as emotional states and imaged memory, in order to form close relationships, make accurate decisions and predict future reward (Strathearn 2007).

Furthermore, each individual was thought to have multiple representations based on different processing pathways (i.e. memory systems) (Schacter & Tulving 1994) that were called 'dispositional representations' (DRs), with the possibility that different DRs could regulate behaviour under different conditions and in different contexts. The degree of integration among the DRs was the other dimension of the DMM.

Crittenden expected that threatened children and adults would show organised attachment strategies that reflected more complex Type A or C organisations than found in Ainsworth's A1-2, B, and C1-2 patterns. The new patterns were numbered A3-8 and C3-8 and included organised A/C combinations (Crittenden 1985; Radke-Yarrow *et al.* 1985) (see Figure 4.1). According to Crittenden's DMM, A3-4 and C3-4 attachment strategies were only available developmentally from the early preschool years, and A5-6 and C5-6 strategies were available during the school years, eventually incorporating sexuality into the maturational strategy. The most severe forms of psychopathology, described in A7-8 and C7-8 patterns, were only seen in adulthood. These additional patterns were labelled as either 'compulsive A+' or 'obsessive C+' strategies, describing strategies with increasingly distorted levels of cognition and affect, respectively; with the higher subscript strategies tending to integrate *falsified* cognitive and affective information.

In the DMM, there was no 'disorganised' category and, in fact, fear was treated as a powerful *organising* affect (cf. Ledoux 1996). This differed from Main, who

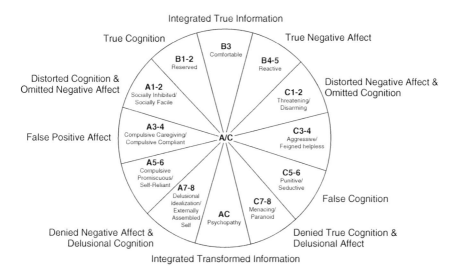

Figure 4.1 Dynamic-Maturational Model of Attachment and Adaptation (Dr Patricia Crittenden: with permission)

considered fear to be a disorganising mechanism (Main & Hesse 1990). Further, events occurring after infancy could affect a person's strategy; that is, attachment was biased toward constancy, but could change if the environment also changed (Crittenden 2000, 2006; Hamilton 2000; Lewis *et al.* 2000; Thompson & Raikes 2003; Weinfeld *et al.* 2000). Patterns of attachment were conceptualised as self-protective strategies that developed through interaction with attachment figures. The learning itself was based on both temporally ordered information ('cognition') and the intensity of stimulation (or 'affect'). That is, information processing yielded DRs that, in turn, organised self-protective behavioural strategies. Infant behaviour of all types was presumed to be a functional aspect of the infant–caregiver relationship and to maximise the infant's likelihood of survival, given the caregiver's sometimes threatening or neglectful behaviour (Crittenden 2008).

In the DMM, information that requires little transformation to yield protective behaviour (Type B strategy) promotes balanced relationships, whereas information that needs to be distorted to yield protective behaviour (Types A, C and A/C) promotes anxious relationships. These distortions of true information can be observed and classified through coding AAI transcripts or SSP videotapes. For example, a frightened child may give a paradoxical smile ('false positive affect') in order to appease his mother, or an adult may describe a neglectful parent in idealising terms. In more severe psychopathology, true affective or cognitive information may be completely omitted, falsified or denied.

When the mother is sensitively responsive (B), the infant is expected to be secure or balanced (B). However, when the mother is predictably unresponsive to the child's negative affect (e.g. displays of anger or fear), as might be seen in a Type A adult pattern, the infant may utilise a *reverse* strategy (e.g. a Type C strategy with an even more exaggerated display of affect) to reach an affectively distant mother (Crittenden *et al.* 1991; Hautamäki *et al.* 2010; Shah *et al.* 2010). For example, the child of a predictably unresponsive depressed mother might need to exaggerate negative affect (Type C strategy) in order to elicit maternal caregiving, thus presenting as a 'colicky' or irritable baby. In contrast, in the face of unpredictable danger, such as random acts of physical abuse at the hands of a drug-addicted parent (Type C), the infant or child may learn to inhibit any display of negative affect (Type A strategy) in order to prevent further abuse. While this strategy may be adaptive in one particular context, it may lead to maladaptive behaviour in a future context, such as in a school classroom setting. Here, the strategy might manifest as withdrawn behaviour, inattention or eventual learning problems, despite an environment that is now safe and predictable. Thus, these strategies may be adaptive in the face of danger, but highly maladaptive in a safe environment.

Similarities and differences between the ABC + D and DMM models of attachment classification

The similarities

Having presented an overview of the two classification systems of infant and adult attachment, we are better able to identify similarities and differences between the ABC + D and DMM models of attachment. Both models are formulated on Ainsworth's original ABC classification, and are predicated on the belief that patterns of maternal sensitive responsiveness influence subsequent infant attachment, with the strongest continuity demonstrated with secure (B) patterns of attachment (Shah *et al.* 2010). Both models classify infant attachment using Ainsworth's SSP, identify patterns of security (B) and insecurity (A, C), and incorporate an expansion of Ainsworth's original classification system to explain anomalous behaviour of infants. Both models incorporate a focus on developmental processes by which patterns of infant attachment play a substantive role on later developmental trajectories and outcomes, but the models place differential emphasis on the predictive capacity of infant attachment on later emotional development. Finally, both models expanded Ainsworth's work in infant attachment by exploring the association between adult representations of attachment and subsequent infant attachment patterns

The crucial differences

Continuity vs. discontinuity

There are several substantive differences between the ABC + D and DMM approaches to attachment (Crittenden 2004; Landa & Duschinsky 2013) (see Table 4.2). One of the critical differences between the ABC + D model and the DMM is the degree to which infant attachment is thought to predict later patterns of attachment. Although the ABC + D model has accounted for discontinuity of attachment classification over time, especially with changes in caregiver availability (Weinfeld et al. 2000), initial conceptualisation of infant attachment using the Ainsworth classification was predicated on the belief that when viewed organisationally, patterns

Table 4.2 Comparison of ABC + D and DMM classification systems (Crittenden 2004; Shah et al. 2010).

	ABC + D	DMM
Original intent of classification system	Prediction of infant patterns of attachment	Description of self-protective strategies and patterns of mental processing
Categorical/ dimensional outcome	Categorical outcomes	Dimensional outcomes along a cognitive/affective continuum
Continuity vs. discontinuity	Prediction of continuity of attachment pattern across generations, based on enduring 'internal working models'	Prediction of discontinuity of attachment, based on maturational shifts and developmental experience across the lifespan, and multiple, situation-specific 'dispositional representations' (DRs)
Role of fear	Disorganising effect on attachment categorisation	Highly organising effect on attachment strategy
Meaning of infant 'security'	Response to sensitive and responsive maternal caregiving	Integration of cognitive and affective information processing
Changes in attachment over time	Early experiences determine later outcomes (developmental trajectory), whereby attachment classification in infancy is largely predictive of adult attachment classification	Early experiences have a cumulative and dynamic effect (developmental pathways) allowing for attachment classifications to change over time
Internal Working Model (IWM)	Infant has one IWM which persists over time and is shaped by the quality of early caregiving	Infant has multiple, situation-specific DRs rather than one enduring IWM
Intergenerational transmission of attachment	ABC + D model presumes that patterns of infant attachment are predictable across circumstances, and are largely stable over time, although has accounted for discontinuity of attachment classification with changes in caregiver availability	DMM model anticipates that sentinel life events may catalyse a change in attachment classification, resulting in some infants manifesting opposite patterns of attachment from their caregivers

of infant attachment were predictable across circumstances, and largely stable over time (Sroufe & Waters 1977; Waters 1978). The DMM differed in this belief that an infancy-based model could describe human behaviour in adulthood. Thus, the DMM approach was formulated on the premise that attachment patterns over time were influenced by maturational shifts and neurological changes that resulted in variable developmental pathways (in which discontinuity is expected), rather than a continuity of individual patterns (Crittenden 2000).

The ABC + D and DMM models also differ in their organisational conceptualisation of attachment patterns. The ABC + D model describes patterns of infant attachment categorically (A: avoidant; B: secure; C: ambivalent; D: disorganised) whereas the DMM describes patterns of attachment that vary dimensionally along a cognition–affect continuum. In the DMM, patterns of attachment are conceptualised as self-protective strategies that are learned through interaction with attachment figures. The learning itself is based on both temporally ordered information (termed 'cognition') and the intensity of stimulation (or 'affect'), as these are processed through various parts of the brain (Strathearn 2007, 2011; Strathearn *et al.* 2009). That is, information processing yields DRs that, in turn, organise self-protective behavioural strategies (Crittenden 1990). In the DMM model, a 'cognitive' pattern of attachment is used to describe attachment that emerges in response to predictable, temporal contingencies. Conversely, an 'affective' pattern develops when feelings and emotions appear to organise and motivate behaviour. A Type B (balanced) pattern is seen when infants utilise both affective and cognitive strategies to organise behaviour.

The DMM model in infancy describes attachment patterns that progress along a continuum from primarily cognitive to affective strategies: $A_{1-2} \rightarrow B_{1-2} \rightarrow B_3 \rightarrow B_4 \rightarrow C_{1-2}$, with the classification A/C used to describe patterns of attachment that are unintegrated or where different strategies are employed in different contexts (Crittenden 2000).

Both models also address the role of fear shaping infant patterns of attachment, but the ABC + D model views fear as a 'disorganising' strategy, wherein fear of the caregiver prevents the infant from formulating a coherent (i.e. organised) pattern of attachment, and a disorganised pattern emerges. Conversely, in the DMM model, fear is conceptualised as an organising strategy to foster self-protection, and the infant's behavioural strategies will vary based on the caregiver's behaviour and on which memory system is activated most strongly (Crittenden 1999).

Development and definition of 'secure' attachment

In addition, the ABC + D and DMM models differ in their conceptualisation of the process of becoming securely attached. Both Main and Crittenden conceptualise Type B attachment as the most balanced, and the least vulnerable to psychopathology (Crittenden 2006; Main 2000). Main believed that secure infant attachment emerged in the context of maternal contingency and sensitive responsiveness to the infant's signals, which was manifest by the infant's organised ability to seek proximity to the mother when distressed, and engage in exploration of the environment when not distressed (Main 2000). In addition, however, Crittenden conceptualised that infants develop organised strategies through a process of integration of both cognitive and affective information, involving a relative reliance on the two types of information (affect or cognition) and a degree of integration of the information and corresponding representations. In this regard, in the DMM, the distinction between security and insecurity is not as sharply dichotomised as in a categorical ABC + D model but, rather, varies along a dimensional continuum.

Changes in attachment over time

Other differences between the Main and Crittenden models include whether early conditions largely determine later outcomes (developmental trajectory) or whether experience has a cumulative and dynamic effect (developmental pathways); whether individuals have a single enduring IWM or multiple, situation-specific DRs; and whether a four-category model based on infancy can describe attachment at later ages, or whether additional patterns are needed (Shah *et al.* 2010).

Intergenerational transmission

Regarding the mother-to-infant (intergenerational) transmission of attachment patterns or strategies, the ABC + D model differs most notably from the DMM in its presumption of continuity of attachment patterns from caregiver to child (Van IJzendoorn 1995), whereas the DMM model anticipates that sentinel life events may catalyse a change in attachment classification (e.g. after childbirth, or with effective psychotherapy). Infants may adopt a different pattern of attachment from their caregiver, if that is most adaptive for them. In fact, rather than demonstrating continuity with caregiver attachment, some infants have been shown to organise the opposite pattern from their mothers (Shah *et al.* 2010).

Conclusion

From a common theoretical foundation established by John Bowlby and Mary Ainsworth, two models of attachment across the lifespan have emerged. Both the ABC + D model and the Dynamic-Maturational Model of Attachment and Adaptation assert that patterns established in infancy form an important foundation upon which future attachment strategies are built during childhood, adolescence and adulthood, although the tools used to describe these patterns and their meaning may differ. Crittenden has expanded the range of assessment tools to include the preschool and childhood years, as well as adolescence (Crittenden & Landini 2011). Although several studies have directly compared these two models (Crittenden *et al.* 2007; Crittenden & Newman 2010; Spieker & Crittenden 2010), additional studies are needed which incorporate long-term outcomes associated with each.

Understanding the meaning and function of these attachment strategies will also assist us to move beyond the simplistic notion of 'secure is good' and 'insecure is bad', to a realisation of how attachment can be adaptive and help to compensate for trauma and adversity throughout life.

References

Ainsworth, M.D.S. (1979). Infant–mother attachment. *American Psychologist, 34*(10), 932–937.

Ainsworth, M.D.S., Blehar, M.C., Waters, E., & Wall, S. (1978). *Patterns of Attachment: A psychological study of the Strange Situation.* Hillsdale, NJ: Erlbaum.

Bowlby, J. (1969). *Attachment and Loss, Vol. 1 Attachment.* New York: Basic Books.

Bowlby, J. (1980). *Attachment and Loss, Vol. 3 Loss.* New York: Basic Books.

Carlson, E.A. (1998). A prospective longitudinal study of attachment disorganization/disorientation. *Child Development, 69*(4), 1107–1128.

Crittenden, P.M. (1981). Abusing, neglecting, problematic, and adequate dyads: Differentiating by patterns of interaction. *Merrill Palmer Quarterly, 28*(1), 18.

Crittenden, P.M. (1985). Social networks, quality of child rearing, and child development. *Child Development, 56,* 1299–1313.

Crittenden, P.M. (1990). Internal representational models of attachment relationships. *Infant Mental Health Journal, 11,* 259–277.

Crittenden, P.M. (1999). *Attaccamento in etâ adulta. L'approccio dinamico maturativo alla Adult Attachment Interview. Edizione Italiana a cura di Graziella Fava Vizziello e Andrea Landini.* Milan: Cortina.

Crittenden, P.M. (2000). A dynamic-maturational approach to continuity and change in pattern of attachment. In P.M. Crittenden & A. H. Claussen (eds), *The Organization of Attachment Relationships: Maturation, culture, and context* (pp. 343–357). New York: Cambridge University Press.

Crittenden, P.M. (2004). *Patterns of Attachment in Adulthood: A Dynamic-Maturation approach to analyzing the Adult Attachment Interview.* Unpublished manuscript, Miami, FL.

Crittenden, P.M. (2006). A Dynamic-Maturational Model of Attachment. *Australian and New Zealand Journal of Family Therapy, 27*(2), 105–115.

Crittenden, P.M. (2008). *Raising Parents: Attachment, parenting, and child safety.* Cullompton, UK: Willan Publishing.

Crittenden, P.M., & Ainsworth, M.D.S. (1989). Child maltreatment and attachment theory. In D. Cicchetti & V. Carlson (eds), *Handbook of Child Maltreatment* (pp. 432–463). New York: Cambridge University Press.

Crittenden, P.M., & Landini, A. (2011). *Assessing Adult Attachment.* New York: W. W. Norton.

Crittenden, P.M., & Newman, L. (2010). Comparing models of borderline personality disorder: Mothers' experience, self-protective strategies, and dispositional representations. *Clinical Child Psychology and Psychiatry, 15*(3), 433–451.

Crittenden, P.M., Partridge, M.F., & Claussen, A.H. (1991). Family patterns of relationship in normative and dysfunctional families. *Development and Psychopathology, 3,* 491–512.

Crittenden, P.M., Claussen, A.H., & Kozlowska, K. (2007). Choosing a valid assessment of attachment for clinical use: A comparative study. *Australian and New Zealand Journal of Family Therapy, 28*(2), 78–87.

George, C., Kaplan, N., & Main, M. (1985). *Adult Attachment Interview*. Department of Psychology, University of California, Berkeley.

George, C., Kaplan, N., & Main, M. (1996). *Adult Attachment Interview, 3rd Edition.* Department of Psychology, University of California, Berkeley.

Hamilton, C.E. (2000). Continuity and discontinuity of attachment from infancy through adolescence. *Child Development, 71*(3), 690–694.

Hautamäki, A., Hautamäki, L., Neuvonen, L., & Maliniemi-Piispanen, S. (2010). Transmission of attachment across three generations. *European Journal of Developmental Psychology, 7*(5), 618–634.

Hesse, E. (1996). Discourse, memory, and the Adult Attachment Interview: A note with emphasis on the emerging cannot classify category. *Infant Mental Health Journal, 17*(1), 4–11.

Hesse, E., & Main, M. (2000). Disorganized infant, child, and adult attachment: Collapse in behavioral and attentional strategies. *Journal of the American Psychoanalytic Association, 48*(4), 1097–1127.

Landa, S., & Duschinsky, R. (2013). Crittenden's Dynamic-Maturational Model of Attachment and Adaptation. *Review of General Psychology, 17*(3), 326–338.

Ledoux, J. (1996). *The Emotional Brain: The mysterious underpinnings of emotional life.* New York: Simon & Schuster.

Lewis, M., Fearing, C., Rosenthal, S. (2000). Attachment over time. *Child Development, 71*(3), 707–720.

Lyons-Ruth, K. (1996). Attachment relationships among children with aggressive behavior problems: The role of disorganized early attachment patterns. *Journal of Consulting and Clinical Psychology, 64*(1), 64–73.

Lyons-Ruth, K. (1999). Maternal frightened, frightening or atypical behavior and disorganized infant attachment patterns. *Monographs of the Society for Research in Child Development, 64*(3), 67–96.

Main, M. (1995). Recent studies in attachment: Overview, with selected implications for clinical work. In S. Goldberg, R. Muir, & J. Kerr (eds), *Attachment Theory: Social, developmental and clinical perspectives.* Hillsdale, NJ: Analytic Press.

Main, M. (1996). Introduction to the special section on attachment and psychopathology: 2. Overview of the field of attachment. *Journal of Consulting and Clinical Psychology, 64*(2), 237.

Main, M. (2000). The organized categories of infant, child, and adult attachment: Flexible vs. inflexible attention under attachment related stress. *Journal of the American Psychoanalytic Association, 48*, 1055–1096.

Main, M. (2010). Cross-cultural studies of attachment organization: Recent studies, changing methodologies, and the concept of conditional strategies. *Human Development, 33*(1), 48–61.

Main, M., & Goldwyn, R. (1995). Interview-based adult attachment classifications: Related to infant-mother and infant–father attachment. *Developmental Psychology, 19*, 227–239.

Main, M., & Hesse, E. (1990). Parents' unresolved traumatic experiences are related to infant disorganized attachment status: Is frightened and/or frightening parental behavior the linking mechanism? In M.T. Greenberg, D. Cicchetti, & E.M. Cummings (eds), *Attachment in the Preschool Years: Theory, research, and intervention* (pp. 161–182). Chicago: University of Chicago Press.

Main, M., & Solomon, J. (1990). Procedures for identifying infants as disorganized/disoriented during the Ainsworth Strange Situation. In M.T. Greenberg, D. Cicchetti, & E.M. Cummings (eds), *Attachment in the Preschool Years: Theory, research, and intervention* (pp. 121–160). Chicago: University of Chicago Press.

Main, M., & Weston, D. (1981). The quality of the toddler's relationship to the mother and father. *Child Development, 52*, 932–940.

Main, M., Kaplan, N., & Cassidy, J. (1985). Security in infancy, childhood and adulthood: A move to the level of representation. *Monographs of the Society for Research in Child Development, 50*(1/2), 66–104.

Radke-Yarrow, M., Cummings, E.M., Kuczynski, L., & Chapman, M. (1985). Patterns of attachment in two- and three-year-olds in normal families and families with parental depression. *Child Development, 56*, 884–893.

Schacter, D.L., & Tulving, E. (1994). What are the memory systems of 1994? In D.L. Schacter & E. Tulving (eds), *Memory Systems* (pp. 1–38). Cambridge, MA: Bradford.

Shah, P.E., Fonagy, P., & Strathearn, L. (2010). Is attachment transmitted across generations? The plot thickens. *Clinical Child Psychology and Psychiatry, 15*(3), 329–346.

Spieker, S., & Crittenden, P.M. (2010). Comparing two attachment classification methods applied to preschool strange situations. *Clinical Child Psychology and Psychiatry, 15*(1), 97–120.

Sroufe, L.A., & Waters, E. (1977). Attachment as an organizational construct. *Child Development, 48*(4), 1184–1199.

Strathearn, L. (2007). Exploring the neurobiology of attachment. In L.C. Mayes, P. Fonagy, & M. Target (eds), *Developmental Science and Psychoanalysis: Integration and innovation* (pp. 117–130). London: Karnac Press.

Strathearn, L. (2011). Maternal neglect: Oxytocin, dopamine and the neurobiology of attachment. *Journal of Neuroendocrinology, 23*(11), 1054–1065.

Strathearn, L., Fonagy, P., Amico, J.A., & Montague, P.R. (2009). Adult attachment predicts mother's brain and oxytocin response to infant cues. *Neuropsychopharmacology, 34*(13), 2655–2666.

Thompson, R.A., & Raikes, H.A. (2003). Toward the next quarter-century: Conceptual and methodological challenges for attachment theory. *Development and Psychopathology, 15*(03), 691–718.

Van IJzendoorn, M.H. (1995). Adult attachment representations, parental responsiveness, and infant attachment: A meta analysis on the predictive validity of the Adult Attachment Interview. *Psychological Bulletin, 117*(3), 387–403.

Waters, E. (1978). The reliability and stability of individual differences in infant-mother attachment. *Child Development, 49*(2), 483–494.

Weinfeld, N.S., Sroufe, L.A., & Egeland, B. (2000). Attachment from infancy to early adulthood in a high risk sample: Continuity, discontinuity, and their correlates. *Child Development, 71*, 695–702.

Chapter 5

Disorganised attachment and reactive attachment disorders

David Shemmings

Introduction

Persistent and often deep-rooted disagreements exist between researchers and clinicians over the difference between *disorganised attachment* – DA (Main & Hesse 1998) and *reactive attachment disorder* – RAD (e.g. Zeanah 1996); indeed in 2003 a special edition of the journal *Attachment and Human Development* was devoted to the exploration of these differences. This chapter seeks not to reconcile them but to examine their distinctive features and emphases as it is 'quite clear that that disorganized attachment is not synonymous with RAD' (Zeanah & Gleason 2010: 9).

One of the obvious differences between DA and RAD is that the former emerged from attachment theory and research, rooted in ethology and developmental psychology (see Holmes 2001) whereas RAD was developed by psychiatrists and clinicians following the medical model that studies symptom groups to reach diagnoses. The medical model diagnostic process is discussed by Gutjahr in Chapter 8.

It is generally accepted, for example, that before 1998 (see Zeanah & Gleason 2010: 2) almost no empirical research or theoretical derivation informed the nosology of RAD. This led Van IJzendoorn & Bakermans-Kranenburg (2003: 315) to conclude that 'it is astonishing that a widely used diagnostic system for attachment disorders seems almost not to be informed by attachment theory'.

Another difference is that much of the early work on RAD concerned the relatively small number of children from institutions and orphanages when no selective attachment had been made, and it often focused on how the child responded to strangers, whereas the initial research into DA was (and still is) concerned with major disruptions within a child's existing primary caregiving relationships and has been studied in the general population. The infrequency of RAD is often overlooked; the prevalence levels in the general population tend to be reported at around 1.5 per cent (23 children with RAD from 1,646 children from a 'deprived' sector of an urban centre in the UK; Minnis *et al.* 2013). It is commonplace, for example, to hear non-clinicians – but practitioners who should know better – using the term 'attachment disorders' to include a variety of behaviours which, while experienced often as troublesome, occur within most normative populations.

Prevalence among higher risk groups – typically children in the care of the state – tends to be higher, but

> using a narrow definition that maps well onto ICD-10 disorders, only 2% of (children cared for by the state) were identified as having a possible attachment disorder, whereas about 20% were identified with a broader set of attachment-related problems that went beyond the ICD-10 diagnoses.
>
> (Woolgar & Scott 2013: 4)

Theoretical and research background

What is reactive attachment disorder?

According to Zeanah and Shah (2005: 3) 'Reactive attachment disorder (RAD) describes a constellation of aberrant attachment behaviours and other social behavioural anomalies that are believed to result from "pathogenic care".' Such behaviours can be observed and then used in the diagnostic process.

This diagnosis first appeared in the third version of the *Diagnostic and Statistical Manual of Mental Disorders of the American Psychiatric Association* (*DSM-III*) in 1980. *DSM-IV* (1994) sub-divided RAD into two separate parts: the *inhibited* and *disinhibited* attachment disorders. The new *DSM-5* (American Psychiatric Association 2013) now proposes two different disorders: the *Reactive Attachment Disorder of Infancy and Early Childhood* and the *Disinhibited Social Engagement Disorder*.

Using the *DSM-IV* terminology, children diagnosed with an *inhibited* attachment disorder appear very uncommunicative and emotionally withdrawn. They regularly experience difficulties controlling their feelings but do not seek (or accept) comfort when stressed. They are hypervigilant but show non-responsive, almost pathological resistance to being comforted. Highly distrusting of close relationships, they become hostile and aggressive.

Children diagnosed with a *disinhibited* attachment disorder approach or respond to 'strangers' indiscriminately but they have an unnerving facility with unfamiliar adults to make them feel they are 'special'; but their non-selective, random intimacy-seeking is a visage hiding a very troubled child. They show a lack of preference for their own caregivers, and they often behave significantly younger than their years. They are usually chronically anxious.

Overall the *DSM-IV* RAD criteria were felt to be 'too focused on aberrant social behaviors and not specifically enough focused on aberrant attachment behaviors' (Zeanah & Gleason 2010: 7). Also, '[it] includes both excessive familiarity with relative strangers (which does not describe attachment behaviors) and lack of selectivity in choice of attachment figures (which does describe attachment behaviors)' (2010: 10).

Table 5.1 Indicators of reactive attachment disorder and disorganised attachment: DSM-5 criteria for reactive attachment disorder of infancy or early childhood

A A pattern of markedly disturbed and developmentally inappropriate attachment behaviours, evident before 5 years of age, in which the child rarely or minimally turns preferentially to a discriminated attachment figure for comfort, support, protection and nurturance. The disorder appears as a consistent pattern of inhibited, emotionally withdrawn behaviour in which the child rarely or minimally directs attachment behaviours towards any adult caregivers, as manifest by both of the following:

  1 Rarely or minimally seeks comfort when distressed.
  2 Rarely or minimally responds to comfort offered when distressed.

B A persistent social and emotional disturbance characterised by at least two of the following:

  1 Relative lack of social and emotional responsiveness to others.
  2 Limited positive affect.
  3 Episodes of unexplained irritability, sadness, or fearfulness which are evident during nonthreatening interactions with adult caregivers.

C Does not meet the criteria for Autistic Spectrum Disorder
D Pathogenic care as evidenced by at least one of the following:

  1 Persistent disregard of the child's basic emotional needs for comfort, stimulation, and affection (i.e. neglect).
  2 Persistent disregard of the child's basic physical needs.
  3 Repeated changes of primary caregiver that prevent formation of stable attachments (e.g. frequent changes in foster care).
  4 Rearing in unusual settings such as institutions with high child/caregiver ratios that limit opportunities to form selective attachments.

E There is a presumption that the care in Criterion C is responsible for the disturbed behaviour in Criterion A (e.g. the disturbances in Criterion A began following the pathogenic care in Criterion C).
F The child has a developmental age of at least 9 months'

Additionally, it is now clear that 'the disinhibited' type behaviour

> occurs in children who lack attachments, in children who have attachments, and even in children who have secure attachments. Further, on closer inspection, it is not necessarily attachment behaviors that are disinhibited but rather social engagement or affiliative behaviors that are expressed non-selectively.
>
> (Zeanah & Gleason 2010: 10)

See DeJong (Chapter 9) for a discussion of other affiliative processes. In the new proposed *DSM-5* criteria the definition of RAD is now 'warranted when a child who is developmentally capable of forming attachments, does not because of an aberrant caregiving environment' (American Psychiatric Association 2013).

Table 5.2 DSM-5 criteria for disinhibited social engagement disorder

A A pattern of behaviour in which the child actively approaches and interacts with unfamiliar adults by exhibiting at least two of the following:

   1 Reduced or absent reticence to approach and interact with unfamiliar adults.
   2 Overly familiar behaviour (verbal or physical violation of culturally sanctioned social boundaries).
   3 Diminished or absent checking back with adult caregiver after venturing away, even in unfamiliar settings.
   4 Willingness to go off with an unfamiliar adult with minimal or no hesitation.

B The behaviour in A is not limited to impulsivity as in ADHD but includes socially disinhibited behaviour.
C Pathogenic care as evidenced by at least one of the following:

   1 Persistent failure to meet the child's basic emotional needs for comfort, stimulation, and affection (i.e. neglect).
   2 Persistent failure to provide for the child's physical and psychological safety.
   3 Persistent harsh punishment or other types of grossly inept parenting.
   4 Repeated changes of primary caregiver that limit opportunities to form stable attachments (e.g. frequent changes in foster care).
   5 Rearing in unusual settings that limit opportunities to form selective attachments (e.g. institutions with high child to caregiver ratios).

D There is a presumption that the care in Criterion C is responsible for the disturbed behaviour in Criterion A (e.g. the disturbances in Criterion A began following the pathogenic care in Criterion C).
E The child has a developmental age of at least 9 months

Furthermore,

> what was formerly called reactive attachment disorder, disinhibited type in DSM-IV . . . does not appear to reflect disordered attachment but rather a deviant tendency to violate culturally sanctioned social boundaries in inter-actions with others. Both of these disorders have been much more carefully studied and characterized in early childhood, but a small body of evidence suggests the persistence of signs of disinhibited social engagement disorder into middle childhood and adolescence.
>
> (Zeanah & Gleason 2010: 28–9)

What is disorganised attachment?

The category of disorganised attachment (D) was described when Main and her colleagues observed, on rating Strange Situation procedures (SSP), children that could not be adequately coded in the existing ABC system. (See Van Rosmalen, Van IJzendoorn and Bakermans-Kranenburg in Chapter 1).

Table 5.3 Indicators of disorganised attachment behaviours in the Strange Situation

1   Sequential display of contradictory behaviour patterns – such as very strong attachment behaviour suddenly followed by avoidance, freezing or dazed behaviour.
2   Simultaneous display of contradictory behaviours – such as strong avoidance with strong contact-seeking, distress, or anger.
3   Undirected, misdirected, incomplete and interrupted movements and expressions – for example, extensive expressions accompanied by movement away from, rather than toward the carer.
4   'Stereotypies' – such as asymmetrical movements or mistimed movements; and anomalous postures – such as stumbling for no apparent reason and only when the carer is present.
5   Freezing, stilling, and slowed 'underwater' movements and expressions.
6   Direct indices of apprehension regarding the carer – such as hunched shoulders or a fearful facial expression.
7   Direct indices of disorganisation and disorientation – such as disoriented wandering, confused or dazed expressions, or multiple rapid changes in affect.

DA is not a psychiatric diagnosis like RAD (albeit it has been used as such) but has been developed within the framework of classical attachment theory.

DA is not an attachment 'style' but a description of very specific, temporarily immobilised behaviours displayed by a child when their attachment system is activated in the presence of their caregiver. This state could also be described as one in older children and adults in which the individual ceases 'mentalising'. In psychoanalytic terms a regression to an earlier developmental mode of psychic functioning (see Luyten & Fonagy in Chapter 6). Main and Hesse's (1998) powerful phrase 'fear without solution' captures the essence of DA. It occurs when the child is frightened 'of' or occasionally 'for' a primary caregiver. Such responses could not be classified under the classic ABC system. Lyons-Ruth and Jacobvitz (2008: 676) describe the behaviours when this happens as follows (note the 'shutting down' feature of each one):

> [U]nclassified infants were observed approaching the parent with head averted; rocking on hands and knees following an abortive approach; or screaming by the door for the parent, then moving away on reunion. What unclassified infants appeared to have in common were contradictory intentions (approaching a parent with head averted), or behaviours that involved apprehension, either directly (fearful facial expressions, oblique approaches), or indirectly e.g. disoriented behaviours, including dazed or trance-like expressions; or freezing of all movement at the parent's entrance.

Such behaviour is consistently seen in about 10–15 per cent of children in low-risk, non-clinical samples of children (for example, Out *et al*. 2009).

*What behaviours, traits and influences are associated with DA
and what are its key consequences and developmental sequelae?*

Because at present there is far less research on RAD compared to DA, especially given its proposed new criteria for inclusion in *DSM-5*, this section applies only to the field of disorganised attachment. Nevertheless, it is possible that some of the findings would also apply to RAD. A meta-analysis conducted at Leiden University (Van IJzendoorn *et al.* 1999; N = 248) found that compared to the normative 15 per cent figure for DA in non-clinical populations its prevalence was elevated among children with autism, cerebral palsy or Down syndrome (around 35%). Children with physical conditions such as congenital heart disease and cleft palate were no more likely to exhibit DA than low-risk groups. Similarly, children diagnosed with ADHD tended not to show DA. Nor were temperamental differences found.

Instead, 'the findings . . . indicate that attachment disorganisation emerges *within a particular relationship*; they do not support the notion of attachment disorganisation as an individual trait or inborn characteristic of the child' (Lyons-Ruth and Jacobvitz 2008: 699, emphasis added). This is not the case with RAD, where children with ADHD, Williams disease and fetal alcohol syndrome (Zeanah & Gleason 2010), for example, can exhibit attachment disorders. In groups of children with maltreating parents (N = 165) 48 per cent were found to show DA behaviour compared with the normative 15 per cent within low-risk groups, but this percentage rose to nearly 80 per cent when the more sensitive Main and Solomon codings were used (Van IJzendoorn *et al.* 1999). This is because their coding 'includes more index behaviours than other classifications available when most of the research was undertaken' (Shemmings & Shemmings 2011: 43). The high combined effect size across all five samples for maltreatment is perhaps not surprising because this is centrally what DA means: the paradox for the child that the very person who they expect will love, care for and protect them is, at one and the same time, the source of danger. Van IJzendoorn *et al.* concluded that DA is 'an early sign of psychopathology' (1999: 244). This meta-analysis and a more recent one by Fearon *et al.* (2010, N = 5,947), which reviewed 69 samples, found more externalising behaviour – such as harming or attacking other people or property rather than oneself – among those children assessed as showing DA behaviour. Some writers argue that as children showing DA behaviour in infancy and toddlerhood get older they try to gain mastery of their caregiver/s in two opposing ways: either by excessive, role-reversed caregiving to the adult or by becoming hostile and punitive. However, as such descriptions describe on occasions the behaviour of most teenagers (not all of whom, of course, have disorganised attachments) it is argued here that the more precise markers observable in *Story Stem Completion* methods and the *Child Attachment Interview* (see below) are to be preferred in order to avoid over-identifying DA behaviour. Although attachment insecurity (the 'anxious-ambivalent' or 'anxious-avoidant' patterns) in itself tends not to lead to mental health disorders, Dozier *et al.* believe that 'the only clear connections between infant attachment and adult psychopathology are between disorganised attachment and dissociative symptoms in adolescence and early adulthood. They conclude that part of the reason is that the child quickly develops a 'sensitized neurobiology' (Dozier *et al.* 2008: 736). There is also a connection between DA behaviours observed in childhood and the diagnosis of a borderline personality disorder in adult life. This important association is discussed by Fonagy and colleagues in Chapters 2 and 6. In summary, Van IJzendoorn and Bakermans-Kranenburg state: 'Disorganised attachment has been shown to be indexed with clear-cut behavioral markers . . . and have serious developmental consequences . . . Extreme indications of disorganisation may be regarded as psychiatric disturbance with more or less severe symptoms and consequences' (2003: 317).

Neurobiological and biochemical explanations

McCrory, de Brito and Viding (2010) offer the best summary of neurobiological and biochemical findings to date, and illustrate how maltreatment and, by implication, given their association, behaviour seen with DA, can affect the structure of the brain. Maltreated children may have smaller cranial and cerebral volume, as well as reduced 'white matter' in key parts of the brain. The amygdala, hypothalamus and hippocampus are also affected, which can result in losses of dendritic branching. There may also be biochemical consequences of DA, especially in the way the body deals with stress. The Hypothalamic-Pituitary-Adrenal (HPA) axis is involved centrally in cortisol production by activating stored glucose for secretion into the blood. The HPA axis has to produce the *optimal* amount of cortisol. Under- or over-production of cortisol produces so called 'toxic stress' (National Scientific Council on the Developing Child 2005), the consequences of which can lead to psychopathological sequelae in adulthood. These complex issues are discussed further by Music in Chapter 7.

Identification and assessment of reactive attachment disorders

As discussed above RAD is a psychiatric diagnosis in which behaviours ('symptoms') are clustered into a syndrome which, if other symptoms are present can lead to a diagnosis being given. In the 'medical model' diagnosis of a disease assumes there is a root cause or aetiology. This process is discussed further in this book by Gutjahr (Chapter 8).

RAD is now divided into two different disorders rather than as a sub-division of the one disorder (American Psychiatric Association 2013). The proposal is to label them *Reactive Attachment Disorder of Infancy and Early Childhood* and *Disinhibited Social Engagement Disorder*. The diagnosis of an attachment disorder is made by a clinical practitioner, usually but not always a child psychiatrist. However, children warranting this diagnosis occur very infrequently.

Identification and assessment of disorganised attachment

Individuals with a disorganised attachment are encountered much more frequently but it is only observable in infants, toddlers, younger children and adolescents. In adulthood behaviours associated with disorganised attachments 'transform' into similarly disorganised features that can be observed within close relationships. Such individuals may receive an adult psychiatric diagnosis of a borderline personality disorder if their behaviour is sufficiently dysfunctional (see *DSM-IV* for diagnostic criteria).

Child behaviours

The difficulties associated with DA can be observed both clinically and in more formal assessments. The measures of attachment in children of different ages, each of which requires training to administer and code, are discussed in more detail in *The Routledge Handbook of Attachment: Assessment* (Farnfield & Holmes 2014).

Infants/toddlers

STRANGE SITUATION PROCEDURE (SSP) – APPROX. 11 MONTHS–3.5 YEARS

The SSP (Ainsworth *et al.* 1979) remains the 'gold standard' with which to assess attachment patterns. It is a powerful indicator of DA because it involves the infant directly experiencing a reunion experience with a caregiver when they are simultaneously experiencing the mildly anxiety-provoking situation of having been left on their own for a short period of time. Seven behaviours are indicative of DA (see Table 5.3). Some of these behaviours could be seen when, for example, a child is involved in 'pretend' play, so care must be taken to accurately assess DA behaviours.

Younger children

STORY STEM COMPLETION (SSC) – APPROX. 3–8 YEARS

Toddlers learn more complex and sophisticated strategies to handle stressful situations. An elegant way of exploring their state of mind with regard to attachment was developed by asking the child to finish a number of story beginnings which all include elements of mild anxiety ('spilled juice', 'lost pig' are two examples). They are asked 'Can you *show me* and *tell me* what happens next?' (the use of *both* verbs is important). The stories are 'brought to life' by means of *Play People*, animals and other 'props' to help make them more concrete.

Methods include the *MacArthur Story Stem Battery* (MSSB: Bretherton *et al.* 1990) developed in 1990 for children between 3 to 8 years; the *Story Stem Assess-*

ment Profile (SSAP: Hodges *et al.* 2003) developed in 1990; and the *Manchester Child Attachment Story Task* (MCAST: Green *et al.* 2000) developed in 2000 for children aged around 4 to 8 years.

DA is indicated by three 'markers' in a Story Stem, each of which captures vividly the essential experience for the child of 'fear without solution'.

Marker 1   *Catastrophic Fantasy* (e.g. people and characters die inexplicably and there is little or no resolution to the beginning of the story)

Marker 2   *Bizarre/Atypical Responses* (e.g. speaking in a strange voice or walking off – but this is different from a child becoming bored with the assessment process)

Marker 3   *'Good/Bad' Shift* (where one character is portrayed as 'good' and then 'bad' but without any explanation in the narrative for the shift).

Pre/young adolescents

CHILD ATTACHMENT INTERVIEW – APPROX. 7–11 YEARS

The *Child Attachment Interview* (CAI) was devised in 2003 by Target, Fonagy and Shmueli-Goetz for children aged 7 to 11. Its underpinning principles are very similar to those informing the *Adult Attachment Interview* (AAI; George *et al.* 1996). The AAI asks adults to reflect on their past to see how they access, narrate and explore early memories (hence, it is a measure of their current attachment organisation *not their childhood pattern*). Children aged between 7 and 11 are still firmly located in their childhood so the CAI assesses their current attachment organisation (the DA markers are similar to those with the Story Stem Completion assessment but with additions to reflect the child's developing cognition). Remembering that DA is marked by a fleeting set of temporary behaviours under conditions of mild attachment activation, a child's attachment behaviour will eventually resolve into a more organised 'style', even including an overall secure pattern. An example of this, at first sight, inconsistent anomaly – how can a child who shows DA also be securely attached? – was described to me as follows:

A 3 year old boy from a war-torn area was forced to witness his father hacked to death and then his two sisters tortured, raped and murdered in front of him. Prior to this horrific event his relationship with both his parents had been very secure, but soon afterwards he showed strong indications of DA behavior during the relatively short time his mother could not be emotionally available for him. But her 'absence' was short-lived, and only periodic, so in most situations and circumstances he remained securely attached to her: his default position was that of secure attachment, but there were occasions when he was frightened for (but not 'of') his mother, so he displayed, albeit fleetingly, 'fear without solution'.

Identifying and assessing intervening factors leading to reactive attachment disorders

Due to the paucity of research in the field of RAD it is more difficult to identify precisely the mediating factors. The key determinant in DSM-5 is 'pathogenic care' (see Table 5.1). The criteria are similar for the two disorders except for the replacement of 'disregard' in caregiving (D2) in RAD for caregiving 'failure' in disinhibited social engagement disorder (C2) which, while not entirely the same, could potentially lead to definitional problems when conducting research. Although the evidence base for RAD is less clear than for DA, the most detailed study to date by Lyons-Ruth *et al.* (2009):

> determined that indiscriminate behavior was present among family reared, high-risk infants only if they had been maltreated or if their mothers had had psychiatric hospitalizations. They found that mothers' disrupted emotional interactions with the infant mediated the relationship between caregiving adversity and indiscriminate behaviour.
>
> (Zeanah & Gleason 2010: 16)

Thus it is likely that there are also overlaps between the caregiving dimensions involved in DA and RAD.

Identifying and assessing intervening factors leading to disorganised attachments

There are now strong indications that three key intervening variables in caregivers – *unresolved loss, disconnected/extremely insensitive parenting* and *low mentalisation* – mediate to produce DA behaviour in children (Shemmings & Shemmings 2011). Both *unresolved loss and trauma* and *mentalisation* are assessed using the AAI.

The AAI is a complex interviewing process using a narrative approach to elicit working models of attachment by 'surprising the unconscious'. Specifically:

> the 60- to 90-minute interview asks interviewees to choose five adjectives to describe their relationship with their mother/father, to supply anecdotes illustrating why these adjectives are appropriate, to speculate about why their parents behaved as they did, and to describe changes over time in the quality of their relationships with their parents.
>
> (Shaver & Mikulincer 2002: 136)

There are now two versions of the AAI with different coding systems. These are discussed in Farnfield and Holmes (2014).

The Main and Goldwyn system uses:

five continuous rating scales intended to capture the probable quality of early experiences, separately with mother/father (e.g. loving, rejecting, neglecting), and on 12 scales that describe the individual's current state of mind regarding those experiences (e.g. idealising, continuing anger, derogation of attachment, coherence of the narrative). A primary attachment category is then assigned.

(Shaver & Mikulincer 2002: 136)

In Crittenden's Dynamic-Maturational Model (DMM) coders classify transcripts according to the different memory systems to arrive at a DMM attachment strategy together with any lack of resolution of loss and/or trauma and modifiers.

Understanding and recognising unresolved trauma and loss

The emphasis here is on the word 'unresolved' because the lack of psychological resolution is a more powerful predictor of infant DA than the loss itself. This was originally postulated by Ainsworth and Eichberg (1991) and was confirmed by a meta-analysis by Van IJzendoorn, Juffer and Duyvesteyn (1995). A strong indicator of the lack of resolution during the AAI is low capacity for 'meta-cognitive monitoring', seen in an individual's lapses in the monitoring of speech or thinking. Examples include 'falling silent in mid-sentence but then completing the sentence 20 seconds or more later as if no time had passed, or failing to finish the sentence entirely' (Lyons-Ruth & Jacobvitz 2008: 672).

When parenting, if the unresolved loss relates to a bereavement, for example, the carer may become 'bombarded with intrusive images, thoughts, feelings and memories about the deceased and this, in turn makes them likely candidates for complicated or prolonged grief' (Shaver & Fraley 2008: 59). It is this unresolved 'feel' during the AAI which, in adults, most closely corresponds to DA behaviour in children; it is this sense of disorganisation and lack of coherence in the narrative that resembles a child's experience of 'fear without solution'. If the adult is also a parent then unresolved loss or trauma is likely to limit their ability to be attuned and sensitive to their child's psychological state of mind. Prolonged and extreme emotional 'unpresence' can leave a child chronically frightened of, or for, their carer.

Initially, one of the limitations of research looking at unresolved loss using the AAI was that, if when asked if they recall any loss or trauma an individual states that they do not, then the transcript was coded 'cannot classify' (or CC). To overcome the problem Lyons-Ruth and her colleagues developed the construct of the 'hostile-helpless' (HH) state of mind (Lyons-Ruth et al. 2005) which refers to 'the extent to which an individual has positively identified with the psychological stance of the infant caregiver whom he or she globally devalues elsewhere in the interview' (Lyons-Ruth & Jacobvitz 2008: 674). An example is 'We were friends . . . we were enemies. We're just alike, but we fought all the time' (Lyons-Ruth &

Jacobvitz 2008: 674). The researchers refer to three studies in 'high-risk' samples which explored the relationship between adults classified as HH in the AAI and the subsequent effect on DA behaviour in their children, which all revealed significant associations.

Disconnected or insensitive caregiving

DISCONNECTED PARENTAL BEHAVIOUR

Disconnected caregiving is a precise term indicating far more than 'disinterest'. It refers to 'sudden and unpredictable changes in behaviour which are not preceded by explanatory gestures or vocalizations and are unaccompanied by signs of affection or playfulness'. It also includes: 'dissociated, anomalous or disrupted caregiving, accompanied by frightened or frightening behaviour and disruptive emotional communication' (Shemmings & Shemmings 2011: 60). Even studies of low-risk samples 'have demonstrated that anomalous parenting, involving (often only brief episodes of) parental dissociative behaviour . . . is related to the development of attachment disorganization' (Van IJzendoorn & Bakermans-Kranenburg 2009: 2).

EXTREMELY INSENSITIVE PARENTING

On its own, parental insensitivity does not reliably predict DA behaviour. For example, Van IJzendoorn et al.'s (1999) meta-analysis established a non-significant effect size (r = 0.10) when investigating associations between DA and parental insensitivity (N = 1,951). As Lyons-Ruth concluded 'surprisingly, parental behaviour that is coded as insensitive . . . has only been weakly correlated with infant disorganised attachment behaviour' (Lyons-Ruth 2003: 889). While correlated with attachment insecurity, parental insensitivity is only mildly associated with attachment *disorganisation*. It is only when the level of insensitivity is extreme that the connection to DA is strengthened.

THE DISCONNECTED AND EXTREMELY INSENSITIVE PARENTING MEASURE

Unresolved loss and trauma interrupt mind-minded and sensitively attuned caregiving to their child. The result 'is an inability to comfort and soothe children when their attachment system is activated' (Out et al. 2009: 420–1). 'Other-relatedness' is seriously impaired if a parent is self-referentially preoccupied; they then become emotionally unavailable, sometimes frighteningly. The Disconnected and Extremely Insensitive Parenting Measure (DIP) builds on the work of Main and Hesse (1992) who initially developed five Frightening or Frightened (FR) scales, to which a sixth was added by 2006 to produce a coding system which is often used in research into DA. Similar to the FR scales, Lyons-Ruth and her colleagues developed the Atypical Maternal Behavior Instrument for Assessment and Classification (AMBIANCE) (Bronfman *et al.* 2004). The measurement of caregiving behaviours is constantly developing and the latest extension comes from Dorothée Out and her colleagues at Leiden University. The DIP (Out *et al.* 2009) builds upon the FR and AMBIANCE by distinguishing more clearly between *disconnected parenting* and *extremely insensitive parenting*.

Mentalisation

Although the precise links between disconnected and extremely insensitive parental behaviour and DA are elusive, there is also a growing belief that the 'missing link' (see Fonagy & Target 2005) is to be found in the process of 'mentalisation'. Mentalisation refers to the notion that most people can appreciate that others have different perceptions of the same event and can experience different feelings during or after the same event; most also understand that others hold different expectations and assumptions from their own. But some individuals cannot do so and are not curious about the minds of others. Those on the autistic spectrum comprise one such group, but so too do maltreating and chronically unavailable caregivers and adults with personality disorders. As we have seen, this may be the result of reduced amygdalic activity, itself the result of not having received enough mentalised experiences as a child. Fonagy and Target (2005) contend that low mentalisation is likely to produce DA behaviour in children because the caregiver simply does not appreciate the harm they could be causing. Consequently, low mentalising capacity is regularly found among parents who maltreat their children (see, for example, Allen *et al.* 2008; Crittenden 2008; Slade 2008). Such parents tend significantly to misattribute feelings and intensions to young children that they cannot have or they hold persecutory attributions such as 'my baby hates me'.

Mentalisation is discussed by Fonagy and his colleagues in Chapters 2 and 6 of this volume. The assessment of mentalisation is discussed by Luyten and Fonagy in Farnfield and Holmes (2014).

Theory and research into practice – clinical implications

Which interventions offer most potential for attenuating the negative effects of DA and RAD and for replacing maltreating caregiving with more sensitive and attuned parenting?

Disorganised attachment

Over the past decade, two meta-analyses have been conducted: one covering attachment-based interventions generally, the other one devoted to DA. Again, it is likely that some of the findings will transfer to RAD.

Less is more: Meta-analyses of sensitivity and attachment interventions in early childhood (Bakermans-Kranenburg et al. 2003)

This review analysed 70 published studies, including 88 intervention effects on sensitivity (N = 7,636) and attachment (N = 1,503). Interventions were coded as aiming to:

i   increase *carer sensitivity* by helping the parent become more attuned to their child's needs;

ii   re-evaluate the carer's *representations of their own early relationships* by exploring internal working models of attachment relationships in general, but also specifically with their children;

iii provide *social* support through practical help and advice using relationship-based interventions derived from trust-building approaches; or

iv   combine any of these approaches.

The results showed that interventions can enhance parental sensitivity and infant attachment security but change in parent sensitivity is more responsive to treatment than child attachment (Bakermans-Kranenburg *et al.* 2003; Juffer, *et al.*, 2014).

Very specific and clear interventions were far more effective than what the authors term 'broad-band interventions': 'less is more'. Family characteristics, such as single parenthood, social isolation, etc. had little effect on treatment outcomes.

This topic is considered in more detail by Juffer *et al.* in *The Routledge Handbook of Attachment: Implications and Interventions* (Holmes & Farnfield 2014: Chapter 5).

Disorganised infant attachment and preventive interventions: A review and meta-analysis (Bakermans-Kranenburg et al. 2005)

Ten studies with 15 interventions were analysed to review specifically whether interventions could be related directly to DA. They were partitioned into those that were 'sensitivity-based' and those that were 'representationally based'. The review included narrative detail about the approaches meta-analysed. The findings mirrored the first study: the most effective interventions were those using *sensitivity-based* approaches.

Reactive attachment disorder

Apart from work by Becker-Weidman and Hughes (2010) in respect of *dyadic developmental psychotherapy* there is less evidence of systematic analyses or meta-analyses of interventions in the field of RAD. This is not to say that there are not many anecdotal examples of interventions aimed at ameliorating RAD.

Concluding remarks

Disorganised attachment and the two categories of *reactive attachment disorders* are clearly different: they are used by different professional groups with different philosophical and theoretical backgrounds. Their histories are different as is their reliance upon evidence-based research. Nevertheless, their adherents share a commitment to stress their distinctiveness while accepting the inevitable overlap between them. One distinction that does not appear in the literature, however, is that the way in which RAD and DA are determined is dissimilar in one other respect: DA can only be determined by creating a situation such as the Strange Situation procedure, Story Stem Completion or the Child Attachment Interview which involves mildly stressing the child in an attachment-based situation, either literally or in the child's mind. This requirement is essential and it is unreliable to deduce the presence of DA behaviour from 'naturally occurring', serendipitous situations. It is the presence of the 'fear without solution' that is always the focus of attention.

The dysfunctional behaviour or symptoms associated with RAD may also only occur when the child experiences similar attachment-related stress in everyday life events, albeit that the full psychological significance of such events for the child might not be obvious to the observer (for example, parent, carer or professional).

The problem with both RAD and DA, though, is that quite a few practitioners use these terms indiscriminately to describe almost any and every troublesome behaviour in children. Some may or may not have insecure attachments, indeed almost 50 per cent of the population are insecurely attached (Howe *et al.* 1999). These descriptions should only be used following a detailed assessment by an adequately trained professional and, as discussed above, can only be applied to quite a small proportion of the population.

References

Ainsworth, M., Blehar, M., Waters, E., & Wall, S. (1979) *Patterns of Attachment: A psychological study of the Strange Situation*, Hillsdale, NJ: Lawrence Erlbaum Associates.

Ainsworth, M.D.S., & Eichberg, C.G. (1991) 'Effects on infant–mother attachment of mother's unresolved loss of an attachment figure, or other traumatic experience'. In C.M. Parkes, J. Stevenson-Hinde, & P. Marris (eds), *Attachment across the Life Cycle* (pp. 160–183), New York: Tavistock/Routledge.

Allen, J.G., Fonagy, P., & Bateman, A.W. (2008) *Mentalising in Clinical Practice*, Arlington, VA: APP.

American Psychiatric Association (2013) *The Diagnostic and Statistical Manual for Mental Disorders 5*, Arlington, VA: American Psychiatric Association.

Bakermans-Kranenburg, M.J., & Van IJzendoorn, M.H. (2007) Research review: 'Genetic vulnerability or differential susceptibility in child development: The case of attachment', *Journal of Child Psychology and Psychiatry and Allied Disciplines*, 48: 1160–1173.

Bakermans-Kranenburg, M.J., Van IJzendoorn, M.H., & Juffer, F. (2003) 'Less is more: Meta-analysis of sensitivity and attachment interventions in early childhood', *Psychological Bulletin*, 129: 195–215.

Bakermans-Kranenburg, M.J., Van IJzendoorn, M.H. & Juffer, F. (2005) 'Disorganized infant attachment and preventative interventions: A review and meta-analysis', *Infant Mental Health Journal*, 26: 191–216.

Becker-Weidman, A., & Hughes, D. (2010) 'Dyadic Developmental Psychotherapy: An effective and evidence-based treatment – comments in response to Mercer and Pignotti', *Child & Family Social Work*, 15(1): 6–11.

Bretherton, I., Ridgeway, D., & Cassidy, J. (1990) 'Assessing internal working models of the attachment relationship: An attachment story completion task for 3-year-olds'. In M. Greenberg, D. Cicchetti, & M. Cummings (eds), *Attachment in the Preschool Years: Theory, research and intervention* (pp. 273–308), Chicago: University of Chicago Press.

Bronfman, E., Parsons, E., & Lyons-Ruth, K. (2004) *Atypical Maternal Behavior Instrument for Assessment and Classification (AMBIANCE): Manual for coding disrupted affective communication*, unpublished manual, Department of Psychiatry, Cambridge Hospital, Massachusetts.

Crittenden, P.M. (2008) *Raising Parents: Attachment, parenting and child safety*, Portland, OR: Willan.

Dozier, M.K., Stovall-McClough, C., & Albus, K.E. (2008) 'Attachment and psychopathology in adulthood'. In J. Cassidy & P.R. Shaver (eds), *Handbook of Attachment: Theory, research and clinical applications*, 2nd edition (pp. 637–665), New York: The Guilford Press.

Farnfield, S., & Holmes, P. (eds) (2014) *The Routledge Handbook of Attachment: Assessment*, London and New York: Routledge.

Fearon, R.M.P., Bakermans-Kranenburg, M.J., Van IJzendoorn, M.H., Lapsley, A., & Roisman, G.I. (2010) 'The significance of insecure attachment and disorganization in the development of children's externalizing behavior: A meta-analytic study', *Child Development*, 81: 435–456.

Fonagy, P., & Target, M. (2005) 'Bridging the transmission gap: An end to an important mystery of attachment research?' *Attachment and Human Development*, 7: 333–343.

George, C., Kaplan, N., & Main, M. (1996) *The Attachment Interview for Adults*, unpublished manuscript, Department of Psychology, University of California, Berkeley (3rd ed.).

Green, J., Stanley, C., Smith, V., & Goldwyn, R. (2000) 'A new method of evaluating attachment representations in young school-aged children: The Manchester Child Attachment Story Task (MCAST)', *Attachment and Human Development*, 2: 48–70.

Hodges, J., Steele, M., Hillman, S., & Henderson, K. (2003) 'Mental representations and defences in severely maltreated children: A story stem battery and rating system for clinical assessment and research applications'. In R. Emde, D. Wolk, C. Zahn-Waxler, & D. Oppenheim (eds), *Narrative Processes and the Transition from Infancy to Early Childhood* (pp. 240–267), New York: Oxford University Press.

Holmes, J. (2001) *The Search for a Secure Base: Attachment theory and psychotherapy*, London: Routledge.

Holmes, P., & Farnfield, S. (eds) (2014) *The Routledge Handbook of Attachment: Implications and interventions*, London and New York: Routledge.

Howe, D., Brandon, M., Hinings, D., & Schofield, G. (1999) *Attachment Theory, Child Maltreatment and Family Support: A practice and assessment model*, London: Macmillan.

Juffer, F., Bakermans-Kranenburg, K. J., and Van Ijzendoorn, M. H. (2014) 'Attachment-based interventions: sensitive parenting is the key to positive parent–child relationships', In P. Holmes and S. Farnfield (eds). *The Routledge Handbook of Attachment: Implications and Interventions*, (pp. 83–103), Abingdon: Routledge.

Lyons-Ruth, K. (2003) 'Dissociation and the parent-infant dialogue: A longitudinal perspective', *Journal of the American Psychoanalytic Association*, 51: 883–911.

Lyons-Ruth, K., & Jacobvitz, D. (2008) 'Attachment disorganisation: Genetic factors, parenting contexts, and developmental transformation from infancy to adulthood'. In J. Cassidy & P.R. Shaver (eds), *Handbook of Attachment: Theory, research and clinical applications*, 2nd edition (pp. 666–697), New York: The Guilford Press.

Lyons-Ruth, K., Yellin, C., Melnick, S., & Atwood, G. (2005) 'Expanding the concept of unresolved mental states: Hostile/helpless states of mind on the Adult Attachment Interview are associated with disrupted mother–infant communication and infant disorganization', *Development and Psychopathology*, 17: 1–23.

Lyons-Ruth, K., Bureau, J.-F., Riley, C.D., & Atlas-Corbett, A.F. (2009) 'Socially indiscriminate attachment behavior in the strange situation: Convergent and discriminant validity in relation to caregiving risk, later behavior problems, and attachment insecurity', *Development and Psychopathology*, 21: 355–367.

Main, M., & Hesse, E. (1992) 'Disorganized/disoriented infant behavior in the Strange Situation, lapses in the monitoring of reasoning and discourse during the parent's Adult Attachment Interview, and dissociative states'. In M. Ammaniti & D. Stern (eds), *Attachment and Psychoanalysis* (pp. 86–140), Rome: Gius, Laterza and Figl.

Main, M., & Hesse, E. (1998) *Frightening, frightened, dissociated, deferential, sexualized and disorganized parental behavior: A coding system for parent–infant interactions*, 6th edition. Unpublished manual, University of California at Berkeley.

Main, M., & Solomon, J. (1990) 'Procedures for identifying infants as disorganized/disoriented during the Ainsworth Strange Situation'. In M.T. Greenberg, D. Cicchetti, & E.M. Cummings (eds), *Attachment in the Preschool Years: Theory, research, and intervention*. The John D. and Catherine T. MacArthur Foundation series on mental health and development (pp. 121–160). Chicago, IL: The University of Chicago Press.

McCrory, E., De Brito, S.A., & Viding, E. (2010) 'Research Review: The neurobiology and genetics of maltreatment and adversity', *Journal of Child Psychology and Psychiatry*, 51(10): 1079–1095 (accessed online, February 2010).

Minnis, H., Macmillan, S., Pritchett, R., Young, D., Wallace, B., Butcher, J., *et al.* (2013) *British Journal of Psychiatry*, 202(5): 342–346.

National Scientific Council on the Developing Child (2009) *Excessive stress disrupts the architecture of the developing brain* (Working Paper 3), Cambridge, MA: Center on the Developing Child, Harvard University. Available online at: http://developingchild. harvard.edu/library/reports_and_working_papers/wp3/ (accessed 4 December 2009).

Out, D., Bakermans-Kranenburg, M.J., & Van IJzendoorn, M.H. (2009) 'The role of disconnected and extremely insensitive parenting in the development of disorganized attachment: The validation of a new measure', *Attachment and Human Development*, 11: 419–443.

Shaver, P.R., & Fraley, R.C. (2008) 'Attachment, loss and grief: Implications for theory, research and clinical intervention'. In J. Cassidy & P.R. Shaver (eds), *Handbook of*

Attachment: Theory, research and clinical applications, 2nd edition (pp. 666–697), New York: The Guilford Press.

Shaver, P.R., & Mikulincer, M. (2002) 'Attachment-related psychodynamics', *Attachment and Human Development*, 4: 133–161.

Shemmings, D., & Shemmings, Y. (2011) *Understanding Disorganised Attachment: Theory and practice of working with children and families*, London: Jessica Kingsley.

Slade, A. (2008) 'Working with parents in child psychotherapy: Engaging the reflective function'. In F.N. Busch (ed.), *Mentalisation: Theoretical considerations, research findings and clinical implications* (pp. 207–234), New York: Taylor & Francis.

Target, M., Fonagy, P., & Schmueli-Goetz, Y. (2003) 'Attachment representations in school-age children: The development of the Child Attachment Interview (CAI)', *Journal of Child Psychotherapy*, 29(2): 171–186.

Van IJzendoorn, M.H. (1995) 'Adult attachment representations, parental responsiveness, and infant attachment: A meta-analysis on the predictive validity of the adult attachment interview', *Psychological Bulletin*, 117: 387–403.

Van IJzendoorn, M.H., & Bakermans-Kranenburg, M.J. (2003) 'Attachment disorders and disorganised attachment: Same or different?' *Attachment & Human Development*, 5(3): 313–320.

Van IJzendoorn, M.H., & Bakermans-Kranenburg, M.J. (2009) 'Attachment security and disorganization in maltreating families and orphanages'. Available online at: http://www.enfant-encyclopedie.com/pages/PDF/van_IJzendoorn-Bakermans-KranenburgANGxp-Attachment.pdf.

Van IJzendoorn, M.H., Juffer, F., & Duyvesteyn, M.G.C. (1995) 'Breaking the intergenerational cycle of insecure attachment: A review of the effects of attachment-based interventions on maternal sensitivity and infant security', *Journal of Child Psychology and Psychiatry*, 36: 225–248.

Van IJzendoorn, M.H., Schuengel, C., & Bakermans-Kranenburg, M.J. (1999) 'Disorganized attachment in early childhood: Meta-analysis of precursors, concomitants, and sequelae', *Development and Psychopathology*, 11: 225–249.

Woolgar, M., & Scott, S. (2013) 'The negative consequences of over-diagnosing attachment disorders in adopted children: The importance of comprehensive formulations', *Clinical Child Psychology and Psychiatry*. Published online at: http://ccp.sagepub.com/content/early/2013/04/08/1359104513478545 (accessed 23 June 2013).

Zeanah, C.H. (1996) 'Beyond insecurity: A reconceptualization of attachment disorders in infancy', *Journal of Consulting and Clinical Psychology*, 64: 42–52.

Zeanah, C.H., & Gleason, M.M. (2010) *Reactive Attachment Disorder: A review for DSM-V*, American Psychiatric Association. Available online at: http://www.nrvcs.org/nrvatachmentresources/documents/APA%20DSM-5%20Reactive%20Attachment%20Disorder%20Review%5b1%5d.pdf (accessed 30 June 2012).

Zeanah, C.H., & Shah, P. (2005) 'Attachment and its impact on child development: Comments on Van IJzendoorn, Grossmann and Grossmann, and Hennighausen and Lyons-Ruth', *Encyclopedia of Early Child Development*, Institute of Infant and Early Childhood Mental Health, Tulane University Health Sciences Center, USA. Available online at: http://www.child-encyclopedia.com/pages/PDF/attachment.pdf (accessed 30 June 2012).

Chapter 6

Mentalising in attachment contexts

Patrick Luyten and Peter Fonagy

Introduction

Attachment and mentalising are two notions that are often mentioned in the same breath; and correctly so. Mentalising or reflective functioning is the capacity to envision ourselves and others in terms of intentional mental states such as feelings, desires, wishes, goals, values, and attitudes (Allen *et al.* 2008; Luyten *et al.* 2012b). This capacity, which is fundamental in our ability to navigate what is essentially an interpersonal world, has its roots in attachment relationships. It first develops in the context of attachment relationships and remains intimately tied to attachment relationships across the life span. It is therefore most appropriate that this volume includes a discussion of their relationships.

First, we briefly discuss the relationship between attachment and mentalising. Next, we discuss the different dimensions of mentalising, the importance of considering variations in mentalising in the context of different relationships, and modes of experiencing subjectivity when mentalising fails.

Attachment and mentalising

Attachment and mentalising are so intimately intertwined that it is hard to think about mentalising and its development without considering the attachment contexts in which this capacity unfolds and manifests itself. Conversely, it is hard to think of attachment without considering the attachment figure's capacity to consider the other person – and particularly the child – as a mental agent. As explained in more detail in Chapter 2 (Fonagy *et al.*) in this volume, the development of mentalising is thought to depend on a combination of the quality of attachment relationships, caregivers' emotional availability, and the extent to which our subjective experiences are adequately mirrored (i.e. in marked and contingent ways) by our attachment figures (Slade 2005; Ensink and Mayes 2010; Sharp and Fonagy 2008).

It is important to note, however, that there is no one-to-one relationship between attachment and mentalising, but rather what has been termed a 'loose coupling'. Specifically, it is the attachment figure's capacity to treat the child as a psychological agent with his/her own mental states that is seen as crucial in the development of the capacity for mentalising. Indeed, it is not secure attachment or high levels of emotional availability per se, but a socialising context that focuses upon mental states, that is thought to foster the development of mentalisation in children (Fonagy *et al.* 2007, 2011). Secure parental attachment and high levels of emotional availability, as such, are not necessarily associated with high levels of parental reflective functioning, although of course in most parents they are positively related (Sharp and Fonagy 2008).

Yet, within securely attached parents there is a considerable range of mentalising capacities. High levels of parental reflective functioning are typically characterised by (a) interest and curiosity in mental states of the child, (b) a recognition of the opacity of mental states, and (c) the recognition that one's own mental states influence the mental states of the child in increasingly complex ways during development and that, in turn, one's own mental states are related to one's own developmental history with attachment figures.

In contrast, parental insecure attachment is almost invariably related to low levels of infant mentalising. Because of their history of attachment disruptions and, in more extreme cases, attachment trauma, insecurely attached parents typically experience a range of problems in envisioning the mental states of their child. Low levels of parental mentalising can be expressed in different ways, but mostly involve (a) a tendency to be overly certain about the mental states of the child, failing to recognise the opacity of mental states (often expressed in intrusive hyper-mentalising), or, conversely, to be completely at a loss with regard to the mental states of the child, (b) a tendency to make malevolent attributions, (c) impairments in the capacity to join in pretend play and enter into the child's internal subjective world, and (d) a lack of genuine interest in the mental states of the child (Ensink and Mayes 2010; Leckman *et al.* 2007; Sadler *et al.* 2006; Suchman *et al.* 2010; Luyten *et al.* 2014b).

The implications of this intricate, yet complex, relationship between attachment and mentalising are clear. It follows that it is crucially important when assessing mentalising to take into account its roots in past and current attachment relationships.

Dimensions of mentalising

Before addressing the relationships between attachment and mentalising in more detail, it is vital to point out that mentalising is not a unitary construct: it has different facets. For some time now, we have organised these facets according to four underlying dimensions:

1   automatic – controlled
2   internally focused – externally focused
3   self-oriented – other-oriented
4   cognitive – affective

(Fonagy and Luyten 2009; Luyten *et al.* 2012b)

The distinction between these dimensions has both research and clinical merits. While extant research findings suggest that these four dimensions or polarities involve relatively distinct neural circuits (Lieberman 2007; Uddin *et al.* 2007; Satpute and Lieberman 2006), clinically, it is important to distinguish between these dimensions, as patients may have a wide range of mentalising impairments, necessitating a targeted treatment approach and focus (Fonagy and Luyten 2009; Luyten *et al.* 2012b).

Patients' mentalising abilities should, therefore, be assessed in detail with respect to these four dimensions underlying mentalising. Detailed knowledge of the specific types of impairments in mentalising – and the specific attachment contexts in which they manifest – might not only inform the focus of treatment but also indicate to the assessor and therapist the type of relationship and associated deficits in mentalising that are likely to develop; thus, they could serve as important 'transference tracers' later in treatment (Bateman and Fonagy 2006). Evaluation of individuals' mentalising capacity thus depends on detailing their *mentalising profile*, that is, their functioning with respect to each of the four polarities underlying mentalising, particularly since an individual may show different degrees of mentalising ability on each of these dimensions (see Figure 6.1).

Automatic versus controlled mentalising

For most of the time, in our daily interactions with others, mentalising proceeds in an automatic or implicit manner. Neuroimaging research suggests that this capacity

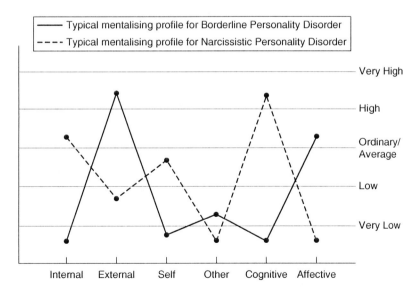

Figure 6.1 Mentalising profiles for borderline and narcissistic personality disorder

is underpinned by neurocircuits that allow fast, parallel processing of social information that is reflexive, and requires little or no attention, intention, awareness, and
effort (Lieberman 2007; Uddin *et al.* 2007; Satpute and Lieberman 2006). Recent
studies suggest that infants are probably born with a biologically pre-wired capacity to envision and encode mental states automatically from very early on, which
clearly attests to the intricate relationships between the development of mentalising
and attachment, pointing to our fundamental orientation towards others as a source
for both safety and social information (Kovacs *et al.* 2010).

By contrast, more controlled or explicit mentalising is a serial and relatively
slow process, which is typically verbal and requires reflection, attention, intention,
awareness, and effort, and therefore develops more slowly. Moreover, it has been
shown that mentalising that initially requires controlled efforts becomes increasingly automatic and thus does not involve conscious and deliberate reflection (Satpute and Lieberman 2006). It might, therefore, be particularly difficult to change
deeply ingrained dispositional attributions that are reliant on automatic, precon-
ceived judgements of the self and others. Importantly, as discussed in greater detail
below, stress or arousal facilitates automatic mentalising, but tends to impair the
capacity for controlled mentalising (Mayes 2006; Lieberman 2007).

This impact of emotional arousal also creates challenges for the assessment of
mentalising capacity. For instance, patients with borderline personality disorder
(BPD) might be able to carry out experimental mentalising tasks relatively well
when they are not emotionally aroused (Arntz *et al.* 2006), but may show considerable difficulty when under higher levels of stress; in the latter situation, automatic
mentalisation predominates, and BPD patients are typically dominated by overly
schematic assumptions about the internal states of others and find it challenging to
reflect on and moderate these assumptions.

Internally versus externally based mentalising

The second polarity is that of internally focused versus externally focused mentalising (Lieberman 2007). Internally focused mentalising refers to mental processes that are inferred from a focus on one's own or another's mental interior
(e.g. thoughts, feelings, wishes), while externally focused mentalising refers to
mental processes derived from observations of visible physical and features and/
or actions of oneself or someone else (e.g. facial expressions or posture). This
polarity is distinct from the self–other dimension discussed below, since internally
and externally focused mentalising might focus on either the self or another.

The internal versus external distinction might be particularly relevant to understanding how some patients may show difficulties in 'reading the mind' of others
based on more internal features, but show hypersensitivity to emotions based on
facial expressions or bodily posture, or other similar dissociations. For instance,
while recent studies suggest that BPD patients show considerable impairment in
understanding the intentions of others, an internally based task (e.g. King-Casas
et al. 2008), other studies suggest that these patients are often as sensitive as nor-

mal controls or even more sensitive to facial expressions, an externally based task (Domes *et al.* 2008, 2009; Lynch *et al.* 2006). In contrast, individuals with antisocial personality disorder (ASPD) might be unable to read fearful emotions from facial expressions (an externally based task) (Marsh and Blair 2008), but may show particular ability to read the inner states of others, in some cases to the extent that they make use of this capacity to manipulate others (Bateman and Fonagy 2008).

The presence of discontinuity between internally based and externally based mentalising might, in part, be explained by the fact that two relatively different neural networks underpin these capacities (Luyten *et al.* 2012b). This might also shed light on the development of mentalising in relation to attachment, and could help to explain dissociations in parental mentalising based on external versus internal features of young parents. In early development, and particularly given that infants under the age of 24 months are largely nonverbal, parental mentalising is mainly based on external features such as the infant's behaviours and facial expressions (Beebe *et al.* 2007, 2008). Some parents show considerable difficulty with this process but do better at reflecting on the internal mental states of their children once they are older, when they can make greater use of internally directed mentalisation processes (Sharp and Fonagy 2008). In contrast, other parents show the opposite problem (Luyten *et al.* 2014b).

This might also partly explain the effects of video-feedback parent–infant intervention programmes (Bakermans-Kranenburg *et al.* 2008; Slade and Sadler 2007). In these interventions, parents work with a therapist and reflect upon the possible meanings of the child's behaviour and expressions; this intervention helps the parents develop their ability to read the mind of others based on external features and also links this ability to their capacity to reflect on the others' minds based on internal features.

Mentalisation with regard to self versus others

Many forms of psychopathology, most notably psychosis and BPD (e.g. Bender and Skodol 2007; Blatt and Auerbach 1988; Clarkin *et al.* 2001), are associated with severe impairments in mentalising with regard to both the self and others. Evidence from recent neuroimaging studies supports the assumption that the capacity to mentalise about others is closely linked to the ability to reflect on the self, as common neural substrates underpin both capacities (Dimaggio *et al.* 2008; Lieberman 2007; Lombardo *et al.* 2007; Uddin *et al.* 2007). However, while some types of psychopathology might be associated with impairment in the capacity to reflect about both self and other, other forms may be characterised by a gross imbalance between these capacities. For example, as noted earlier, whereas patients with ASPD often appear to be expert in 'reading the mind' of others, and may misuse this ability to coerce others, they typically are unable to understand their own inner world (Bateman and Fonagy 2006, 2008). Similarly, patients with paranoid or narcissistic personality disorder are often overly concerned about their own internal mental states, and may even appear to have exceptional self-reflective capacities, but concurrently lack interest in or ability to conceive of the mental states of others.

Importantly, neuroimaging research has suggested another possible dissociation in relation to the self–other distinction in that there are two distinct ways of knowing the self and others, which are supported by distinct neural networks (Lieberman 2007; Uddin *et al.* 2007). A developmentally more basic, earlier neural system consists of a more bodily based, frontoparietal mirror neuron system that is involved in understanding the multimodal embodied self (e.g. face and body recognition) and others through motor-simulation mechanisms (Gallese *et al.* 2004; Rizzolatti and Craighero 2004). One fundamental mechanism that allows us to understand the actions and emotions of others thus involves activation of the mirror neuron system for actions, and activation of visceromotor centres for the understanding of affect. Studies of this mirror neuron system (Molnar-Szakacs *et al.* 2006; Gazzola *et al.* 2006; Lotze *et al.* 2006; Calmels *et al.* 2006) thus suggest that one specific pathway to understanding the actions, emotions, and sensations of others involves *a direct sharing of their actions* (Keysers and Gazzola 2006; Rizzolatti *et al.* 2006). Hence, a single mechanism underpinned by shared neural circuits applies both to witnessing the actions, sensations, and emotions of others and to performing the same actions oneself (Calvo-Merino *et al.* 2005, 2006) and appears to provide immediate 'other-to-self' (and 'self-to-other') mapping.

Second, a cortical midline system that relies less on bodily information, and processes information about the self and others in more symbolic ways, consists of the medial prefrontal cortex, anterior cingulate cortex, and precuneus (Frith and Frith 2006; Frith 2007; Uddin *et al.* 2007). This system appears to play a key role in distinguishing between one's own experiences and those of others. This cortical midline system is also more experience-based and thus emerges later in development compared with the frontoparietal system.

Studies have suggested that a subregion within the lateral prefrontal cortex inhibits one's own reactions while one is thinking about the mind of someone else. Impairments in this capacity may be related to naive realism (Pronin *et al.* 2004), a tendency to ignore intentional states underpinning behaviour and actions that we have termed the 'psychic equivalence mode' (Fonagy and Bateman 2006b). Reflective or controlled mentalising maintains self–other differentiation by enabling differentiation between our own and others' intentions and by inhibiting the tendency for overly concrete experience of the other as if it was a part of the self. The close association of self-cognition and social cognition implies a closeness and intertwining of representations of self and other; with the risk of the experience of losing the integrity of the self, an experience that is typical for many patients with borderline features, for instance, when confronted with the wishes of others.

Cognitive versus affective mentalisation

The fourth polarity refers to the integration of cognitive and affective aspects of mentalising. Within this dimension, some aspects of mentalisation are more related to cognition, including belief-desire reasoning and perspective taking, while others are more related to affect, such as affective empathy and mentalised affectivity (Fonagy *et al.* 2002; Jurist 2005). Theory of mind research typically tends to focus on the former, while research on (affective) empathy primarily focuses on the latter. As with the other three dimensions, there is increasing evidence that distinct, albeit to some extent overlapping, neurocognitive systems are involved in these capacities (Sabbagh 2004; Shamay-Tsoory and Aharon-Peretz 2007). While cognitively oriented mentalisation depends on several areas in the prefrontal cortex, affectively oriented mentalising seems to be particularly dependent on the ventromedial prefrontal cortex.

It is important to keep in mind that different types of psychopathology are characterised by overemphasis on either the cognitive or the affective aspects of mentalisation and/or by impairments in the integration of the two. There is increasing evidence that these impairments are related to the use of attachment deactivation versus hyperactivation strategies (Mikulincer and Shaver 2007), which are discussed in the next section.

Relationship-specific mentalising and individual differences in attachment history

A central tenet of attachment approaches is that internal working models of self and others are generalised cognitive–affective structures that are relatively stable over time (Bowlby 1973, 1980). These internal working models are presumed to be activated in interpersonal contexts, such as in relationships with parents, romantic partners, and friends (Fraley 2007).

Similarly, mentalising is often depicted as a general, stable capacity. For example, the Reflective Functioning Scale (Fonagy *et al.* 1998), as scored on the Adult Attachment Interview (AAI), the Child Attachment Interview (Shmueli-Goetz *et al.* 2008), and the Parent Development Interview (Slade *et al.* 2007), is assessed using an aggregate score of mentalising across different attachment relationships and contexts.

Yet, given the close links between attachment and mentalising, although mentalising undoubtedly has trait-like features, context, and attachment contexts in particular, influences mentalising (Allen *et al.* 2008; Luyten *et al.* 2012b). Just as there is substantial variation in the nature and quality of attachment relationships and internal working models of others (e.g. Pierce and Lydon 2001; Fraley 2007), there can be considerable fluctuations in mentalising depending on the (attachment) context. Moreover, again pointing to the intricate links between attachment and mentalising, the quality of mentalising is often determined by the quality of the attachment relationship and mentalising capacities of the person with whom one interacts. Generally, poor mentalising pulls for poor mentalising.

It is here that psychotherapists, and mental health professionals more generally, can make a difference, by breaking these vicious cycles. Mentalising, therefore, should be assessed from a fundamentally interactionistic perspective. Diamond and colleagues (2003), for instance, showed that the quality of mentalising in patient–therapist dyads is bidirectional, with the therapist's level of mentalising determining in part the level of mentalising observed in the patient and vice versa. Interviews such as the AAI (Hesse 2008) the CAI (Shmueli-Goetz *et al.* 2008), and the Object Relations Interview (Diamond *et al.* 1991), which elicit narratives about different significant others, allow for assessing mentalising with regard to self and others as well as mentalising in specific relationships; these measures therefore provide a promising route for further research in this area.

Elsewhere, we have discussed the effect of attachment strategies, and attachment deactivation versus hyperactivation strategies in particular (Mikulincer and Shaver 2007), on mentalising in the context of a biobehavioural model of the relationships among attachment, stress and mentalising (Fonagy and Luyten 2009; Luyten *et al.* 2012b). Based on Arnsten's (1998) dual process model and Mayes' (2000, 2006) elaboration of this model, we have proposed that with increasing stress, there is a switch from more prefrontal, controlled and executive mentalising to more automatic mentalising (see Figure 6.2).

Attachment hyperactivation and deactivation strategies determine three key parameters in the switch from controlled to automatic mentalising: (a) the threshold at which this switch happens, (b) the strength of the relationship between stress and the activation of controlled versus automatic mentalising, and (c) the time to recovery from stress (i.e. return to controlled mentalising) (see Table 6.1).

Attachment hyperactivation strategies in response to stress (Mikulincer and Shaver 2007) are associated with a low threshold for the deactivation of areas of the brain involved in controlled mentalisation; thus, more automatic, subcortical regions, including the amygdala, have a low threshold for responding to stress. This combination of features explains the tendency of anxiously attached

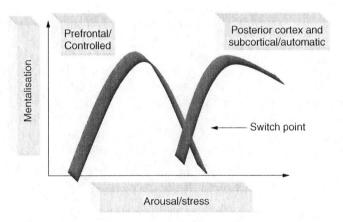

Figure 6.2 A biobehavioural model of the relationship between stress and mentalising

Table 6.1 Relationships among attachment strategies and mentalising

Attachment strategies	Threshold for switch	Strength of automatic response	Recovery of controlled mentalisation
Secure	High	Moderate	Fast
Hyperactivating	Low: hyperresponsivity	Strong	Slow
Deactivating	Relatively high: hyporesponsive, but failure under increasing stress	Weak, but moderate to strong under increasing stress	Relatively fast
Disorganised	Incoherent: hyperresponsive, but often frantic attempts to downregulate	Strong	Slow

individuals to attach to others readily; this often results in disappointment because these individuals also have a low threshold for deactivation of the neural systems associated with controlled mentalising, including those involved in judging the trustworthiness of others (Allen *et al.* 2008). Furthermore, there is evidence for excitatory feedback loops that lead to increased vigilance for stress-related cues in individuals who use hyperactivating strategies (Mikulincer and Shaver 2007), suggesting that these individuals also show an increased time to recovery of lapses in mentalising in high-arousal contexts. Hence, they might require considerable time to be able to recover capacity for controlled mentalising.

Clinicians should interpret such instances of loss of controlled mentalising during assessment (e.g. as a result of actively probing or challenging automatic assumptions, see below) as a clear warning against referring these patients to a treatment that is highly interpretive.

In contrast, individuals who primarily use *attachment deactivation strategies* are able to keep the neural systems involved in controlled mentalising 'on-line' for longer, including the neural systems that are recruited when judging the trustworthiness of others (i.e. the 'pull mechanism' associated with attachment) (Vrticka *et al.* 2008; Vrticka and Vuilleumier 2012). This may make it particularly difficult to differentiate pseudomentalisation driven by deactivation strategies from genuine mentalising. As well as the often excessive, overly cognitive, and pretend mode quality of this pseudomentalising (Sharp *et al.* 2011), it has been shown that these deactivating strategies tend to fail under increasing levels of stress, resulting in strong feelings of insecurity, heightened reactivation of negative self-representations, and increased stress (Mikulincer *et al.* 2004). Hence, mentalising deficits in dismissive or avoidant individuals are more likely to be observed in the context of settings that are strongly challenging and thus cause strong activation of the attachment system.

An example of such a setting would be the AAI (e.g. Fonagy *et al.* 1996; Levinson and Fonagy 2004), which includes many demanding questions concerning affectively charged issues such as the individual's attachment history, and experiences of loss and abuse in particular. Deactivating strategies are also associated with a relatively brief time to recovery of mentalising (Mikulincer and Shaver 2007), which makes it sometimes even more difficult to distinguish between pseudomentalising and genuinely high levels of mentalising. Research has also shown that while individuals who use deactivating strategies may show considerable biological indications of stress (such as increases in blood pressure), at the same time they not only appear to be calm but also report that, subjectively, they do not *feel* distressed (Luyten *et al.* 2012c, 2014a; Dozier and Kobak 1992). Potential indicators of such a dissociation between subjective and biological distress include the observation that an individual appears too calm for the situation (e.g. showing no signs of discomfort when talking about a history of emotional neglect), or is unable to provide examples to illustrate general statements (e.g. cannot describe specific attachment experiences), or may at first appear to be calm but then suddenly becomes extremely uncomfortable (e.g. starts sweating or reports suddenly feeling dizzy). Typically, these individuals often attribute such sudden changes not to the topic of discussion, but to external circumstances (e.g. that they feel dizzy because they have not eaten enough that day).

Disorganised attachment is associated with both marked impairments in mentalising as well as a tendency for hypermentalising (Bateman and Fonagy 2004); this is related to their use of attachment deactivating strategies when hyperactivating strategies fail, or vice versa, often resulting in notable oscillations between absent and hypermentalising. The use of hyperactivating strategies is associated with a decoupling of controlled mentalising; this leads to failures in understanding the mental states of self and other as a result of overreliance on models of social cognition that pre-date full mentalising (Bateman and Fonagy 2006). On the other hand, because deactivating strategies are typically associated with attempts to minimise and avoid affective contents, individuals with disorganised attachment also show a tendency for hypermentalising, that is, continuing but unsuccessful mentalising attempts.

Secure attachment, in contrast to the above three strategies, is related to the capacity to retain high levels of mentalising even during stressful situations, and to recover mentalising capacities relatively rapidly. Temporary lapses in mentalisation are a normal part of normal functioning, but the ability to switch from automatic to controlled mentalising in an adaptive fashion, to continue to mentalise even in stressful circumstances, and to recover relatively quickly from such lapses, are characteristic of genuine mentalising capacities. Moreover, the ability to continue to mentalise even when under considerable stress is associated with what have been termed 'broaden and build' cycles of attachment security (Fredrickson 2001): these reinforce feelings of secure attachment, personal agency, and affect regulation ('build'), which enable the individual to move into different and more adaptive environments ('broaden') (Mikulincer and Shaver 2007).

Thus, individuals with high levels of mentalising not only show considerable resilience in the face of stressful conditions, but are often able to gain a different perspective on their lives as a result of adversity. Congruent with the assumption that there are close ties between attachment and mentalising, they also show a good capacity for relationship-recruiting – the capacity to become attached to caring and helping others (Hauser *et al.* 2006) – and effective co-regulation of stress and adversity (Luyten *et al.* 2014a). These individuals typically also show a good capability to explore both the external world and their own internal world, expressed, for instance, in notable creativity, capacity for symbolisation, the ability to shift their perspective on their own lives and others', and attention to and interest in dreams and fantasies, art or music, and the internal world of people in general.

This genuine 'mind-mindedness' is one of the best indicators of high levels of mentalising, and is associated with a sense of internal freedom to explore thoughts, feelings, desires, and experiences. Such individuals feel internally secure in a way that enables them to explore and verbalise even difficult memories or experiences, and they show a clear desire and curiosity to explore these issues. This security of mental exploration (Allen *et al.* 2008), which may be driven by either positive or negative experiences, thus entails the freedom to call for, and accept, help; a key feature of secure attachment (Grossman *et al.* 1999).

Attachment hyperactivation and deactivation strategies limit the ability to 'broaden and build', and inhibit other behavioural systems that are involved in resilience, such as exploration, affiliation, and caregiving (Insel and Young 2001; Neumann 2008; Mikulincer and Shaver 2007). Hence, individuals who use such strategies typically show difficulties in entering lasting relationships (including relationships with mental health care professionals), show limited interest in or ability to explore their own and others' internal worlds, and often seem to have become 'stuck' in major life tasks such as intimacy or generativity (Luyten *et al.* 2008). People who predominantly use attachment hyperactivation strategies often show a 'centralised' pattern of relationships with considerable vulnerability for self versus other confusion (Fonagy and Luyten 2009). They are either overly clinging when in a stressful situation or show a pattern of idealisation and subsequent denigration.

Conversely, individuals who primarily make use of attachment deactivating strategies tend to show a more 'distributed' relationship pattern characterised by distancing oneself from others, strong approach-avoidance conflicts, and often frantic attempts to assert autonomy in the face of stress (see Bateman and Fonagy 2006; Luyten *et al.* 2012a). These individuals might appear to have high levels of mentalising, but lack the genuine capacity to reflect on the self and others. Although people with either a centralised or a distributed pattern of relationships may be interested in their own internal world and their dreams and fantasies, they often seem to lack true creativity. As a result, their dreams and fantasies are often barren, or may seem creative on the surface, but on closer examination reflect rather poor, clichéd images and ideas ('pseudosymbolisation').

When mentalising fails: pre-mentalising modes of experiencing subjectivity

With the loss of mentalising, pre-mentalising modes of experiencing subjectivity re-emerge. These developmentally earlier modes of thinking about the self and others typically emerge in contexts of high arousal, most often in attachment contexts (Allen *et al.* 2008).

In the *psychic equivalence mode*, subjective experience (thoughts and beliefs) become too real. What the individual thinks is real, there is no room for doubt (e.g. 'I know that he has never liked me'), while the *pretend mode* severs the connection with reality, often giving rise to hypermentalising and even dissociative experiences ('I can't stop thinking about what he said to me, I have thought about it over and over again, but I still can't figure out what he meant'). The *teleological mode*, in turn, is a mode of thinking in which mental states are equated with or reduced to observable reality/behaviour ('If you really like me, you will not leave me alone now').

Individuals with a history of severe attachment disruptions are particularly likely to show these pre-mentalising modes. Typically, such individuals shut off mentalising as a means of self-protection to avoid thinking about traumatic experiences (often in combination with self-harming behaviour or substance abuse), or alternatively are prone to hypervigilance regarding the mental states of others, and/or tend to recreate frightening states of mind in others (e.g. by shouting, humiliating, or threatening others). Individuals with antisocial features might use this latter strategy purposefully to control others and/or to undermine others' capacities to think and mentalise.

An attachment theory of borderline personality disorder based on mentalisation ideas

To show how psychoanalytic and attachment theory ideas can usefully be integrated to address clinical problems, we will briefly review the mentalisation-based theory and treatment of BPD (Bateman and Fonagy 2004, 2006; Fonagy and Bateman 2006b; Fonagy *et al.* 2003). We consider the failure of mentalisation within the attachment context to be the core pathology of BPD (Bateman and Fonagy 2004) and our treatment package aims to assist in its recovery (Bateman and Fonagy 2006b).

Individuals with BPD have schematic, rigid, and sometimes extreme views, which make them vulnerable to powerful emotional storms and apparently impulsive actions, and which can create profound problems of behavioural regulation, including affect regulation. In our model of the failure of mentalisation in BPD, the role of the attachment environment is considered alongside constitutional vulnerabilities. The vulnerability reflected in the heritability of BPD (Torgersen 2000) may be directly linked to the capacity for mentalisation or might represent the fragility of this capacity in situations of environmental deficiency, as exemplified by severe neglect, psychological or physical abuse, childhood molestation, or other forms of maltreatment.

As we considered above, mentalisation can be temporarily inhibited by strong emotional arousal, by the intensification of attachment needs, or by a defensive turning away from the world of hostile and malevolent minds in the context of severe maltreatment. Mentalisation deficit associated with maltreatment might not necessarily reflect incapacity but, rather, a form of decoupling, inhibition, or even a phobic reaction to mentalising in maltreated individuals.

There are multiple possibilities:

1   We have suggested above that the reluctance to conceive of mental states on the part of maltreated individuals might be understandable given the hostile and malevolent thoughts and feelings that the abuser must realistically hold to explain his/her actions against a vulnerable young person (e.g. Fonagy 1991). Consistent with this assumption, forms of maltreatment that are most clearly malevolent and clearly target the child have greatest impact on mentalisation (i.e. physical, sexual, and psychological abuse).

2   It could be argued that adversity undermines cognitive development in general (Cicchetti and Lynch 1995; Cicchetti and Toth 1995). Certainly, there is strong evidence to suggest that addressing issues of maltreatment in parent–child relationships can facilitate the child's cognitive development (Cicchetti et al. 2000).

Our current model stresses that minor experiences of loss or relatively small emotional upsets without expectation of comforting might be enough to cause intense activation of the attachment system in these individuals. Their attachment system is hyperactivated, probably due to interpersonal experiences associated with childhood trauma. This state of arousal inhibits mentalisation and, combined with an unstable capacity for affect regulation, triggers the typical symptoms of the disorder.

There is ample evidence that maltreatment puts children at risk of profound deficits in the skills required to negotiate social interactions with peers and friends. These are broad-ranging and include verbal ability, the comprehension of emotional stimuli and situations, and possibly also theory of mind. We have seen that the level of mental state understanding (particularly emotion understanding) is closely linked to the extent that emotions are openly discussed in the mother–child dyad or can be discussed given the child's disabilities and the parents' ability to overcome these. We may then argue that maltreatment acts on mentalisation in many ways; it compromises the unconstrained, open reflective communication between parent and child or, indeed, between child and child.

Maltreatment undermines the parent's credibility in linking internal states and actions. This limitation in communication is not hard to comprehend, and could hardly be otherwise if the maltreatment is perpetrated by a family member. But, even in cases where it is not, the centrality of the maltreatment experience for the child, coupled with the oversight on the part of the parent of an experience of maltreatment that the child encounters outside the home, could serve to invalidate the child's communications with the parent concerning the child's subjective state. Thus, apparently reflective discourse will not correspond to the core of the child's subjective experiences, and this moderates or reduces the facilitative effect of mentalising verbal rationalisations of actions in generating an intentional as opposed to a teleological orientation. The formulations advanced here imply that therapeutic interventions should aim to engage maltreated children in causally coherent psychological discourse within appropriate contexts. The more reliable processing of pedagogical information in the context of secure attachment would account for the broad and generic intellectual benefits that appear to accrue from secure attachment in infancy.

Insecure and unpredictable attachment relationships between parent and infant may create an adverse social environment for the acquisition of mentalisation or 'mind-reading' in the child. This might to a limited extent be adaptive in that within extreme social contexts mentalisation is a less useful strategy. If parent–child interaction is in crucial respects not genuine, the child might well be deconditioned from using this as his/her predictive strategy. Severely insecure, abusive, inconsistent, and disorganised attachment relations could well be detrimental for mentalisation to survive as a dominant, predictive interpersonal strategy. However, within the same contexts of deprivation and risk, mentalisation could hold the key to breaking the cycle of abuse and deprivation for that child growing up, and for the children he/she produces.

We see the capacity to mentalise as particularly helpful when people have been traumatised. Mentalisation of experiences of adversity can moderate their negative sequelae (Fonagy et al. 1996). The capacity to mentalise enables those who are subjected to traumatic experiences to hold back modes of primitive mental functioning. It makes conceptual sense, therefore, for mentalising to be a focus for therapeutic intervention if we are to help BPD patients bring primitive modes of mental functioning under better regulation and control.

Conclusions

This chapter reviewed the intrinsic relationships between the development of attachment bonds and mentalising, our ability to interpret and understand ourselves and others in terms of internal mental states, across the life span. We have argued that the evaluation of an individual's ability to mentalise depends on their functioning with respect to each of the four polarities entailed in mentalising (automatic–controlled, internal–external, self–other, cognitive–affective), which are influenced by individual differences in the use of attachment strategies that might differ depending upon the specific attachment context.

Hence, assessing an individual's mentalising capacities should entail close attention to the nature of the tie between the individual and his/her past and current attachment figures, in research as well as clinical contexts. This is not a moot point as it seems that our past and current attachment figures have provided us not only with internal working models of ourselves and others, but also with a greater or lesser capacity to reflect on these internal working models, their roots in the past, their influence on our current ways of experiencing ourselves and others, and their potential for change in the future.

This view has important implications for the conceptualisation of psychosocial treatments from an attachment perspective. Although, as noted, several intervention approaches have been developed and systematically evaluated on the basis of the mentalising approach, it could well be that all effective treatment approaches foster mentalising, albeit in different ways, to the point that increases in the capacity for mentalising might be a common factor explaining, in part, the effects of current psychosocial interventions (Allen *et al.* 2008). Moreover, while traditionally psychosocial interventions took place in the context of a new attachment relationship with a mental health professional, there is increasing evidence that for many individuals, considerable therapeutic change can be achieved without having to establish an attachment relationship, as is, for instance, demonstrated by studies showing the efficacy of internet-based treatments or self-help programmes.

Similarly, there is some evidence to suggest that treatments that involve frequent and intense attachment relationships may be iatrogenic for some patients, as they might overstimulate the attachment system, resulting in a decoupling of mentalising (Fonagy and Bateman 2006a). Future research should thus be aimed at identifying the optimal balance in interventions between the stimulation of the attachment system and the extent to which mentalising is promoted. Hence, much as parents attempt to do in normal psychological development, psychosocial interventions should aim at finding the optimal balance between the formation of an attachment bond and fostering mentalisation.

From a mentalising perspective, it can be predicted that the epistemic trust (meaning the particular trust required for someone to learn from another, entailing a confidence in the 'teacher's' reliability and intentions) and the ability to call for and accept help that are typical of individuals with good mentalising capacities allows many of these individuals to benefit from interventions that require little or no attachment bond (as well as interventions that require forming an attachment relationship, of course). As we have seen, these individuals are open to change their assumptions about the self and others – demonstrating the close bonds between secure attachment, mentalising and epistemic trust.

However, in individuals with a history of (marked) insecure attachment experiences and serious impairments in mentalising, the establishment of a new and often corrective attachment relationship might be a requirement to be able to restore epistemic trust, and hence foster mentalising and psychological change, further emphasising the parallel between therapeutic processes and the developmental origins of attachment, mentalising and epistemic trust.

Somewhat paradoxically, we are all too familiar with the difficulties these individuals often have in establishing new and trusting attachment relationships, as well as with the dangers of overstimulation of the attachment system and subsequent decoupling of mentalising in many of these individuals.

References

Allen, J., Fonagy, P. and Bateman, A. (2008) *Mentalizing in clinical practice*, Washington, DC: American Psychiatric Press.

Arnsten, A. F. T. (1998) 'The biology of being frazzled', *Science*, 280: 1711–12.

Arntz, A., Bernstein, D., Oorschot, M., Robson, K. and Schobre, P. (2006) *Theory of mind in borderline and Cluster-C personality disorder: No evidence for deficits*, Maastricht: Maastricht University, the Netherlands, unpublished.

Bakermans-Kranenburg, M. J., Van IJzendoorn, M. H., Mesman, J., Alink, L. R. A. and Juffer, F. (2008) 'Effects of an attachment-based intervention on daily cortisol moderated by dopamine receptor D4: A randomized control trial on 1- to 3-year-olds screened for externalizing behavior', *Development and Psychopathology*, 20: 805–20.

Bateman, A. W. and Fonagy, P. (2004) *Psychotherapy for borderline personality disorder: Mentalization based treatment*, Oxford: Oxford University Press.

Bateman, A. W. and Fonagy, P. (2006) *Mentalization based treatment for borderline personality disorder: A practical guide*, Oxford: Oxford University Press.

Bateman, A. and Fonagy, P. (2008) 'Comorbid antisocial and borderline personality disorders: Mentalization based treatment', *Journal of Clinical Psychology: in session*, 64: 1–14.

Beebe, B., Jaffe, J., Buck, K., Chen, H., Cohen, P., Blatt, S., *et al.* (2007) 'Six-week postpartum maternal self-criticism and dependency and 4-month mother-infant self- and interactive contingencies', *Developmental Psychology*, 43: 1360–76.

Beebe, B., Badalamenti, A., Jaffe, J., Feldstein, S., Marquette, L., Helbraun, E., *et al.* (2008) 'Distressed mothers and their infants use a less efficient timing mechanism in creating expectancies of each other's looking patterns', *Journal of Psycholinguistic Research*, 37: 293–307.

Bender, D. S. and Skodol, A. E. (2007) 'Borderline personality as a self-other representational disturbance', *Journal of Personality Disorders*, 21: 500–17.

Blatt, S. J. and Auerbach, J. S. (1988) 'Differential cognitive disturbances in three types of borderline patients', *Journal of Personality Disorders*, 2: 198–211.

Bowlby, J. (1973) *Attachment and Loss, Vol. 2: Separation: Anxiety and Anger*, London: Hogarth Press and Institute of Psycho-Analysis.

Bowlby, J. (1980) *Attachment and Loss, Vol. 3: Loss: Sadness and Depression*, London: Hogarth Press and Institute of Psycho-Analysis.

Calmels, C., Holmes, P., Jarry, G., Hars, M., Lopez, E., Paillard, A. and Stam, C. J. (2006) 'Variability of EEG synchronization prior to and during observation and execution of a sequential finger movement', *Human Brain Mapping*, 27: 251–66.

Calvo-Merino, B., Glaser, D. E., Grezes, J., Passingham, R. E. and Haggard, P. (2005) 'Action observation and acquired motor skills: An FMRI study with expert dancers', *Cerebral Cortex*, 15: 1243–9.

Calvo-Merino, B., Grezes, J., Glaser, D. E., Passingham, R. E. and Haggard, P. (2006) 'Seeing or doing? Influence of visual and motor familiarity in action observation', *Current Biology*, 16: 1905–10.

Cicchetti, D. and Lynch, M. (1995) 'Failures in the expectable environment and their impact on individual development: The case of child maltreatment', in D. Cicchetti and D. J. Cohen (eds), *Developmental Psychopathology*, New York: John Wiley & Sons, Vol. 2, pp. 32–71.

Cicchetti, D. and Toth, S. L. (1995) 'A developmental psychopathology perspective on child abuse and neglect', *Journal of the American Academy of Child and Adolescent Psychiatry*, 34: 541–565.

Cicchetti, D., Rogosch, F. A. and Toth, S. L. (2000) 'The efficacy of toddler–parent psychotherapy for fostering cognitive development in offspring of depressed mothers', *Journal of Abnormal Child Psychology*, 28: 135–148.

Clarkin, J. F., Foelsch, P. A., Levy, K. N., Hull, J. W., Delaney, J. C. and Kernberg, O. F. (2001) 'The development of a psychodynamic treatment for patients with borderline personality disorder: A preliminary study of behavioral change', *Journal of Personality Disorders*, 15: 487–95.

Diamond, A., Blatt, S. J., Stayner, D. and Kaslow, N. (1991) *Self-other differentiation of object representations*, Unpublished research manual, Yale University.

Diamond, D., Stovall-McClough, C., Clarkin, J. F. and Levy, K. N. (2003) 'Patient–therapist attachment in the treatment of borderline personality disorder', *Bulletin of the Menninger Clinic*, 67: 227–59.

Dimaggio, G., Lysaker, P. H., Carcione, A., Nicolo, G. and Semerari, A. (2008) 'Know yourself and you shall know the other . . . to a certain extent: Multiple paths of influence of self-reflection on mindreading', *Consciousness and Cognition*, 17: 778–89.

Domes, G., Czieschnek, D., Weidler, F., Berger, C., Fast, K. and Herpertz, S. C. (2008) 'Recognition of facial affect in borderline personality disorder', *Journal of Personality Disorders*, 22: 135–47.

Domes, G., Schulze, L. and Herpertz, S. C. (2009) 'Emotion recognition in borderline personality disorder: A review of the literature', *Journal of Personality Disorders*, 23: 6–19.

Dozier, M. and Kobak, R. (1992) 'Psychophysiology in attachment interviews: Converging evidence for deactivating strategies', *Child Development*, 63: 1473–80.

Ensink, K. and Mayes, L. C. (2010) 'The development of mentalisation in children from a theory of mind perspective', *Psychoanalytic Inquiry*, 30: 301–37.

Fonagy, P. (1991) 'Thinking about thinking: Some clinical and theoretical considerations in the treatment of a borderline patient', *International Journal of Psycho-Analysis*, 72: 639–656.

Fonagy, P. and Bateman, A. (2006a) 'Progress in the treatment of borderline personality disorder', *British Journal of Psychiatry*, 188: 1–3.

Fonagy, P. and Bateman, A. W. (2006b) 'Mechanisms of change in mentalization-based treatment of BPD', *Journal of Clinical Psychology*, 62: 411–30.

Fonagy, P. and Luyten, P. (2009) 'A developmental, mentalization-based approach to the understanding and treatment of borderline personality disorder', *Development and Psychopathology*, 21: 1355–81.

Fonagy, P., Leigh, T., Steele, M., Steele, H., Kennedy, R., Mattoon, G., *et al.* (1996) 'The relation of attachment status, psychiatric classification, and response to psychotherapy', *Journal of Consulting and Clinical Psychology*, 64: 22–31.

Fonagy, P., Target, M., Steele, H. and Steele, M. (1998) *Reflective-functioning manual, version 5.0, for application to Adult Attachment Interviews*, London: University College London.

Fonagy, P., Gergely, G., Jurist, E. and Target, M. (2002) *Affect regulation, mentalization and the development of the self*, New York: Other Press.

Fonagy, P., Target, M., Gergely, G., Allen, J. G. and Bateman, A. (2003) 'The developmental roots of borderline personality disorder in early attachment relationships: A theory and some evidence', *Psychoanalytic Inquiry*, 23: 412–459.

Fonagy, P., Gergely, G. and Target, M. (2007) 'The parent–infant dyad and the construction of the subjective self', *Journal of Child Psychology and Psychiatry*, 48: 288–328.

Fonagy, P., Luyten, P. and Strathearn, L. (2011) 'Borderline personality disorder, mentalization, and the neurobiology of attachment', *Infant Mental Health Journal*, 32: 47–69.

Fraley, R. C. (2007) 'A connectionist approach to the organization and continuity of working models of attachment', *Journal of Personality*, 75: 1157–80.

Fredrickson, B. L. (2001) 'The role of positive emotions in positive psychology. The broaden-and-build theory of positive emotions', *American Psychologist*, 56: 218–26.

Frith, C. D. (2007) 'The social brain?', *Philosophical Transactions of the Royal Society of London. Series B, Biological Sciences*, 362: 671–8.

Frith, C. D. and Frith, U. (2006) 'The neural basis of mentalizing', *Neuron*, 50: 531–4.

Gallese, V., Keysers, C. and Rizzolatti, G. (2004) 'A unifying view of the basis of social cognition', *Trends in Cognitive Sciences*, 8: 396–403.

Gazzola, V., Aziz-Zadeh, L. and Keysers, C. (2006) 'Empathy and the somatotopic auditory mirror system in humans', *Current Biology*, 16: 1824–9.

Grossman, K. E., Grossman, K. and Zimmermann, P. (1999) 'A wider view of attachment and exploration', in J. Cassidy and P. R. Shaver (eds), *Handbook of attachment: Theory, research and clinical applications*, New York: Guilford Press, pp. 760–86.

Hauser, S., Allen, J. and Golden, E. (2006) *Out of the woods: Tales of resilient teens*, London: Harvard University Press.

Hesse, E. (2008) 'The Adult Attachment Interview: Protocol, method of analysis, and empirical studies', in J. Cassidy and P. R. Shaver (eds), *Handbook of attachment: Theory, research and clinical applications*, 2nd ed., New York: Guilford Press, pp. 552–58.

Insel, T. and Young, L. (2001) 'The neurobiology of attachment', *Nature Reviews. Neuroscience* 2: 129–36.

Jurist, E. L. (2005) 'Mentalized affectivity', *Psychoanalytic Psychology*, 22: 426–44.

Keysers, C. and Gazzola, V. (2006) 'Towards a unifying neural theory of social cognition', *Progress in Brain Research*, 156: 379–401.

King-Casas, B., Sharp, C., Lomax-Bream, L., Lohrenz, T., Fonagy, P. and Montague, P. R. (2008) 'The rupture and repair of cooperation in borderline personality disorder', *Science*, 321: 806–10.

Kovacs, A. M., Teglas, E. and Endress, A. D. (2010) 'The social sense: Susceptibility to others' beliefs in human infants and adults', *Science*, 24: 1830–34.

Leckman, J. F., Feldman, R., Swain, J. E. and Mayes, L. C. (2007) 'Primary parental preoccupation: Revisited', in L. C. Mayes, P. Fonagy and M. Target (eds), *Developmental science and psychoanalysis: Integration and innovation*, London: Karnac, pp. 89–108.

Levinson, A. and Fonagy, P. (2004) 'Offending and attachment: The relationship between interpersonal awareness and offending in a prison population with psychiatric disorder', *Canadian Journal of Psychoanalysis*, 12: 225–51.

Lieberman, M. D. (2007) 'Social cognitive neuroscience: A review of core processes', *Annual Review of Psychology*, 58: 259–89.

Lombardo, M. V., Barnes, J. L., Wheelwright, S. J. and Baron-Cohen, S. (2007) 'Self-referential cognition and empathy in autism', *PLoS ONE*, 2: e883.

Lotze, M., Heymans, U., Birbaumer, N., Veit, R., Erb, M., Flor, H. and Halsband, U. (2006) 'Differential cerebral activation during observation of expressive gestures and motor acts', *Neuropsychologia*, 44: 1787–95.

Luyten, P., Vliegen, N., Van Houdenhove, B. and Blatt, S. J. (2008) 'Equifinality, multifinality, and the rediscovery of the importance of early experiences: Pathways from early adversity to psychiatric and (functional) somatic disorders', *Psychoanalytic Study of the Child*, 63: 27–60.

Luyten, P., Fonagy, P., Lemma, A. and Target, M. (2012a) 'Depression', in A. Bateman and P. Fonagy (eds), *Handbook of mentalizing in mental health practice*, Washington, DC: American Psychiatric Association, pp. 385–417.

Luyten, P., Fonagy, P., Lowyck, B. and Vermote, R. (2012b) 'The assessment of mentalization', in A. Bateman and P. Fonagy (eds), *Handbook of mentalizing in mental health practice*, Washington, DC: American Psychiatric Association, pp. 43–65.

Luyten, P., Van Houdenhove, B., Lemma, A., Target, M. and Fonagy, P. (2012c) 'An attachment and mentalization-based approach to functional somatic disorders', *Psychoanalytic Psychotherapy*, 26: 121–40.

Luyten, P., Mayes, L., Fonagy, P. and Van Houdenhove, B. (2014a) 'The interpersonal regulation of stress', Manuscript submitted for publication.

Luyten, P., Mayes, L. C., Nijssens, L. and Fonagy, P. (2014b) 'The Parental Reflective Functioning Questionnaire: Development and preliminary validation', Manuscript submitted for publication.

Lynch, T. R., Rosenthal, M. Z., Kosson, D. S., Cheavens, J. S., Lejuez, C. W. and Blair, R. J. (2006) 'Heightened sensitivity to facial expressions of emotion in borderline personality disorder', *Emotion*, 6: 647–55.

Marsh, A. A. and Blair, R. J. (2008) 'Deficits in facial affect recognition among antisocial populations: A meta-analysis', *Neuroscience and Biobehavioral Reviews*, 32: 454–65.

Mayes, L. C. (2000) 'A developmental perspective on the regulation of arousal states', *Seminars in Perinatology*, 24: 267–79.

Mayes, L. C. (2006) 'Arousal regulation, emotional flexibility, medial amygdala function, and the impact of early experience: Comments on the paper of Lewis et al.', *Annals of the New York Academy of Sciences*, 1094: 178–92.

Mikulincer, M. and Shaver, P. R. (2007) *Attachment in adulthood: Structure, dynamics and change*, New York: The Guilford Press.

Mikulincer, M., Dolev, T. and Shaver, P. R. (2004) 'Attachment-related strategies during thought suppression: Ironic rebounds and vulnerable self-representations', *Journal of Personality and Social Psychology*, 87: 940–56.

Molnar-Szakacs, I., Kaplan, J., Greenfield, P. M. and Iacoboni, M. (2006) 'Observing complex action sequences: The role of the fronto-parietal mirror neuron system', *Neuroimage*, 33: 923–35.

Neumann, I. D. (2008) 'Brain oxytocin: A key regulator of emotional and social behaviours in both females and males', *Journal of Neuroendocrinology*, 20: 858–65.

Pierce, T. and Lydon, J. E. (2001) 'Global and specific relational models in the experience of social interactions', *Journal of Personality and Social Psychology*, 80: 613–31.

Pronin, E., Gilovich, T. and Ross, L. (2004) 'Objectivity in the eye of the beholder: Divergent perceptions of bias in self versus others', *Psychological Review*, 111: 781–99.

Rizzolatti, G. and Craighero, L. (2004) 'The mirror-neuron system', *Annual Review of Neuroscience*, 27: 169–92.

Rizzolatti, G., Ferrari, P. F., Rozzi, S. and Fogassi, L. (2006) 'The inferior parietal lobule: Where action becomes perception', *Novartis Foundation Symposia*, 270: 129–40; discussion 40–5, 64–9.

Sabbagh, M. A. (2004) 'Understanding orbitofrontal contributions to theory-of-mind reasoning: Implications for autism', *Brain and Cognition*, 55: 209–19.

Sadler, L. S., Slade, A. and Mayes, L. C. (2006) 'Minding the baby: A mentalization-based parenting program', in J. G. Allen and P. Fonagy (eds), *Handbook of mentalization-based treatment*, London: John Wiley & Sons, pp. 271–88.

Satpute, A. B. and Lieberman, M. D. (2006) 'Integrating automatic and controlled processes into neurocognitive models of social cognition', *Brain Research*, 1079: 86–97.

Shamay-Tsoory, S. G. and Aharon-Peretz, J. (2007) 'Dissociable prefrontal networks for cognitive and affective theory of mind: A lesion study', *Neuropsychologia*, 45: 3054–67.

Sharp, C. and Fonagy, P. (2008) 'The parent's capacity to treat the child as a psychological agent: Constructs, measures and implications for developmental psychopathology', *Social Development*, 17: 737–54.

Sharp, C., Pane, H., Ha, C., Venta, A., Patel, A. B., Sturek, J. and Fonagy, P. (2011) 'Theory of mind and emotion regulation difficulties in adolescents with borderline traits', *Journal of the American Academy of Child and Adolescent Psychiatry*, 60: 563–73.

Shmueli-Goetz, Y., Target, M., Fonagy, P. and Datta, A. (2008) 'The Child Attachment Interview: A psychometric study of reliability and validity', *Developmental Psychology*, 44: 939–56.

Slade, A. (2005) 'Parental reflective functioning', *Attachment and Human Development*, 7: 269–81.

Slade, A. and Sadler, L. (2007) 'Minding the baby', in L. C. Mayes, P. Fonagy and M. Target (eds), *Developmental science and psychoanalysis*, London: Karnac, pp. 271–288.

Slade, A., Bernbach, E., Grienenberger, J., Levy, D. and Locker, A. (2007) *Addendum to Reflective Functioning scoring manual for use with the Parent Development Interview. Version 3.0'*, New York: The City College and Graduate Center of the City University of New York.

Suchman, N. E., DeCoste, C., Leigh, D. and Borelli, J. (2010) 'Reflective functioning in mothers with drug use disorders: Implications for dyadic interactions with infants and toddlers', *Attachment and Human Development*, 12: 567–85.

Torgersen, S. (2000) 'Genetics of patients with borderline personality disorder', *Psychiatric Clinics of North America*, 23: 1–9.

Uddin, L. Q., Iacoboni, M., Lange, C. and Keenan, J. P. (2007) 'The self and social cognition: The role of cortical midline structures and mirror neurons', *Trends in Cognitive Sciences*, 11: 153–7.

Vrticka, P. and Vuilleumier, P. (2012) 'Neuroscience of human social interactions and adult attachment style', *Frontiers in Human Neuroscience*, 6.

Vrticka, P., Andersson, F., Grandjean, D., Sander, D. and Vuilleumier, P. (2008) 'Individual attachment style modulates human amygdala and striatum activation during social appraisal', *PLoS ONE*, 3: e2868.

Chapter 7

Attachment, our brains, nervous systems and hormones

Graham Music

Introduction

We need to tread with caution when thinking about what light brain science can shed on human emotional development. It is true that the exciting development of new forms of brain scanning has accelerated our understanding in ways we could not have predicted. It was not long ago that all we knew about brains was almost entirely gleaned from examining those of the deceased. Since the 'decade of the brain' in the 1990s there has been a huge proliferation of studies and many dramatic claims have been made. In this chapter I will outline some of these, and look at findings that might illuminate our understanding of attachment and what happens in intimate relationships. However, this is done with awareness that neuroscience is in its infancy still, and that it can be too easy to claim too much, especially when insufficient care is taken in analysing the results of scans, as too often happens, as several papers have recently flagged up (e.g. McCabe and Castel 2008; Weisberg *et al.* 2008).

Of course neuroscience is by no means new to psychotherapy. Freud himself, with his neurological training, showed enormous prescience in predicting the kind of developments that would not actually occur for another century: 'We must recollect that all our provisional ideas in psychology, will presumably someday be based on an organic superstructure' (Freud 1914: 78). Bowlby too, of course, was very concerned to identify the instinctual brain and nervous system patterns central to attachment dynamics, even speculating about the role of brain regions such as the prefrontal lobes in emotional control (Bowlby 1969).

Some of the new findings chime extremely well with attachment theory. Of particular relevance is the ever-growing evidence that the way children are parented has a huge impact on their later development and, we have discovered, on the ways in which their brain architecture takes shape. What we have learnt about the plasticity of the human brain confirms what we know from attachment theory; the human infant adapts to their particular emotional environment, and attachment strategies are generally appropriate adaptations to a child's earliest environments. Such adaptability is not only seen in brain architecture, but also in the ways in which our hormonal systems become programmed very early on, in response to the kinds of experiences we have with our earliest caregivers. We have also learnt that while our genetic inheritance is important, genetic potentials will be turned on or off by the specific kinds of experiences that we have, as the burgeoning field of epigenetics is illustrating (e.g. Champagne and Curley 2009; Miller 2010; Labonté *et al.* 2012). Bowlby, of course, did not have the detailed knowledge that we have today, but one suspects he might have been pleased that so many of the new findings fit so neatly with his original theories. In the ensuing sections I will briefly discuss some of these areas of burgeoning research.

Brain exercise and neuroplasticity

One way of thinking about the brain is that it is like a muscle group, albeit an extraordinarily complex one, and the bits that are used are strengthened from being exercised while others can wither from neglect. Our brains are highly complicated and able to make incredibly complex calculations in fractions of seconds. The fundamental units of the brain are 'neurons', which are long entities with a central nucleus (containing genes), and long extensions called axons.

Neurons connect to each other via synapses, which enable the transmission of neurotransmitters, which can then fire neuronal activity further 'downstream'. Incredibly, the average neuron connects directly to 10,000 other neurons and the average brain has 100 billion neurons. Each neuron has one or more axons, which send messages to other neurons, and axons branch so that there are far more synapses than neurons. In fact Pinker (2002) refers to 100 trillion synapses in the human brain. Each neuron has a cell body and tens of thousands of tiny branches (dendrites) which do the receiving via electro-chemical messages. A piece of brain the size of a grain of sand contains 100,000 neurons, 2 million axons and a billion synapses (Siegel 2012).

The human brain is born prematurely, having an overabundance of brain cells at the start but with very few connections between them. In the post-natal period there is a massive process of 'pruning', a process called 'use it or lose it', and cells that are not used simply die off. Schwartz and Begley (2002: 117) quoting a figure of 20 billion synapses pruned every day between childhood and early adolescence, say: 'Like bus routes with no customers, they go out of business.' Once a connection is formed it remains wired, but unused neurons are 'pruned', although new pathways and wiring can still form later in life. New experience is filtered through already-formed pathways, just as water will naturally flow down already-formed channels, hence the phrase 'cells that fire together wire together', coined by the neuroscientist Hebb (1949), and called Hebb's law.

This is what is meant by humans having an 'experience dependent' brain and describes the process whereby particular pathways form at the expense of other potential pathways and become standard ways by which one experiences the world. Attachment styles can be seen as developing in this way.

The human brain learns fast, and is an extraordinarily powerful predictor of the future. If the presence of adults triggers either fear or dissociative processes, as it does in many children who have suffered early and ongoing trauma, these same fear responses will in all likelihood also be triggered by other more benign adults, such as kindly teachers or adoptive parents. The human brain, and particularly the infant brain, is very malleable, a capacity that Schore (2012) and others have described as 'neuroplasticity'. The period from the last trimester of pregnancy through to the second year of life is crucial, although thankfully some plasticity remains throughout the lifespan, particularly during adolescence. Schore states the parent is the psychobiological regulator of the developing infant brain, and that in the first two years attachment styles are developing through communication between the infant and child's right brains, so that the mother's face is effectively the environment that stimulates particular neuronal circuitry and hormonal baselines.

Memory

Thus early experiences are remembered and, as Bruce Perry wrote (1995), states can become traits, or in attachment patterns, responses can become behavioural patterns and expectations of relationships. The neuroscience describes such patterns in terms of how we learn from experiences. A simple starting point is to outline two different forms of memory. The first is often called declarative or explicit memory and is concerned with memories of facts and events that can be actually, consciously recalled and spoken about. Recalling a date or name would fall into this category, as would recalling a recent event. The other kind of memory, central to attachment theory, is procedural or implicit memory.[1]

Procedural memory is a kind of knowledge which describes non-conscious bodily based memories such as 'how we do' things, and also describes the residues of certain traumas remembered at a somatic, non-conscious level. Procedural memories include skills such as riding a bike or playing an instrument, and also memories of how relationships are likely to go, based on previous experience. Attachment patterns are based on such procedural learning. If I cry and no one comes or shows any interest in my communications about my feelings, then I will stop expressing my distress in this way. This is what we see in avoidant attachment patterns, for example. We all take our procedural memories of relationships into new social situations and relationships. Therapeutic work these days is often about uncovering, making sense of and then helping clients to unlearn such patterns, or at least to learn new ones alongside old ones.

The well-known 'still-face' experiments that Tronik (2007) and others undertook illustrate procedural expectations in young babies. When an interacting mother is suddenly asked to keep a still face, babies become disturbed, self-soothe and try every trick they know to get their mothers back. These babies show that they already have expectations of relationships that are suddenly being challenged by the still face and, for example, babies whose mothers are very depressed and for whom a flat still face is not unusual, do not show such distress. Beebe and Lachmann (2013) found that the way babies interact with their mothers at four months predicts attachment patterns at a year. She found that four-month-olds who have intrusive and impinging mothers will look warily at their mothers, and when their mother smiles at them, they have their heads turned away and tend to resort to bodily self-comforting, like holding their hands together. These are the babies who later show disorganised attachment patterns, whereas those who will become securely attached meet the mother's face full on, seemingly with confidence. As a result of early interactions young infants have already developed clear behavioural patterns and internal representations of relationships, albeit laid down far outside consciousness.

Psychotherapy has taken much of this on board already, with an emphasis on the 'here-and-now' transference relationship (Casement 1990), and the idea that the therapist might be a new 'developmental object' (Hurry 1998) and so aid patients to learn new expectations of relationships. We also work less with attempting to lift the veil of repression to reveal actual memories, and also less with cognitive-based insights 'about' the patient, and more with procedural expectations about relationships as manifested in therapeutic interactions. It makes sense that what the Adult Attachment Interview reveals is not 'facts' about an adult's childhood, but rather information about how they process emotional experiences and make sense of them. The narrative styles of adults as measured in the interview might also be seen as an example of procedural ways of being, deeply engrained ways of making sense of and processing what has happened in relationships when the attachment system is triggered. Early experiences build deep beliefs about people and relationships.

Nervous systems

We use very different parts of our brains when in different moods, or in different contexts, such as when in a loving environment or under threat. When in danger we tend to become very aroused, and resort to primitive survival responses such as fight or flight, or even freeze. Our whole being and physiology then is geared to coming through the threat, as we tense up and prepare for trouble, while other bodily functions, such as digestion or immune responses, temporarily go into abeyance, as do higher order thought processes. Children who have suffered extreme trauma, such as many with disorganised attachments, tend to develop a predisposition to go into such states very quickly.

Furthermore, different parts of our complex brains have evolved at different stages in our evolutionary history and serve different functions. Although slightly simplified, MacLean's (1990) concept of the triune brain is a useful starting point. This theory states that human brains can be related to three main stages in our evolutionary history and uses the metaphor of the reptilian brain, the limbic system and the neo-cortex. While some of the details of this theory do not stand close scrutiny, it still provides a helpful metaphor for making sense of different brain processes.

Many aspects of our brain functioning have changed little since the reptilian parts of our brain reached their most advanced stage some 250 million years ago in reptiles. As well as controlling things like heart-rate, breathing, temperature and balance, structures such as the brain stem control ancient but vital survival instincts for dominance and aggression. Some 100 million years later, with mammals, the limbic system came into existence, maybe the region that psychotherapists particularly interact with as it is really the seat of our emotional life, and concerns how we make judgements, learn whether an experience is likely to be pleasurable or not, and how we form emotional memories. It also contains vital structures that I will return to later, such as the amygdala and the hippocampus. The 'new kid on the block' is the neo-cortex, a mere two or three million years old, and its most complex form is seen in humans with our two cerebral hemispheres, responsible for human thought, language, imagination and consciousness.

An exercise I quite often undertake with myself when working with clients is to ask whether it is the reptilian or mammalian brains or the cerebral cortex that is active at a particular moment. Basic instinctual responses emanate from the reptilian brain, responses such as hate, lust, aggression, and particularly the powerful defensive strategies of fight, flight or freeze. If one is confronted by massive anger or hatred in a child who at that moment has a highly active brain stem and is in 'fight' mode, it is folly to make an intellectually complex comment that only the cerebral cortex could make sense of, as those more complex parts of the brain are not active at such moments.

In reality there are not three separate brain areas, and in fact complex relationships and pathways have developed between them over the millennia. Indeed, Daniel Siegel (2012) has argued firmly that psychological health is marked by ever-increasing complexity and interdependence of aspects of brain functioning, and that many of the people who have developed psychological 'issues' of one form or another show a less complex and interwoven structure, with more chaos and more rigidity, and less organisation.

Stephen Porges (2011) has taken such an evolutionary view a step further in relation to our autonomic nervous systems. He shows that we have three very different kinds of responses to stress, each rooted in a different stage of our phylogenetic history. Our most primitive reaction is one we share with the least developed of vertebrates and depends on a branch of our vagus nerve, the so-called dorsal vagal branch, an evolutionarily older branch shared with vertebrates, reptiles and amphibians. Its activation leads to complete immobilisation, freezing and the closing down of our systems. Dissociation and metabolic shutdown are typical of this 'rabbit in headlights' system. It is adaptive because predators are not attracted to creatures that seem lifeless. Our bodies only resort to this in the most extreme life or death situations.

An evolutionarily more advanced response comes from our sympathetic nervous system, which includes the fight-flight response, and this is seen in all mammals. Under threat this system's responses include increased heart-rate, sweating, quicker breathing, dilation of the eyes, feeling cold and inhibited digestion. It fires up when we feel anxious, furious or frightened. When our attachment system is triggered and we feel frightened then this system often fires up, and of course it is in mammals we see the behaviours most similar to human attachment. We all need this arousal system and we all experience times when we resort to it, such as when frightened or angry. Some people, though, are highly sympathetically aroused far more easily than others.

The third and evolutionarily most advanced element of our autonomic nervous system is only seen in mammals and in an increasingly complex form in humans, and is central to both feeling good and being open to others. It depends on a sophisticated (ventral) branch of our vagus nerve, sometimes called the 'smart vagus', which connects our brain stem, heart, stomach and our facial muscles. This myelinated branch of the vagus nerve is active in processes such as bonding, attachment, social communication, language use, empathy and care for others. This system stops working when we feel anxious or threatened.

When feeling calm and trusting, such as we see in a child playing happily in the presence of a mother they might even have temporarily forgotten about, then this system involving our 'smart' vagus nerve will be active. This system has an opposite effect to the sympathetic nervous system's arousing mechanisms, and is part of the parasympathetic nervous system which calms us down. Its thousands of nerve endings communicate with many of our internal organs, like the gut. Indeed the gut is termed by some the enteric nervous system or our second brain (Gershon 1999), and functions as a semi-autonomous nervous system containing about 100 million neurons, firing both sympathetic and parasympathetic patterns and rich with neurotransmitters such as serotonin. The vagus nerve is implicated in attachment, bonding, love, team-work, cooperation and working together.

This is a measureable trait linked to something called heart-rate variability, and people who have what is called high vagal tone are more relaxed and open. Premature babies with low vagal tone are more stressed and less likely to survive. Adults with borderline personality disorder have lower vagal tone, and less variable heart rates (Austin et al. 2007). Our heart rates go up when we anxiously take a sharp intake of breath, such as when watching scary films, and lower, for example, when watching films that induce loving feelings. With lower heart rates and more relaxation breathing out becomes deeper (Goetz et al. 2010). At our most healthy we move easily between these states. This is what we see in securely attached children after the Strange Situation test. They are quickly distressed but return to normal easily when their attachment figure returns. Clinicians are worried about children and adults who can only respond within a very narrow range.

It is becoming increasingly clear that there is an important relationship between attachment style and vagal tone (Diamond et al. 2012). Children with high vagal tone are the ones who are friendly, generous and helpful in class, generally the securely attached ones, whereas those with low vagal tone are more likely to have behavioural problems and be unhappy (Eisenberg et al. 1996).

All mammals have a nervous system that initially requires regulation by a parent, something that Bowlby seems to have been uncannily aware of. Those who are not emotionally and physiologically regulated develop systems out of kilter, respond atypically to many experiences and are not able to participate in the richness of life that most children enjoy. Children brought up in a violent environment, for example, will have a much more highly activated sympathetic nervous system; in other words they will be very easily aroused, often in a dramatic way, and will find it hard to calm down, concentrate or feel at ease. While we are designed to resort to sympathetic arousal states when danger looms, we are also designed to calm down quickly afterwards. Chronic bad experiences can lead to people being stuck in these anxious and fearful states. Such hypervigilance and arousal might be adaptive in a violent and abusive home, but less so for the adopted child whose new parents are benign and kindly.

We have two main stress response systems. The fastest to react is SAM (sympathetic adrenomedullary), regulated by the hormone CRF (corticotropin-releasing factor), leading to the fast release of adrenaline and noradrenaline, and stimulating the body's vital organs. Its actions are almost instantaneous but are also short-lived. Slower is the better known HPA (hypothalamic-pituitary-adrenal) axis, involving the stress hormone cortisol, a more slow-burning but long-lasting system.

The heart-rate patterns of the depressed mothers living in violent areas spike when their toddlers are upset and these mothers also struggle to calm down. This is what we see in people with low vagal tone, both higher reactivity and less emotional flexibility. Such mothers also tend to have higher cortisol levels. Mothers suffering extreme trauma, such as those with PTSD symptoms, in fact have extremely low levels of cortisol (Yehuda 2001), as if the system has gone into overload and turned off.

Hormones and opiates

Experiences programme our hormonal systems, as well as our nervous systems, and as we grow older these patterns become well-established and can become biological templates that are hard to shift. We might become predisposed, for example, to be very quickly sympathetically aroused, releasing large amounts of adrenaline and the stress hormone, cortisol, in response to the slightest stimulus, such as a loud noise down the road, and we might not have the buffer of the protective hormones such as oxytocin that can lower fear and increase feelings of ease. Indeed the smart vagus seems to be a kind of oxytocin superhighway, and when vagal tone is high we become calmer, more at ease and open, and release protective hormones.

Indeed the human brain produces many hormones and opiates, some of the best known being the stress hormone, cortisol, and oxytocin, sometimes called the 'love hormone' as well as other endogenous opioids and endorphins, and dopamine. The mother's stress level during pregnancy affects the unborn child (Field 2004), and cortisol in pregnant mothers crosses the placenta and can adversely affect the developing foetus. Cortisol is nowadays easily measured on saliva samples and it is clear that when children are fearful, or when left without their closest attachment figures, their cortisol levels tend to become higher and their blood pressure and heart rates increase. Children starting nursery have higher levels of cortisol than those receiving home-based care, so it seems the attachment system triggers cortisol release (Groeneveld *et al.* 2010), while more sensitive home-based childcare correlates with lower cortisol levels. We also know that children with less secure attachment patterns, such as those whose parents have serious social phobia, tend to have even higher cortisol levels on starting school (Russ *et al.* 2012).

Children who have been subjected to high levels of trauma or suffered consistent anxiety, such as many in our clinical caseloads, can have ongoing elevated cortisol rates. Cortisol has a number of pernicious effects, leading Sue Gerhardt (2004) to dub it 'corrosive cortisol', particularly in light of how it can attack cells in the hippocampus, the part of the brain that is central to memory, so being implicated in memory loss. Occasionally extreme trauma can have the opposite effect and result in extremely low cortisol levels – often seen in PTSD victims such as Holocaust survivors (Yehuda *et al.* 2005). Either way too much or too little cortisol or stress is not what the human body was designed for. As suggested above, if one has been subjected to constant assaults or cumulative trauma it is possible to become either hyper-aroused, sensing danger everywhere and barely ever calming down, or the opposite, a suppressed, closed down, self-protective state that one sees in massive dissociation.

One neuropeptide, oxytocin, is particularly relevant to our understanding of attachment (Zak 2012). Oxytocin is maybe best known as the hormone central to the bonding process, whether between parents and infants or between members of a couple. It is no coincidence that other species who 'pair-bond' and show monogamous traits also have high levels of oxytocin receptors. The most famous scientific analysis of pair-bonding has come from the study of two different kinds of voles, which are mouse-like rodents. There is a meadow vole which is very promiscuous, and also tends to practically ignore its offspring, showing very few loving or nurturing behaviours. Yet there is another kind of vole called a prairie vole which is a monogamous species, and is much more nurturing to its offspring. The major difference between these two species seems to be in the amount of oxytocin they release, as well as another hormone, vasopressin, which is molecularly almost identical. Indeed if the feckless meadow voles are artificially given vasopressin they then tend to become loyal and faithful to their sexual partners, while if one inhibits the release of oxytocin and vasopressin prairie voles become as undependable as their meadow cousins. We see the same pattern in other creatures. If we stop the oxytocin release in rats they become much worse parents.

Oxytocin is known to induce tranquillity, reduce social fear, and increase empathy. Under its influence animals such as rats become calmer, and most creatures feel less pain when their bodies have high levels of it. We humans release it when we have a massage, or are being lovingly touched, and with more oxytocin we become more generous (Morhenn *et al.* 2008). In couples who are encouraged in medical trials to touch each other kindly, the husbands not only have higher oxytocin levels than control groups, but their blood pressure is considerably lower (Holt-Lunstad *et al.* 2008).

Oxytocin works to diminish the effect of the stress hormone cortisol, reducing the likelihood of being anxious and frightened. Experimenters found that when shown pictures of threatening and scary faces, those given a placebo showed much higher activation of the amygdala, a brain area linked with stress and anger, and the group given oxytocin showed much lower activation, suggesting that social fear is lowered by oxytocin (Kirsch *et al.* 2005). Oxytocin is working directly against these kinds of stress reactions such as the release of adrenaline, quicker heart rates, higher blood pressure and tense bodies.

Unfortunately, artificially introducing oxytocin is unlikely to be a medical or psychiatric panacea, particularly as oxytocin, normally introduced via a nasal spray, has a very brief life in the body of only a few minutes and, furthermore, cannot cross the brain–blood barrier. Nonetheless, experiments give some indication of its power and importance. For example, in one study fathers given oxytocin intranasally not only became more sensitive to their infants, but these infants became more responsive in return (Weisman *et al.* 2012). The oxytocin levels of human parents of either gender rises considerably in the months after becoming a parent, and the higher the levels, the more affectionate play we see from mothers and the more stimulating play from fathers (Gordon *et al.* 2010).

Those breast-feeding mothers with the highest levels of oxytocin have also been shown to be calmer, and have less physiological signs of stress, such as having lower blood pressure (Light *et al.* 2000). Mothers with an increased oxytocin response when interacting with their infants have been found to be more sensitive to their infant's moods, emotions and physical sensations (Strathearn *et al.* 2012). Importantly, mothers with a secure attachment style are not only better at picking up infant cues, but also their oxytocin circuitry is far more activated when observing infant emotional expressions, whether of laughing or crying (Strathearn *et al.* 2009). Mothers with more insecure styles have high activation of brain areas such as the insula, which are central to a more rejecting and aversive response.

There are some genetic predictors of how much oxytocin we will release. A recent experiment looked at variants of the oxytocin receptor gene, OXTR. There are two versions of this particular gene, A or G, and we inherit from both parents, thus any of us might be AA, GG or AG. Those with two G's seem to be the most prosocial, so much so that when observers watched less than half a minute of 23 romantic couples in conversation, they consistently tended to say that the listeners who had two G alleles were kinder and more empathic (Kogan *et al.* 2011). Similarly a recent Chinese study (Wu *et al.* 2012) isolated different variants of the oxytocin receptor gene, and found that some genetic variants were predictive of empathy and understanding another's feelings, while other variants predicted more cognitive empathy, such as perspective taking. Another study found that in conditions of perceived threat, those with two G's remained charitable and helpful but having other combinations predicted less commitment to civic duty (Poulin *et al.* 2012).

Something similar has even been found in children. For example pre-schoolers with one variant (RS3) of the arginine vasopressin receptor 1A (AVPR1A) gene were consistently less altruistic (Avinun *et al.* 2011). Looking at the same oxytocin receptor polymorphism (*OXTR*), Americans with either two G's or an AG combination were more likely to seek social support when in trouble, but the same was not the case for Koreans with the same combinations, for whom such support-seeking was less culturally syntonic (Kim *et al.* 2010).

The more good, loving experiences we have early on in life then the more oxytocin receptors we are likely to develop. However, we also know that early stressful life experiences lead to fewer oxytocin receptors, so that stressed childhoods lead to lower baseline levels of oxytocin in men (Opacka-Juffry and Mohiyeddini 2011), and women who were abused as girls similarly have lower oxytocin levels (Heim *et al.* 2008). In rats, for example, less licking or grooming by mothers of their offspring leads to a diminished development of the oxytocin system (Champagne *et al.* 2006).

Lane Strathearn (2011), probably more than anyone, has looked at the effects of early neglect. He found, for example, that in severe emotional neglect and in avoidant attachment we also see a lower activation of the dopamine system which, in turn, is closely related to oxytocin release. These hormonal systems work in tandem. An earlier study of neglected Romanian orphans found that the adopted children did not release as much oxytocin when cuddled by their adoptive mothers as the control group of birth children did (Fries *et al.* 2005). We can assume that this would be due to the lack of good very early nurturing experiences in the adopted group, and one by-product of this would have been the production of fewer oxytocin receptors.

It seems, though, that trauma and abuse might play havoc with one's oxytocin system. For example, for people who are very rejection sensitive, and those with borderline personality disorder or attachment issues, being artificially given oxytocin actually decreases cooperation and trust (Bartz *et al.* 2011), probably because bad early experiences seem to give rise to unusual workings of the oxytocin system. We know anyway that those with borderline personality disorder often struggle with trust and cooperation, compared to control groups, in trust games (King-Casas *et al.* 2008). In terms of attachment, findings suggest that borderline personality disorder is often associated with disorganised parenting styles (Hobson *et al.* 2005).

Secure attachment is linked with more altruism and prosocial behaviour in both children and adults. This makes sense as we know that good, loving experiences in infancy lead to more oxytocin release and more oxytocin receptors, and oxytocin enhances nurturing, thoughtful and empathic behaviours. For example, higher oxytocin levels increase the ability to understand what other people are thinking and feeling (Domes *et al.* 2007). Indeed, artificially giving adults doses of oxytocin leads to them paying more attention to the eye-regions of those around them (Guastella *et al.* 2008), even increasing the ability of autistic people to read other people's minds and emotions (Guastella *et al.* 2010). Oxytocin, it seems, oils the wheels of social life, enhancing trust, generosity, empathy and loyalty.

While I have concentrated on oxytocin, there are other hormones that play a central role in attachment and emotional wellbeing, not least serotonin. Serotonin is, of course, the hormone that is targeted by anti-depressant drugs like Prozac, and is fundamentally linked to feeling good. We see low levels of it in depression, alongside irritability and aggression, both in humans and primates (Carver *et al.* 2008). Bad experiences have a powerful effect on serotonin levels. For example, monkeys removed from their mothers at birth have chronically low levels and tend to become violent and are often ostracised from groups (Shannon *et al.* 2005), and we know that childhood adversity such as maternal depression or trauma gives rise to lower serotonin levels (Field 1995).

Again epigenetics (the study of the effect the environment has on gene expression) plays a role. One can have one of two versions of the 5HT gene, and those with the short version are even more vulnerable to childhood trauma and neglect, releasing even less serotonin (Canli *et al.* 2008) and in the face of bad experiences being more prone to aggression, anxiety and depression. Adverse early experiences have a clear effect on gene expression (Lesch 2011). However, abusive early experience equates generally with lower serotonin levels, even more so if one has a short version of the 5HT gene, and we know that many on the fringes of society, such as aggressive psychiatric patients, prisoners and others, have very low levels of serotonin (Davidson *et al.* 2000). Poor early emotional regulation, and exposure to violence, neglect or abuse, can all have a devastating effect on our hormonal systems.

It is interesting that recent research has been suggesting that even brief stressful experiences in adults, such as a 90-minute mock job interview including difficult arithmetical questions, caused an epigenetic effect whereby the stressful experience actually altered the DNA and thus the action of a gene central to oxytocin production (Unternaehrer *et al.* 2012). The epigenetic research dovetails neatly with our understandings of the psychobiological effects of stress, trauma and anxiety, to explain what affects empathic and altruistic tendencies.

There are countervailing tendencies that work in opposite ways to oxytocin and serotonin, and innate human tendencies towards coldness and aggression also have a hormonal aspect, and this is seen particularly in the hormone associated with males, testosterone. We know, for example, that violent prisoners, both male and female, have higher testosterone levels (Dabbs and Dabbs 2000). While we know that oxytocin enhances cooperation and mutual kindness, it was recently found that giving people testosterone had the opposite effect and made people more egocentric and less collaborative (Wright *et al.* 2012). Similarly we have learnt that people, even infants, with higher levels of testosterone are less able to read the emotions of others, and tend to have less empathy (Baron-Cohen 2011). Artificially giving people testosterone has the same negative effect on empathy levels. With high levels, there is less caring of others, more risk taking and quicker arousal to aggression and conflict. Interestingly males, on becoming fathers, tend to experience a lowering of testosterone levels, presumably to enhance nurturing and loving behaviours that testosterone can inhibit (Kuzawa *et al.* 2009). Thus biology, culture and life-history interweave, and while people can be born with lower or higher levels of testosterone, life events and cultural influences also play a part.

Dopamine, too, deserves a mention. It is central to the reward system, activated when we are positive, excited or eager for something, in what Panksepp calls our 'seeking system' (Panksepp and Biven 2012) but it is also involved in addiction, such as to drugs and alcohol. Depressed mothers have low dopamine levels, but more worryingly so do their babies as young as a month old, and of course such mothers do not feel very rewarded by their infants, and their infants experience less pleasure. Mothers of securely attached children have their dopamine circuitry stimulated by seeing pictures of their infants (Strathearn *et al.* 2009). Many current medical and recreational drugs target the dopamine system, and indeed many mimic the body's own opiates. Cocaine, for example, impacts on the dopamine system, and we know, for example, that it is low-status and highly stressed animals, such as rats and indeed primates, that consume more cocaine when it is placed in front of them (Cruz *et al.* 2011), as if compensating for the lack of naturally produced hormones that make us feel good. What the research increasingly shows is that not only our brains but our whole hormonal systems are powerfully programmed by the kinds of early experiences that we have, and that attachment styles are centrally implicated in this (Galbally *et al.* 2011).

Emotion, empathy and cerebral hemispheres

Brain science has recently discovered many networks centrally involved in the attachment system. Many of these discoveries link with the brain regions involved in empathy and understanding of other minds. A few years ago we had the extraordinary discovery of mirror neurons (Iacoboni and Dapretto 2006; Rizzolatti *et al.* 2006). We now know that these mirror neurons fire up when observing someone undertaking an act, so that complementary neurons to yours fire up in my brain when I watch you doing something. We know, of course, that the capacity for empathy is very linked to attachment, and that mind-minded sensitive parenting predicts secure attachment (Meins *et al.* 2002) and it also predicts developing theory of mind earlier.

It seems that with secure attachment we see more activation of areas crucial to empathy, particularly in the prefrontal cortex, whereas in avoidant attachment we see a deactivation of the medial orbitofrontal cortex (Lenzi *et al.* 2012). One of the consistent findings is that parents who are more intrusive and less sensitive tend to have higher activation of the amygdala, a small brain area central to fear and other strong emotions, and indeed we know that experiences of abuse and trauma will lead to much more active amygdala reactions generally, something that we would expect to see in disorganised attachment, and also in ambivalent patterns (Atzil *et al.* 2011). We see more reactivity in insecure attachment styles, less ability to tolerate distress, less sensitive treatment, and typically we see higher amygdala activation in insecure mothers (Riem *et al.* 2012).

Schore (2005) stresses the importance for brain development of the early months and years of life, when huge developments are taking place in the right hemisphere, which can be viewed as the seat of emotional processing, along with other elements of the limbic system. The part of the brain that deals with logic and thinking, the left brain and parts of the cortex, which in evolutionary terms are relatively new, are in fact not much 'on-line' in the first couple of years when many vital neuronal pathways and synaptic connections are forming. Similarly, the part of the brain that contextualises explicit or declarative memories, the hippocampus, is also not very developed in the first year or so of life. In other words, massive developments are taking place before the human mind is able consciously to remember actual events, and in particular many vital procedural memories and expectations are firmly entrenched well before very much conscious declarative functioning occurs.

Iain McGilchrist (2010) has particularly helped make sense of the laterality of our cerebral hemispheres. He has shown, for example, that strokes in areas of the right hemisphere disable empathy circuits and give rise to calculating, instrumental ways of relating to others, typical of the functioning of the left hemisphere. The right hemisphere is much more involved in emotional experience, in empathy and bonding. The kinds of emotional skills central to parenting, and indeed to therapy, such as empathy, are primarily occurring through the right hemisphere, through which we see another person as a feelingful whole person and identify with their experiences. When cooperating with others, we are using more right hemispheric brain areas, whereas competition links with more left-sided ones. When patients have damage to parts of their right hemisphere, they can lose their ability to empathise and are no longer able to be attuned to their feelings, hopes and concerns. After strokes in the right-sided temporoparietal area, McGilchrist shows that patients tend to have a detached sense of alienation, lack of purpose and interest and indeed feeling for their body, as the right parietal lobe is central to body sense, while the left hemisphere tends to treat the body more as a mechanical thing.

With left hemisphere dominance ones sees much higher levels of optimism, often unwarranted, and after right hemisphere strokes people often have extraordinary levels of optimism which shift into omnipotence. It is interesting that people who are more positive have higher activation of their left prefrontal areas whereas more depressed children and adults have higher right prefrontal activation (Davidson 2008). It is probably no coincidence that we see a false overly optimistic presentation in avoidant attachment, an attachment style that tends to privilege rationality over emotionality and in which we see much less empathy and emotional understanding. In just about every area of emotional functioning it is our right hemisphere that is dominant, although one exception is the left hemisphere dominance when feeling and expressing aggression.

It is important to note that both hemispheres are vital to emotional health, and it is the over-valuation of one or the other that can cause difficulty, as McGilchrist shows. For example, the capacity to develop a coherent narrative about emotional experiences, as seen in adults with secure autonomous styles in the Adult Attachment Interview, requires both the capacity to tell a coherent and consistent story, for which the left hemisphere and language centres are crucial, as well as the ability to take in and process emotional experiences via the right. Story-telling led by the left brain alone can be rather wild when not harnessed by right brain emotional understanding, as evidenced in the remarkable but oddly out of touch stories seen in studies of those with right hemisphere brain damage (Ramachandran 2012) or split-brain patients (Sperry 1971).

A whole host of research is combining to show that trauma and abuse and early levels of stress affect a range of brain areas in a way that we are beginning to understand more (Andersen and Teicher 2008). The main brain areas that have consistently been shown to be affected are the frontal lobes, particularly the prefrontal cortex, as well as the hippocampus, which is central to memory, the amygdala, very involved in fear and other strong emotions, and the corpus callosum, which links left and right hemispheres.

Victims of trauma and abuse have a smaller corpus callosum, with fewer nerve endings, and so less capacity both for the hemispheres to communicate effectively, and to work better in tandem (Teicher et al. 2004). We also know that there is much higher amygdala activation in those subjected to trauma and violence, leading them to be far more reactive and less able to be still and calm (Thomas et al. 2001; Sigurdsson et al. 2007). Similarly, childhood trauma is strongly linked with diminished sized hippocampi in adulthood (Andersen et al. 2008), and the hippocampus is central to forming and retrieving memories, among other things. We also consistently see less activation of prefrontal areas such as the ventromedial prefrontal cortex in children who have suffered trauma and abuse as well as severe neglect (Mehta et al. 2009). These prefrontal areas are vital for capacities such as empathy, but also for emotional regulation. There is a lot more that we are bound to find out in the next few years, not only about the effects of different experiences on particular areas of brain function but also on the connectivity between these brain areas. What the research is clearly showing, even if still in rudimentary form, is that different experiences give rise to very different brain development, and the likelihood that those with different attachment patterns will develop predispositions to respond to experiences via different hormonal activation and brain patterns.

Hope or hopeless?

How hopeful or gloomy should such research leave us? We know that the behavioural patterns that are established early on can be very hard to shift, and that once an experience is burnt into the circuits of the amygdala it is there forever, but we also know that new circuits can also grow and form. Interestingly, this is also what story-stem research (Hodges et al. 2003) has shown; that after good adoptions the old stories and ways of being remain, but new expectations of parental behaviour and new views of the world can grow and become stronger. There are definite windows of opportunity during which certain aspects of brain growth can occur, and the brain can certainly change throughout the lifespan. It is also true that some opportunities can be lost forever if not taken in time. Language development is one well-known example, and it seems the same is also true for certain emotional capacities. The best-known windows of opportunity, when there is massive brain growth and change, are the last trimester of pregnancy through the first few years of life, but also in adolescence when huge changes equally occur in the brain. Maybe it is not surprising that so much therapeutic effort and zeal is directed towards those age-groups.

We also know that change is possible throughout the lifespan. A heartening example is the fact that black cab drivers seem to 'grow' different sized and shaped hippocampi from the rest of the population (Maguire *et al.* 2000). There are also studies showing how professional help such as psychotherapy (Beutel *et al.* 2010; Cozolino 2010; Karlsson 2011) and mindfulness (Davidson *et al.* 2003) give rise to very clear brain changes. Joseph LeDoux (1998) states that change such as in therapy is 'another way of creating synaptic potentiation in brain pathways that control the amygdala'. It also seems fairly clear that other forms of caregiving can facilitate forms of neurobiological reprogramming (Fisher *et al.* 2011; Bick *et al.* 2012; Kroupina *et al.* 2012). Emotional support such as therapy can aid the capacity to interpret experience in new and less frightening ways, which LeDoux argues would enhance cortical processes. Other effects of such help are likely to include the laying down of new procedural memories; strengthened links between left and right hemispheres; enhanced reflective capacities; better understanding of other minds; greater ability to form a coherent narrative about oneself; improved capacity to regulate emotions, to tolerate difficult emotions without acting out and to sustain positive affect; and the capability of course to form and manage attachments better in general.

However, it is important to end, as I began, with a note of caution. This broad brush description is limited not only by my own lack of in-depth understanding, but also by the state of the field, which is changing all the time. There is much that we do not know, and many new discoveries are happening all the time. One important area is the discovery of the Default Mode Network (DMN), an interlinked series of brain areas, particularly in the midline, that work away when we are not actively trying to do anything. This DMN, it seems, is likely to be found to have important links with attachment and emotional health, and we already know that it has a role in relation to self-understanding (Qin and Northoff 2011), and that its functioning is adversely affected by trauma and early-life adversity (Bluhm *et al.* 2009).

There are likely to be even bigger discoveries that will turn our understanding upside down. Some have argued that the science of neuroscience has been wrongly named, that neurons are far outnumbered by another kind of cell, the glia cell, which were until recently seen as only the glue that allowed neurons to do their work, but which some argue are equally, if not more, fundamental, hugely outnumber neurons, and will be what future brain science will focus on more (Fields 2009). It seems that we have come a long way and have learnt a lot, but maybe more than anything we are learning how much we do not yet know. Nonetheless this is an exciting time for brain science and new findings all the time are increasing our understanding of the ways in which humans develop, as well as opening up all manner of challenges to the ways in which we have traditionally worked.

Note

1 I am grossly simplifying here and these definitions can be more subtly defined (e.g. Solms and Kaplan-Solms 2001).

References

Andersen, S.L. and Teicher, M.H., 2008. Stress, sensitive periods and maturational events in adolescent depression. *Trends in Neurosciences*, 31 (4), 183–191.

Andersen, S., Tomada, A., Vincow, E., Valente, E., Polcari, A., and Teicher, M., 2008. Preliminary evidence for sensitive periods in the effect of childhood sexual abuse on regional brain development. *The Journal of Neuropsychiatry and Clinical Neurosciences*, 20 (3), 292–301.

Atzil, S., Hendler, T., and Feldman, R., 2011. Specifying the neurobiological basis of human attachment: Brain, hormones, and behavior in synchronous and intrusive mothers. *Neuropsychopharmacology*, 36 (13), 2603–2615.

Austin, M.A., Riniolo, T.C., and Porges, S.W., 2007. Borderline personality disorder and emotion regulation: Insights from the Polyvagal Theory. *Brain and Cognition*, 65 (1), 69–76.

Avinun, R., Israel, S., Shalev, I., Gritsenko, I., Bornstein, G., Ebstein, R.P., and Knafo, A., 2011. AVPR1A variant associated with preschoolers' lower altruistic behavior. *PloS one*, 6 (9), e25274.

Baron-Cohen, S., 2011. *Zero degrees of empathy: A new theory of human cruelty*. London: Allen Lane.

Bartz, J., Simeon, D., Hamilton, H., Kim, S., Crystal, S., Braun, A., *et al.*, 2011. Oxytocin can hinder trust and cooperation in borderline personality disorder. *Social Cognitive and Affective Neuroscience*, 6 (5), 556–563.

Beebe, B. and Lachmann, F.M., 2013. *The origins of attachment: A microanalysis of four-month mother/infant interaction*. Oxford: Routledge.

Beutel, M.E., Stark, R., Pan, H., Silbersweig, D., and Dietrich, S., 2010. Changes of brain activation pre-post short-term psychodynamic inpatient psychotherapy: An fMRI study of panic disorder patients. *Psychiatry Research: Neuroimaging*, 184 (2), 96–104.

Bick, J., Dozier, M., Bernard, K., Grasso, D., and Simons, R., 2012. Foster mother–infant bonding: Associations between foster mothers' oxytocin production, electrophysiological brain activity, feelings of commitment, and caregiving quality. *Child Development*, 84 (3), 826–840.

Bluhm, R.L., Williamson, P.C., Osuch, E.A., Frewen, P.A., Stevens, T.K., Boksman, K., *et al.*, 2009. Alterations in default network connectivity in posttraumatic stress disorder related to early-life trauma. *Journal of Psychiatry & Neuroscience: JPN*, 34 (3), 187.

Bowlby, J., 1969. *Attachment and loss. Vol. 1, Attachment.* London: Hogarth.

Canli, T., Congdon, E., Todd Constable, R., and Lesch, K.P., 2008. Additive effects of serotonin transporter and tryptophan hydroxylase-2 gene variation on neural correlates of affective processing. *Biological Psychology*, 79 (1), 118–125.

Carver, C.S., Johnson, S.L., and Joormann, J., 2008. Serotonergic function, two-mode models of self-regulation, and vulnerability to depression: What depression has in common with impulsive aggression. *Psychological Bulletin*, 134 (6), 912.

Casement, P., 1990. *Further learning from the patient: The analytic space and process.* London: Routledge.

Champagne, F.A. and Curley, J.P., 2009. Epigenetic mechanisms mediating the long-term effects of maternal care on development. *Neuroscience & Biobehavioral Reviews*, 33 (4), 593–600.

Champagne, F.A., Weaver, I.C.G., Diorio, J., Dymov, S., Szyf, M., and Meaney, M.J., 2006. Maternal care associated with methylation of the estrogen receptor-a1b promoter and estrogen receptor-a expression in the medial preoptic area of female offspring. *Endocrinology*, 147 (6), 2909–2915.

Cozolino, L., 2010. *The neuroscience of psychotherapy: Healing the social brain.* New York: W.W. Norton.

Cruz, F.C., Quadros, I.M., Hogenelst, K., Planeta, C.S., and Miczek, K.A., 2011. Social defeat stress in rats: Escalation of cocaine and 'speedball' binge self-administration, but not heroin. *Psychopharmacology*, 215 (1), 165–175.

Dabbs, J.M.B. and Dabbs, M.G., 2000. *Heroes, rogues, and lovers: Testosterone and behavior.* New York: McGraw-Hill.

Davidson, R.J., 2008. Asymmetric brain function, affective style, and psychopathology: The role of early experience and plasticity. *Development and Psychopathology*, 6 (04), 741–758.

Davidson, R.J., Putnam, K.M., and Larson, C.L., 2000. Dysfunction in the neural circuitry of emotion regulation: A possible prelude to violence. *Science*, 289 (5479), 591–594.

Davidson, R.J., Kabat-Zinn, J., Schumacher, J., Rosenkranz, M., Muller, D., Santorelli, S.F., *et al.*, 2003. Alterations in brain and immune function produced by mindfulness meditation. *Psychosomatic Medicine*, 65, 564–570.

Diamond, L.M., Fagundes, C.P., and Butterworth, M.R., 2012. Attachment style, vagal tone, and empathy during mother–adolescent interactions. *Journal of Research on Adolescence*, 22 (1), 165–184.

Domes, G., Heinrichs, M., Michel, A., Berger, C., and Herpertz, S.C., 2007. Oxytocin improves 'mind-reading' in humans. *Biological Psychiatry*, 61 (6), 731–733.

Eisenberg, N., Fabes, R.A., Murphy, B., Karbon, M., Smith, M., and Maszk, P., 1996. The relations of children's dispositional empathy-related responding to their emotionality, regulation, and social functioning. *Developmental Psychology*, 32 (2), 195–209.

Field, T., 1995. Infants of depressed mothers. *Infant Behavior and Development*, 18 (1), 1–13.

Field, T., Diego, M., Dieter, J., Hern, M., Hernandez-Reif, M., Schanberg, S., *et al.* 2004. Prenatal depression effects on the fetus and the newborn. *Infant Behavior and Development*, 27 (2), 216–229.

Fields, R.D., 2009. *The other brain.* 1st ed. New York: Simon & Schuster.

Fisher, P.A., Van Ryzin, M.J., and Gunnar, M.R., 2011. Mitigating HPA axis dysregulation associated with placement changes in foster care. *Psychoneuroendocrinology*, 36 (4), 531–539.

Freud, S., 1914. On narcissism: An introduction. In *The Standard Edition of the Complete Psychological Works of Sigmund Freud, Volume XIV (1914–1916): On the History of the Psycho-Analytic Movement, Papers on Metapsychology and Other Works*, pp. 67–102.

Fries, A.B.W., Ziegler, T.E., Kurian, J.R., Jacoris, S., and Pollak, S.D., 2005. Early experience in humans is associated with changes in neuropeptides critical for regulating social behavior. *Proceedings of the National Academy of Sciences*, 102 (47), 17237–17240.

Galbally, M., Lewis, A.J., IJzendoorn, M., and Permezel, M., 2011. The role of oxytocin in mother–infant relations: A systematic review of human studies. *Harvard Review of Psychiatry*, 19 (1), 1–14.

Gerhardt, S., 2004. *Why love matters: How affection shapes a baby's brain*. 1st ed. Hove: Routledge.

Gershon, M.D., 1999. The enteric nervous system: A second brain. *Hospital Practice (1995)*, 34 (7), 31.

Goetz, J.L., Keltner, D., and Simon-Thomas, E., 2010. Compassion: An evolutionary analysis and empirical review. *Psychological Bulletin*, 136 (3), 351–374.

Gordon, I., Zagoory-Sharon, O., Leckman, J.F., and Feldman, R., 2010. Oxytocin and the development of parenting in humans. *Biological Psychiatry*, 68 (4), 377–382.

Groeneveld, M.G., Vermeer, H.J., Van IJzendoorn, M.H., and Linting, M., 2010. Children's wellbeing and cortisol levels in home-based and center-based childcare. *Early Childhood Research Quarterly*, 25 (4), 502–514.

Guastella, A.J., Mitchell, P.B., and Dadds, M.R., 2008. Oxytocin increases gaze to the eye region of human faces. *Biological Psychiatry*, 63 (1), 3–5.

Guastella, A.J., Einfeld, S.L., Gray, K.M., Rinehart, N.J., Tonge, B.J., Lambert, T.J., and Hickie, I.B., 2010. Intranasal oxytocin improves emotion recognition for youth with autism spectrum disorders. *Biological Psychiatry*, 67 (7), 692–694.

Hebb, D.O., 1949. *The organisation of behaviour*. New York: Wiley.

Heim, C., Young, L.J., Newport, D.J., Mletzko, T., Miller, A.H., and Nemeroff, C.B., 2008. Lower CSF oxytocin concentrations in women with a history of childhood abuse. *Molecular Psychiatry*, 14 (10), 954–958.

Hobson, P., Patrick, M., Crandell, L., García-Pérez, R., and Lee, A., 2005. Personal relatedness and attachment in infants of mothers with borderline personality disorder. *Development and Psychopathology*, 17 (02), 329–347.

Hodges, J., Steele, M., Hillman, S., and Henderson, K., 2003. Mental representations and defences in severely maltreated children: A story stem battery and rating system for clinical assessment and research applications. *Revealing the Inner Worlds of Young Children*, 240–267.

Holt-Lunstad, J., Birmingham, W.A., and Light, K.C., 2008. Influence of a 'warm touch' support enhancement intervention among married couples on ambulatory blood pressure, oxytocin, alpha amylase, and cortisol. *Psychosomatic Medicine*, 70 (9), 976–985.

Hurry, A., 1998. *Psychoanalysis and developmental therapy*. London: Karnac Books.

Iacoboni, M. and Dapretto, M., 2006. The mirror neuron system and the consequences of its dysfunction. *Nature Reviews Neuroscience*, 7 (12), 942–951.

Karlsson, H., 2011. How psychotherapy changes the brain. *Psychiatric Times*, 28 (8), 1–5.

Kim, H.S., Sherman, D.K., Sasaki, J.Y., Xu, J., Chu, T.Q., Ryu, C., *et al.*, 2010. Culture, distress, and oxytocin receptor polymorphism (OXTR) interact to influence emotional support seeking. *Proceedings of the National Academy of Sciences*, 107 (36), 15717–15721.

King-Casas, B., Sharp, C., Lomax-Bream, L., Lohrenz, T., Fonagy, P., and Montague, P.R., 2008. The rupture and repair of cooperation in borderline personality disorder. *Science*, 321 (5890), 806–810.

Kirsch, P., Esslinger, C., Chen, Q., Mier, D., Lis, S., Siddhanti, S., *et al.*, 2005. Oxytocin modulates neural circuitry for social cognition and fear in humans. *The Journal of Neuroscience*, 25 (49), 11489–11493.

Kogan, A., Saslow, L.R., Impett, E.A., Oveis, C., Keltner, D., and Saturn, S.R., 2011. Thin-slicing study of the oxytocin receptor (OXTR) gene and the evaluation and expression of the prosocial disposition. *Proceedings of the National Academy of Sciences*, 108 (48), 19189–19192.

Kroupina, M.G., Fuglestad, A.J., Iverson, S.L., Himes, J.H., Mason, P.W., Gunnar, M.R., *et al.*, 2012. Adoption as an intervention for institutionally reared children: HPA functioning and developmental status. *Infant Behavior and Development*, 35 (4), 829–837.

Kuzawa, C.W., Gettler, L.T., Muller, M.N., McDade, T.W., and Feranil, A.B., 2009. Fatherhood, pairbonding and testosterone in the Philippines. *Hormones and Behavior*, 56 (4), 429–435.

Labonté, B., Suderman, M., Maussion, G., Navaro, L., Yerko, V., Mahar, I., *et al.*, 2012. Genome-wide epigenetic regulation by early-life trauma. *Archives of General Psychiatry*, 69 (7), 722–731.

LeDoux, J., 1998. *The emotional brain*. New York: Simon & Schuster.

Lenzi, D., Trentini, C., Pantano, P., Macaluso, E., Lenzi, G.L., and Ammaniti, M., 2012. Attachment models affect brain responses in areas related to emotions and empathy in nulliparous women. *Human Brain Mapping*, 34 (6), 1399–1414.

Lesch, K.P., 2011. When the serotonin transporter gene meets adversity: The contribution of animal models to understanding epigenetic mechanisms in affective disorders and resilience. *Molecular and Functional Models in Neuropsychiatry*, 7, 251–280.

Light, K.C., Smith, T.E., Johns, J.M., Brownley, K.A., Hofheimer, J.A., and Amico, J.A., 2000. Oxytocin responsivity in mothers of infants: A preliminary study of relationships with blood pressure during laboratory stress and normal ambulatory activity. *Health Psychology*, 19 (6), 560–567.

MacLean, P.D., 1990. *The triune brain in evolution: Role in paleocerebral functions*. Norwell, MA: Kluwer Academic Publishers.

Maguire, E.A., Gadian, D.G., Johnsrude, I.S., Good, C.D., Ashburner, J., Frackowiak, R.S.J., and Frith, C.D., 2000. Navigation-related structural change in the hippocampi of taxi drivers. *Proceedings of the National Academy of Sciences of the United States of America*, 97 (8), 4398–4403.

McCabe, D.P. and Castel, A.D., 2008. Seeing is believing: The effect of brain images on judgments of scientific reasoning. *Cognition*, 107 (1), 343–352.

McGilchrist, I., 2010. *The Master and his emissary: The divided brain and the making of the Western world*. New Haven, CT and London: Yale University Press.

Mehta, M.A., Golembo, N.I., Nosarti, C., Colvert, E., Mota, A., Williams, S.C.R., *et al.*, 2009. Amygdala, hippocampal and corpus callosum size following severe early institutional deprivation: The English and Romanian Adoptees study pilot. *Journal of Child Psychology and Psychiatry*, 50 (8), 943–951.

Meins, E., Fernyhough, C., Wainwright, R., Gupta, M.D., Fradley, E., and Tuckey, M., 2002. Maternal mind-mindedness and attachment security as predictors of theory of mind understanding. *Child Development*, 73 (6), 1715–1726.

Miller, G., 2010. The seductive allure of behavioral epigenetics. *Science*, 329 (5987), 24–27.

Morhenn, V.B., Park, J.W., Piper, E., and Zak, P.J., 2008. Monetary sacrifice among strangers is mediated by endogenous oxytocin release after physical contact. *Evolution and Human Behavior*, 29 (6), 375–383.

Opacka-Juffry, J. and Mohiyeddini, C., 2011. Experience of stress in childhood negatively correlates with plasma oxytocin concentration in adult men. *Stress*, 15 (1), 1–10.

Panksepp, J. and Biven, L., 2012. *The archaeology of mind: Neuroevolutionary origins of human emotion*. New York: Norton.

Perry, B.D., Pollard, R.A., Blakley, T.L., Baker, W.L., and Vigilante, D., 1995. Childhood trauma, the neurobiology of adaptation, and 'use-dependent' development of the brain: How 'states' become 'traits'. *Infant Mental Health Journal*, 16 (4), 271–291.

Pinker, S., 2002. *The blank slate*. London: Penguin Books.

Porges, S.W., 2011. *The polyvagal theory: Neurophysiological foundations of emotions, attachment, communication, and self-regulation*. New York: Norton.

Poulin, M.J., Holman, E.A., and Buffone, A., 2012. The neurogenetics of nice receptor genes for oxytocin and vasopressin interact with threat to predict prosocial behavior. *Psychological Science*, 23 (5), 446–452.

Qin, P. and Northoff, G., 2011. How is our self related to midline regions and the default-mode network? *Neuroimage*, 57 (3), 1221–1233.

Ramachandran, V.S., 2012. *Tell-tale brain: Tales of the unexpected from inside your mind*. London: Windmill Books.

Riem, M.M.E., Bakermans-Kranenburg, M.J., Van IJzendoorn, M.H., Out, D., and Rombouts, S.A.R.B., 2012. Attachment in the brain: Adult attachment representations predict amygdala and behavioral responses to infant crying. *Attachment & Human Development*, 14 (6), 533–551.

Rizzolatti, G., Fogassi, L., and Gallese, V., 2006. Mirrors in the Mind Mirror neurons, a special class of cells in the brain, may mediate our ability to mimic, learn and understand the actions and intentions of others. *Scientific American*, 295 (5), 54–61.

Russ, S.J., Herbert, J., Cooper, P., Gunnar, M.R., Goodyer, I., Croudace, T., and Murray, L., 2012. Cortisol levels in response to starting school in children at increased risk for social phobia. *Psychoneuroendocrinology*, 37 (4), 462–474.

Schore, A.N., 2005. Back to basics: Attachment, affect regulation, and the developing right brain: Linking developmental neuroscience to pediatrics. *Pediatrics in Review*, 26 (6), 204–217.

Schore, A.N., 2012. *The science of the art of psychotherapy*. New York: W.W. Norton.

Schwartz, J. and Begley, S., 2002. *The mind and the brain: Neuroplasticity and the power of mental force*. New York: Harper.

Shannon, C., Schwandt, M.L., Champoux, M., Shoaf, S.E., Suomi, S.J., Linnoila, M., and Higley, J.D., 2005. Maternal absence and stability of individual differences in CSF 5-HIAA concentrations in rhesus monkey infants. *American Journal of Psychiatry*, 162 (9), 1658–1664.

Siegel, D.J., 2012. *The developing mind: Toward a neurobiology of interpersonal experience*. New York: The Guilford Press.

Sigurdsson, T., Doyère, V., Cain, C.K., and LeDoux, J.E., 2007. Long-term potentiation in the amygdala: A cellular mechanism of fear learning and memory. *Neuropharmacology*, 52 (1), 215–227.

Solms, M. and Kaplan-Solms, K., 2001. *Clinical studies in neuro-psychoanalysis: Introduction to a depth neuropsychology*. New York: Other Press.

Sperry, R.W., 1971. Brain bisection and mechanisms of consciousness. *Synthese*, 22 (3–4), 396–413.

Strathearn, L., 2011. Maternal neglect: Oxytocin, dopamine and the neurobiology of attachment. *Journal of Neuroendocrinology*, 23 (11), 1054–1065.

Strathearn, L., Fonagy, P., Amico, J., and Montague, P.R., 2009. Adult attachment predicts maternal brain and oxytocin response to infant cues. *Neuropsychopharmacology: Official Publication of the American College of Neuropsychopharmacology*, 34 (13), 2655–2666.

Strathearn, L., Iyengar, U., Fonagy, P., and Kim, S., 2012. Maternal oxytocin response during mother–infant interaction: Associations with adult temperament. *Hormones and Behavior*, 61 (3), 429–435.

Teicher, M.H., Dumont, N.L., Ito, Y., Vaituzis, C., Giedd, J.N., and Andersen, S.L., 2004. Childhood neglect is associated with reduced corpus callosum area. *Biological Psychiatry*, 56 (2), 80–85.

Thomas, K.M., Drevets, W.C., Dahl, R.E., Ryan, N.D., Birmaher, B., Eccard, C.H., *et al.*, 2001. Amygdala response to fearful faces in anxious and depressed children. *Archives of General Psychiatry*, 58 (11), 1057–1063.

Tronick, E., 2007. *The neurobehavioral and social emotional development of infants and children*. New York: Norton.

Unternaehrer, E., Luers, P., Mill, J., Dempster, E., Meyer, A.H., Staehli, S., *et al.*, 2012. Dynamic changes in DNA methylation of stress-associated genes (OXTR, BDNF?) after acute psychosocial stress. *Translational Psychiatry*, 2 (8), e150.

Weisberg, D.S., Keil, F.C., Goodstein, J., Rawson, E., and Gray, J.R., 2008. The seductive allure of neuroscience explanations. *Journal of Cognitive Neuroscience*, 20 (3), 470–477.

Weisman, O., Zagoory-Sharon, O., and Feldman, R., 2012. Oxytocin administration to parent enhances infant physiological and behavioral readiness for social engagement. *Biological Psychiatry*, 72 (12), 982–989.

Wright, N.D., Bahrami, B., Johnson, E., Di Malta, G., Rees, G., Frith, C.D., and Dolan, R.J., 2012. Testosterone disrupts human collaboration by increasing egocentric choices. *Proceedings of the Royal Society B: Biological Sciences*, 279 (1736), 2275–2280.

Wu, N., Li, Z., and Su, Y., 2012. The association between oxytocin receptor gene polymorphism (OXTR) and trait empathy. *Journal of Affective Disorders*, 138 (3), 468–472.

Yehuda, R., 2001. Biology of posttraumatic stress disorder. *The Journal of Clinical Psychiatry. Supplement*, 62 (17), 41–46.

Yehuda, R., Engel, S.M., Brand, S.R., Seckl, J., Marcus, S.M., and Berkowitz, G.S., 2005. Transgenerational effects of posttraumatic stress disorder in babies of mothers exposed to the World Trade Center attacks during pregnancy. *Journal of Clinical Endocrinology & Metabolism*, 90 (7), 4115–4118.

Zak, P.J., 2012. *The moral molecule: The new science of what makes us good or evil*. London: Bantam Press.

Chapter 8

All the A's and an O

Attachment is not everything

Cornelia Gutjahr

Introduction

The aim of this chapter is to describe disorders that can be alternative or some-times additional diagnoses to disorders or dysfunctions of attachment. It is writ-ten for professionals who are involved with children and young people around issues of child protection and safeguarding, such as social workers, teachers, legal professionals and members of the police force rather than mental health profes-sionals, who may, at times, be very confused by the technical terms used by some professionals and the sometimes conflicting outcomes of assessments on the same child.

The process of diagnosis

Before describing the disorders in more detail I will briefly talk about some aspects of the diagnostic process, which is considerably more subjective in psychiatry than in other branches of medicine.

Since there are no simple blood tests or X-rays that can reliably identify psychi-atric disorders clinicians are largely confined to observing behaviours, assessing forms and contents of thoughts and patterns of mood from the patient and gath-ering information not only from the patients and/or their families or carers but also from other informants, for example schools. This said, there are a number of evidence-based assessment tools used by clinical psychologists (and, to a lesser extent, psychiatrists). Those developed to assess attachment are discussed in the companion volume: *The Routledge Handbook of Attachment: Assessment* (Farn-field & Holmes 2014).

Subsequently the clinician must organise this material into patterns which can be interpreted with the aim of producing differential diagnoses, one of which hopefully is seen as being the most likely cause of the patient's problems.

This limitation has led to the production of diagnostic manuals which describe and systemise these patterns of behaviour. *ICD-10* (*International Classification of Mental and Behavioural Disorders*; World Health Organization 1992) and *DSM-IV* (*Diagnostic and Statistical Manual of Mental Disorders*; American Psychiatric

Association 1994) are still the most widely used. *DSM-5* was introduced in 2013 but has yet to be used by many clinicians. Shemmings discusses the *DSM-5* and matters of attachment in Chapter 5.

Both *ICD-10* and *DSM-IV* provide lists of categories of disorders, clinical descriptions and diagnostic guidelines. The term 'disorder' (rather than 'illness' or 'disease') implies a clinically recognisable set of symptoms and behaviours associated with distress (for the sufferer and/or others) and interference with personal functions; in other words, the same set of symptoms and behaviours would not be classified as a disorder if they were not associated with distress or functional impairments.

Diagnoses can be of great use in allowing treatment and research into treatments, enabling professionals to communicate about the disorder and helping the family and child to have a name for what is bothering them. These labels, in turn, can help to attract additional resources for treatment, support or education. They may also assist in matters of child welfare and care planning. For example, a psychiatric diagnosis given to a parent by an adult psychiatrist, for example 'borderline personality disorder', may assist professionals in better understanding a family in difficulty and in considering treatment options for the parent or care planning for the children. Further, a disturbed child's difficulties might be explained by constitutional or genetic factors rather than by very poor parenting as, for example, if the child is given a reliable diagnosis of autism.

However, diagnoses can be misleading since the logic of a 'diagnosis' is one of a discontinuous condition (you've either 'got it' or you haven't). The majority of psychiatric symptoms and behaviours lie on a continuum or spectrum of frequency and intensity and clinicians therefore need to define cut-offs to decide whether or not the criteria for a diagnosis are met.

There are ongoing debates about the validity of certain diagnoses and therefore also the rationale for treatments. This is in part due to the difference in the populations seen by researchers as opposed to those seen by clinicians. Researchers work with sets of inclusion and exclusion criteria in order to minimise the number of confounding factors and thus define 'pure cases' of a disorder, used for example when comparing different treatments.

Diagnoses in clinical practice

Frontline clinicians on the other hand often see children who may fulfil criteria for a number of different conditions (including problems associated with 'disordered attachments') and who might not respond, or respond unexpectedly, to the treatments that are recommended based on research evidence. The reverse is also true: it is not unusual for clinicians to see children who present with a complex profile of bewildering, distressing and disabling symptoms, indicating a number of different disorders, yet their scores lie below the cut-offs of each of those disorders and they thus find themselves in a 'no-man's-land' in terms of useful labels, treatments and access to resources (DeJong 2010).

Both children and adults can be hard to live with at times and their behaviour can be confusing and a cause of concern and anxiety. Children with very insecure attachment styles can be even harder to live with, care for or educate.

Parents and foster carers sometimes attend clinics very concerned about a child's emotional or behavioural difficulties and they may have already rather fixed ideas about what is wrong with the child (nowadays supported by easy access to the internet). Quite often they, and even the professionals involved, can become confused about the diagnostic issues raised by children with complex problems. The quality of relationships between professionals and parents can play an important role in the diagnostic process and may at times add to the confusion.

A case example

To illustrate this I will describe one child's experiences with a Child and Adolescent Mental Health Service (CAMHS). This account is a composite but it is based on real case histories.

An 11-year journey through the Child and Adolescent Mental Health Service

Z is now a 15-year-old male adolescent. Both of his parents are unemployed and the family live in a socially deprived area.

Aged 4

He was first seen at CAMHS at the age of 4 at his parents' request. They experienced him as angry, defiant and aggressive. He threw frequent tantrums and had no friends at nursery. They were convinced that Z had attention deficit hyperactivity disorder (ADHD) because he 'ticked all the boxes' in an online test and they were hoping that medication would make life at home more bearable.

At the first interview his mother was very critical of Z and said he was a 'devil's child' and had been 'very hard work' as a baby. The parents said that they would sometimes slap him as a last resort. Both parents came across as hostile, angry and demanding to the assessing clinician, while Z seemed to be on his guard, rarely responded to the clinician, sat quite still and did not play or draw.

Staff at the nursery he attended described his aggressive behaviour and difficulties with other children. They said he often seemed distressed when dropped off by his parents, yet did not seem pleased when they picked him up. They also reported an uneasy relationship between staff and the parents.

In the clinicians' view Z's presentation could best be explained as an attachment disorder rather than by ADHD.

His parents were invited to attend an Intensive Parenting course. His mother attended sessions that used a one-way screen (behind which the clinicians sat) and video feedback. She did make fewer negative comments towards him in the sessions but remained otherwise critical of him.

Aged 6

Z's problematic behaviours at home persisted and he was seen again at the age of 6. His parents now said they thought that he might be autistic. Z's teacher confirmed his defiance and problems getting on with the other children. Her ratings of the nature, frequency and severity of Z's other behaviours at school differed considerably from those of the parents. This seemed to rule out a diagnosis of both ADHD and an autistic spectrum disorder (ASD).

A diagnosis of attachment disorder with symptoms of oppositional defiant disorder (ODD) was made.

Family therapy was suggested; the family attended one session and did not return. They were angry and critical of the CAMHS clinicians they had seen so far.

Aged 8

When he was eight years old Z was assessed for ASD at a different service. His play and non-verbal communication skills were thought to be immature and he did not appear to have learning difficulties. The assessment was inconclusive because Z refused to cooperate. Again the professionals noticed the parents' hostility towards Z and themselves.

It was concluded that Z was showing autistic traits but that he did not meet the full criteria needed for a diagnosis of ASD.

Aged 15

The family remained involved with CAMHS on and off over the next few years, their relationships with the clinicians remained quite strained and they were increasingly perceived as a 'difficult' case.

By the time he was 15 years old Z was barely attending school and still had no friends. His school referred him back to CAMHS with concerns that he might be on the autistic spectrum, commenting that he seemed 'quite similar to some of their Asperger's children' and that 'a diagnosis would help him to access specific help and support at school'.

There was initial reluctance to reassess Z given the outcomes of previous assessments. However, his deteriorating school and social performance clearly needed attention. In the interview Z's mother came across as rather literal and concrete and it emerged that, unbeknown to CAMHS, she had been diagnosed with 'mild ASD' a few years ago. His mother said she had come to understand herself and her children better and could now deal quite well with Z. Both assessing clinicians noted the warmth between Z and his parents.

The parents' account of his early development and behaviours seemed to indicate a 'textbook history' of ASD, and Z's individual assessment revealed his marked difficulties in recognising emotions on faces and his very poor ability to take other people's perspective. Neither had been tested formally before.

Z received a diagnosis of High Functioning Autism.

The clinical implications for Z

Z encountered several different diagnoses on this journey including 'attachment disorder'. The diagnoses of 'attachment disorder' and 'reactive attachment disorder' (RAD), with regard to problems consequent upon a child's life experiences, are considered by David Shemmings in Chapter 5.

The possible differential diagnoses

There are indeed a number of other disorders, with very different aetiologies, that are often confused with problems associated with insecure attachment styles.

I will briefly describe each of these conditions before returning to a discussion of the outcome in this case and what larger conclusions can be drawn. I should stress that I am making no claims at being comprehensive in this discussion and the interested reader should turn to more detailed texts (see References).

Autistic spectrum disorders synonymous with the autistic spectrum continuum (ASC)

The autistic spectrum disorders (ASD) are characterised by abnormalities in three main areas:

1   *Verbal and non-verbal communication:* For example, spoken language may
     be stereotyped and repetitive, conversations may not be initiated or sustained,
     eye contact and gesture may be reduced or absent.
2   *Social interaction:* For example, difficulties in imaginative or pretend play,
     in developing and maintaining friendships and inability or unwillingness to
     share enjoyment or interests.
3   *Ritualistic and stereotyped behaviours and resistance to change:* One exam-
     ple might be incessantly watching TV programmes aimed at much younger
     children and becoming extremely distressed when the programmes are
     interrupted.

These qualitative abnormalities are described as 'pervasive' because they are
features of the individual's functioning in all the circumstances they encounter.

In Infantile Autism the child displays abnormalities in all three defining areas
before the age of 3 years and the development of language is either delayed or
absent as opposed to Asperger's syndrome where the development of language is
seemingly normal.

In Atypical Autism the onset may be later than 3 years and/or the symptoms may
be less severe. This diagnosis does not require impairments across all three areas
and is more often used for children with severe or profound learning difficulties.

Autistic spectrum disorders lie on a spectrum ranging from profound disability
(including Kanner's classical autism) to mild impairment (including high functioning autism and Asperger's syndrome). At least half of the children diagnosed
with childhood autism suffer from moderate to severe learning difficulties and
20–30 per cent will develop epilepsy (Howlin 1998).

Depending on the degree of language and learning difficulties these children
may present with behavioural symptoms ranging from mood dysregulation, temper tantrums and meltdowns (for example, because of sensory hypersensitivities
or changes in their routines) to severe self-injurious behaviour, aggression and
violence towards others.

About a quarter of children with ASD are of normal or above normal intelligence (Charman *et al.* 2011). Those with a diagnosis of high functioning autism
can present very similarly to those diagnosed with Asperger's syndrome in terms
of their psychosocial functioning.

Children with Asperger's syndrome do not show a delay in language development, they do however share some difficulties in their understanding and social
communicative use of language with other children on the autistic spectrum.

The ability to take other people's perspective about what they might know or
what they might be feeling is known as the Theory of Mind and is impaired to
varying degrees in people with ASD. Autistic people might assume that the other
person shares their own level of information and reasoning and therefore ought to
come to the same conclusions.

Executive functions refer to the ability to plan, initiate and carry through actions.
This is impaired, again to varying degrees, in ASD due to a lack of flexibility in

thinking. Consequently people on the autistic spectrum might persist in using the same solutions for different problems. For example, they might insist on using the same route to their school irrespective of new roadworks or other obstacles in their way. Impairment of executive functions is not unique to ASD and can also be found in ADHD, ODD and conduct disorder (CD). It is, however, important to take these difficulties into account when planning treatment or management of the child.

Causation

No single cause of ASD has been identified. Family and twin studies do point towards a significant genetic contribution. In some cases there are associations with specific, but uncommon genetic disorders such as Fragile X Syndrome and Tuberous Sclerosis. Pre- and perinatal complications can also be associated with subsequent ASD (Freitag 2008).

Unless there is sufficient information about the child's early development a diagnosis of ASD may be tentative and differential diagnosis (deciding which if any underlying disorder is most likely to cause the symptoms) can be surprisingly difficult.

Generally an improvement in the quality of care provided to children on the autistic spectrum does not result in any significant improvement in the child's core difficulties which are life-long and pervasive.

In this respect they differ from children with significantly insecure attachment styles in which significant changes in functioning may occur over time. A striking example of where attachment disorders presented with a clinical picture resembling autism was seen in the case of children brought up in Romanian orphanages (Rutter *et al.* 1999). These children suffered neglect on a major scale and exhibited classical autistic symptoms as well as severe developmental and cognitive deficits to the extent that they were described as 'quasi-autistic'. A significant number of those who were subsequently adopted improved to such an extent that they no longer met the criteria for an autistic disorder. Those most likely to improve had suffered from inhibited RAD.

ASD is less commonly diagnosed than some of the other conditions we discuss here, such as ADHD. Baird *et al.* (2006) report the total prevalence of all ASDs as 116.1 per 10,000 and 24.8 per 10,000 when a narrower definition of childhood autism was used. However, the rates appear to be increasing and the reason for this is the subject of much discussion. It is thought that changes in diagnostic practices, public awareness and referral patterns, among other things, are contributing significantly to the increase.

Obsessive compulsive disorder (OCD), anxiety disorders and depression are not uncommon in children with ASD and may need treatment in their own right, depending on the severity of the symptoms and impact on the day-to-day functioning. ADHD and Tourette's syndrome may also occur in children on the autistic spectrum.

Treatment

There is no treatment for ASD based on its underlying cause. This said, there are a number of interventions than can have an impact on the course and the quality of life both for the children and their parents/carers. These include psycho-education for the parents/carers, the school and the child. Addressing the language and learning needs of the child and providing social skills training are of equal importance. If the child has sensory hypersensitivities (e.g. to noise, light, crowds) environmental adaptations can help. Similarly, thoughtful planning can satisfy the child's need for structure, predictability and routines. The provision of emotional and practical support, such as respite can be invaluable for the parents/carers. The most cognitively impaired children with ASD and those without language may need intermittent or full-time residential care and, at times, medication.

ASD is the most important differential diagnosis to 'disordered attachments' because of the apparent overlap of the difficulties which, I must stress, have very different aetiologies. Children on the autistic spectrum and their families require interventions and supportive measures which may differ substantially from those needed for children with disordered attachments.

Attention Deficit Hyperactivity Disorder

ADHD can be diagnosed where at least some of the following features are present.

First: Hyperactivity and impulsivity, for example an inability to sit still or acting as if driven by a motor, fidgeting or fiddling with objects. Impulsivity could include not having a sense of danger, for example running out into traffic (asking how often a child has visited A & E in the last six months could be a diagnostic pointer for such behaviour!).

Second: Inattention, seeming not to listen, forgetfulness, distractibility and a persistent failure to carry through tasks (for example, forgetting to bring PE kit to a gym class).

Age of onset: The onset is before the age of seven and the symptoms need to occur and cause impairment across different settings (most commonly the family and school).

Both the *DSM-IV* and the *ICD-10* criteria provide similar lists of symptoms but recommend different ways of establishing a diagnosis. As a result the prevalence rates based on *DSM-IV* are significantly higher than those based on *ICD-10* and can thus range from 2–18 per cent depending on the country, geographical area, study population and diagnostic criteria used (Polanczyk *et al.* 2007). Döpfner *et al.* (2008) found a five-fold increase in the diagnosis of ADHD in the same study population when *DSM-IV* as opposed to *ICD-10* criteria were used.

The larger problem with reaching a diagnosis of ADHD is that although the list of diagnostic criteria seems quite straightforward, these same symptoms can of course also arise in the context of the quality of relationships of children with adults and other children. Furthermore, complex post traumatic stress disorder in the context of abuse and/or neglect can either contribute to or closely resemble ADHD.

Causation

There is no known single cause of ADHD. There is a growing body of evidence from twin and adoption studies suggestive of a significant genetic contribution to the clinical picture. In addition neurobiological abnormalities have been found and are thought to explain some of the clinical findings (Barkley 2013).

Other child intrinsic factors that make a diagnosis of ADHD more likely include male sex (2 to 4 times more boys than girls are diagnosed), head injury, infections and/or substance use during pregnancy. Family and wider environmental factors such as severe marital discord, maternal history of mental illness, paternal history of criminality, domestic violence, large family size, placement in foster-care, low socioeconomic class and poverty are seen as both associated and contributing factors.

Treatment

The most well-known treatment for ADHD is the use of stimulant medication. This remains controversial (Timimi 2002). It is no longer considered a first line treatment in newly diagnosed moderate ADHD, though remains recommended for severe ADHD (NICE 2008).

Other treatments for ADHD have been shown to be effective (NICE 2008). These include psycho-education for the family, school and the child, parent training programmes and cognitive behavioural treatment for the child. Identifying and addressing learning needs that could be causing or contributing to the behaviours, and the treatment of any other disorders comorbidly occurring in the child are equally important. It is important to address family issues such as parental mental and/or physical illness and domestic violence. Further options are family therapy and multisystemic therapy (especially if comorbid with CD).

Factors predicting a positive outcome include good cognitive functioning, easy temperament, the ability to regulate emotions, the quality of relationships within the family and with teachers and peers. The association with CD tends to carry a poor prognosis.

ADHD as a social construct

It should be noted that some authors argue that externalising disorders such as ADHD, ODD and CD are largely social constructs with little or no nosological validity (i.e. whether they are 'real' disorders or not). They argue that cultural and societal factors and expectations render it more likely for some behavioural patterns to be medicalised and medicated (for a more in-depth discussion see Timimi (2002) and Furman (2008)).

Oppositional defiant disorder and conduct disorder

ICD10 and *DSM-IV* describe ODD as characterised by a pattern of negativistic, hostile and defiant behaviours while CD involves the additional presence of persistent patterns of behaviour in which the basic rights of others or major age-appropriate societal norms or rules are violated.

It is estimated that 90 per cent of children diagnosed with conduct disorder had a previous diagnosis of ODD, suggesting that ODD is a precursor of CD (Loeber *et al.* 1993). I will use the term conduct disorder to encompass both ODD and CD in what follows.

Conduct disorders are the most common reason for referral to CAMHS in the UK (Hill 2002).

There are no diagnostic tools exclusively validated for ODD or CD and when questionnaires about a child's behaviour are returned by both parents and school and the young people, there are often low rates of agreement, raising questions about the validity of the concept (Burt *et al.* 2011).

Causation

There is no single known cause for conduct disorder, however factors contributing to the risk of developing CD have been described. Intrapersonal factors include temperament, speech and language difficulties, reading difficulties and learning difficulties, deficits in executive function and social skills.

Family factors include parental mental illness, parental discord, inconsistent parenting style, harsh discipline, high criticism towards the child and low parental warmth, poor supervision, low parental involvement in the child's activities, abuse and neglect (Frick *et al.* 1992). It is important to note that a number of these aetiological factors are also associated with the development of insecure/disorganised attachment patterns (DeKleyen 1996; Guttman-Steinmetz & Crowell 2006) and that these factors in child-rearing have a significant impact on a child's developing attachment style. Wider environmental factors include low socioeconomic status, poverty, unemployment, social isolation of the family and large family size.

Since CD often runs in families some practitioners argue that there is a genetic contribution. It is indeed well established that children with fathers with antisocial personality are more likely to be conduct disordered, however the risk also increases in adopted children whose adoptive fathers have an antisocial personality (Hill 2002).

Of children in the age range 8–16, 5–10 per cent have significant and persistent oppositional, disruptive or aggressive behavioural problems. Boys are twice as likely to receive the diagnosis as girls. This ratio might be biased as the diagnostic criteria focus more on overt characteristics such as aggressive and violent behaviour which are more often found in males (Hill 2002).

CD has a strong association with depression and with ADHD: 25–30 per cent of boys and 50 per cent of girls with CD also have a diagnosis of ADHD. Early onset CD has a significantly worse prognosis compared to that confined to adolescence. Between 40–50 per cent of CD children may go on to develop antisocial personality disorder (though this means that 50–60 per cent do not!). Early onset and severity are the best predictors for persistence into adulthood. CD combined with ADHD has the worst prognosis.

Treatment

The mainstays of treatment for CD are parent management training, family therapy, problem solving, social skills and anger management training and multisystemic therapy, which is an intensive, family-focused and community-based treatment programme for aggressive and violent young people (Henggeler et al. 2009).

Stimulant medication may be indicated to treat comorbid ADHD, likewise antidepressants for the treatment of comorbid depression. Low doses of antipsychotic medication may be used to treat severely aggressive or violent behaviours.

Diagnostic dilemmas

The alert reader will have noticed that there are quite a few symptoms shared in common between all these conditions and that this could lead to confusion in diagnosis. The situation is further complicated as, from clinical experience, certain clinics or child psychiatrists seem to 'favour' one diagnosis over another. Indeed at times it appears that the greater diagnostic variability lies in the doctors and not the children they see. Table 8.1 tabulates the main behaviours seen in the conditions I have been describing.

It is interesting that many of the standard references on this area of psychiatry do not discuss how to differentiate these conditions. For example, the *Handbook of Attachment* (Cassidy & Shaver 1999) does not mention ASD or ADHD and only has a brief entry on ODD. Similarly, in books on ADHD (Pliszka et al. 1999) and ASD (Howlin 1998) attachment is not referenced. This suggests that these authors may come from quite different schools of thought. The school around ASD and ADHD seemingly thinks mainly in terms of possible biological and genetic aetiologies and explanations, while people with a framework around attachment are mostly interested in early relationships. However, it is important to note that these are not simply incompatible schools of thought seeking to offer differing explanations for the same phenomena.

For example, it would not strike most clinicians as unreasonable or illogical to diagnose a patient with both ASD and attachment disorder. However, it might be very difficult or indeed impossible to decide which 'symptom' could be attributable to which 'disorder'.

Table 8.1 Behaviours that can be associated with the psychiatric diagnoses discussed in this chapter

Behaviour	RAD/DA	ASD	ADHD	ODD	CD
Inattention	(+)	(+)	+	(+)	(+)
Restlessness	(+)	(+)	+	(+)	(+)
Disorganisation/lack of planning	(+)	(+)	+	(+)	(+)
Not following instructions	(+)	(+)	+	+	+
Impulsivity	(+)	(+)	+	(+)	(+)
Loses temper	(+)	(+)	+	+	+
Argumentative	(+)	(+)	(+)	+	+
Defies rules and regulations	(+)	(+)	(+)	+	+
Angry, resentful	(+)	(+)	(+)	+	+
Aggressive	(+)	(+)	(+)	+	+
Violent	(+)	(+)	(+)	(+)	+
Cruel to people/animals	(+)	(+)	(+)	(+)	+
Destructive of property	(+)	(+)	(+)	(+)	+
Sexualised behaviour	(+)	(+)	(+)	—	(+)
Self injurious behaviour	(+)	(+)	(+)	(+)	(+)
Impaired nonverbal communication	(+)	+	—	—	—
Insistence on sameness/routines	(+)	+	—	—	—
Stereotyped behaviour	(+)	+	—	—	—
Prefers own company/social withdrawal	(+)	+	—	—	(+)
Friendship difficulties	(+)	+	(+)	(+)	(+)
Indiscriminate friendliness	+	(+)	—	—	—

Key: RAD/AD = Reactive attachment disorder/Attachment disorder
ASD = Autistic spectrum disorder
ADHD = Attention deficit hyperactivity disorder
ODD = Oppositional defiant disorder
CD = Conduct disorder
+ = Nearly always present (a diagnostic criterion for this condition)
(+) = Can also be found in this condition
— = Rarely found in this condition

This diagnostic dilemma can have very significant implications for a child's future in child care proceedings as the clinical opinion that a child has an insecure attachment (or even an attachment disorder) implicates the quality and style of parenting provided, while a diagnosis of ASD (or perhaps ADHD) indicates that significant constitutional or genetic factors are at play.

Discussion

From Table 8.1 we can see that several of the symptoms occur in more than one disorder. Parents, carers and other professionals can be convinced that their child's difficulties must indicate that they suffer from one or other specific disorder. The problem is that often the child's most marked or disturbing 'symptoms' do not discriminate between the various competing diagnoses.

So how do clinicians arrive at a diagnosis? First they make clinical observations of the child and his parents, collect a detailed history of the development of the behaviours and the circumstances in which they arise, a history of the child's overall development, a family history, not only in terms of disorders and diseases but also of experiences (e.g. a trans-generational history of neglect or abuse) and family scripts (Byng-Hall 1995), a social and educational history and, importantly, a description of the family functioning and relationships. They should then seek feedback from school and other relevant settings, where possible direct observations of the child in those settings will add important information. Factors specific to the child, for example temperament or learning difficulties need consideration.

Much of the art of diagnosis in child and adult psychiatry lies in considering the potential interplay of all those factors.

And what might get in the way of this comprehensive process? As Coghill (2012: 816) says:

It might be easy to miss those kinds of links in day-to-day clinical practice if you were either focussed on the particular part of a person's difficulties or if you failed systematically to assess all aspects of a person's life rather than those that they themselves identify as important.

What can we learn from Z?

In the case of Z, viewed in retrospect, it seems reasonable to say that when he first presented, his reported symptoms probably arose from a combination of both an insecure (or disordered) attachment and ASD.

Was 'attachment disorder' a misdiagnosis?

The first presentation of Z at CAMHS showed several features that suggested an insecure attachment disorder. For example, we know that a parent's style of negative attributions and hostility towards their child can have a negative influence on the child's quality and security of attachment. Further intrusive behaviours are associated with attachment difficulties, as can be harsh and inconsistent discipline from either one or both parents.

Z showed little affect during the initial interview. He barely moved, did not look at the clinician or his parents and did not answer questions. He did not seem overtly distressed by his mother's insensitive and hostile comments. His father admitted that he often lost his temper and that he shouted and punished Z. All in all there seemed to be sufficient though not extensive information to justify a diagnosis of attachment disorder.

However, it is also apparent that children who have constitutional difficulties (for example ASD) are not easy to look after and might not bring out the most emotionally attuned or good quality care from their parents.

The nursery's observations around separations and reunions added weight to the diagnosis of attachment disorder. Close readers of the other chapters in this book will probably see several other indications in this vignette that justified that initial diagnosis.

However, this diagnosis could be seen as attributing Z's difficulties to the quality of care he had received as an infant.

Was ADHD dismissed wrongly?

The pervasiveness of the symptoms is a crucial part of a diagnosis of ADHD. This means that they have to be observable in at least two settings, commonly at home and in school. All Z's behaviours reported by his parents could, of course, signify ADHD; he did indeed tick all the boxes where symptoms at home were concerned. However, neither the feedback from nursery nor later from primary school matched the parents' description of the severity of Z's difficult behaviours. He was seen as rather isolated with tantrums, aggression and defiance but, crucially, neither hyperactivity nor inattention or impulsivity featured strongly. It seemed unlikely therefore that his behaviours could be explained by ADHD.

Were there early subtle hints pointing towards a diagnosis of ASD?

Z did not seem to make friends, or perhaps want to make friends, either in school or outside of school.

Some of his tantrums might have been happening in the context of sensory over-stimulation or a disturbance of his rigid sense of order. The difficulty is that these symptoms in isolation could indicate one of several disorders (see Table 8.1) and more indicators are needed, for example in the family history, before a secure diagnosis can be made. When his mother received a diagnosis of ASD this emerging family history did add weight to the probability of ASD as a diagnosis for Z.

What happened to the problems associated with an insecure attachment later on? Did they simply vanish?

Attachment patterns are dependent on the quality of the relationships with attachment figures. The patterns might be different with different figures at the same time, they might be stable over time or they might change in response to the qualitative changes in the relationships with the attachment figures.

In Z's case the last clinicians seeing the family clearly observed a substantial change in the level of warmth and empathy from the parents towards Z at his last visit to the clinic. His mother especially seemed better in tune with Z's needs. She said that her own diagnosis had helped her to understand Z better. The parents reported a good working relationship and father described himself as an 'interpreter' for both his wife and Z. This was borne out in the session.

Z's anger and tantrums seemed to have diminished and had less of an impact on the family. The family relationships had thus vastly improved. However, his 'core' difficulties remained.

Did relationships between the parents and the clinicians influence diagnostic process and its duration?

Up until the detailed reassessment when Z was 15 the parents were invariably perceived and described as 'hostile and demanding' by professionals in CAMHS, the paediatric service and sometimes in verbal feedback from school. Their behaviour may have reflected the power of the 'labels' the professionals are empowered to apply or withhold. Labels such as ASD, ADHD, depression, psychosis are often perceived as 'proper medical conditions' by parents, and sometimes by professionals too, whereas attachment disorder, ODD and CD are frequently seen as 'diagnoses by default' and, considering the associated factors, ultimately as due to 'bad parenting'.

The feeling that we are a bad parent and being seen as bad parents is often accompanied by literally unmentionable shame which can turn into anger or rage. This can impact on the clinicians' ability to think clearly, 'remain on board' and allow a working relationship to develop. Joint working, good supervision and/or reflective practice are invaluable tools under such circumstances.

In Z's case the family was increasingly perceived as difficult and attachment 'filled the diagnostic screen' rather than being seen as one facet in a complex picture. Consequently therapeutic interventions did not work or were rejected. This process only came to an end when Z was re-referred by school at the age of 15, implicitly validating the parents' earlier concerns.

How helpful (or unhelpful) is this diagnosis?

High functioning autism (HFA) is on the mild end of the autistic spectrum and in some cases the symptoms might not influence the patient's ability to function, nor cause much distress. The diagnosis, though valid, might be considered as a negative label and so the decision about receiving or not receiving a diagnosis of HFA or Asperger's syndrome should be up to the individuals and/or their parents. The diagnosis can bring resources with it though: in Z's case his school offered tailored, special support and he gained access to therapy from a specialist service to tackle his anxieties and obsessions. He would also be able to access special support later at college.

Conclusions

Issues of how professionals understand a child's difficulties can be of the greatest importance not only to providing the most effective treatment but sometimes to the whole future life and care of that child. Consider the child, subsequently diagnosed with severe autism by a senior specialist, who was removed from his mother by a local authority because a CAMHS clinician, on the basis of a very few clinical interviews (and using no formal evidence-based assessment tools), diagnosed an attachment disorder, thus implicating the mother's capacity as a parent. This child's young mother had other emotional and social difficulties which compounded her problems in offering her child adequate care, a combination of factors and conflicting diagnoses which understandably confused many of the professionals involved in this case.

A diagnostic assessment in child psychiatry needs to be broad and comprehensive and should not only be a matter of achieving a quick consensus on a specific diagnosis. Assessments are often nevertheless subjective processes with judgements about the nature, degree and the relative importance of symptoms and where they should be placed in different syndrome patterns. The appreciation of family relationships and environments are, equally, a matter of judgement. This is often a lengthy and time consuming process and unlikely to sit easily with the pressures on services to see patients faster and 'more efficiently' and with targets, for example higher throughput, becoming the 'clinical' outcomes (Coghill 2012).

Both clinicians and parents can have 'preferred diagnoses'. I am aware of clinical services that nearly always seem to give a child referred to them the same diagnosis regardless of the complexities of the clinical presentation. All clinicians need to be mindful of this.

Increasingly there are evidence-based diagnostic tools to assist the clinicians. For example, for children who may fall on the autistic spectrum the Autism Diagnostic Observation Schedule (ADOS) (Lord *et al.* 1989) or the Autism Diagnostic Interview-Revised (ADI–R) (Lord *et al.* 1994).

There are now a number of evidence-based assessments for attachment for use across the whole age range from infancy to adulthood. These are discussed in detail in the companion volume (Farnfield & Holmes 2014).

Not surprisingly clinicians can find themselves in that 'grey area' where either diagnostic criteria are met but a diagnosis would not be deemed to be particularly helpful or add anything to a young person's quality of life (for example, in patients with HFA or Asperger's who do not experience significant distress in their social network and would prefer not to be labelled), or the criteria are not quite met but there are high levels of distress and a diagnosis could afford the patients a degree of support, both psychological and practical, that could significantly improve their quality of life and relationships.

It could be argued that in such cases pragmatic diagnoses and, at times, treatments might be indicated, particularly where the young person is caught up in entrenched negative cycles with the parents and/or school. A diagnosis in these circumstances can create a breathing space for the child, the parents and sometimes school and, in turn, improve the relationships. This process could allow virtuous cycles to develop and, over time, render both the diagnosis and the treatment superfluous.

Acknowledgements

My special thanks go to Paul Holmes for suggesting I write this chapter and to my partner David Parish for kick-starting the process.

References

American Psychiatric Association (1994) *Diagnostic and Statistical Manual of Mental Disorders: Fourth Edition; DSM-IV.* Washington, DC: American Psychiatric Association.

Baird G., Simonoff, E., Pickles, A., Chandler, S., Loucas, T., Meldrum, D., & Charman, T. (2006). Prevalence of disorders of the autism spectrum in a population cohort of children in South Thames: The Special Needs and Autism Project (SNAP). *Lancet*, 368(9531), 210–215.

Barkley, R.A. (2013) ADHD: Nature, Course, Outcomes, and Comorbidity. Available online at: http://www.continuingedcourses.net/active/courses/course303.php

Burt, S.A., Klahr, M., Rueter, M.A., McGue, M., & Iacono, W.G. (2011) Confirming the etiology of adolescent acting-out behaviors: An examination of observer-ratings in a sample of adoptive and biological siblings. *Journal of Child Psychology and Psychiatry*, 52(5), 519–526.

Byng-Hall, J. (1995) *Rewriting Family Scripts: Improvisation and systems change.* New York: The Guilford Press.

Cassidy, J., & Shaver, P.R. (eds) (1999) *Handbook of Attachment: Theory, research and clinical applications.* New York: The Guilford Press.

Charman, T., Pickles, A., Simonoff, E., Chandler, S., Loucas, T., & Baird, G. (2011) IQ in children with autism spectrum disorders: Data from the Special Needs and Autism Project (SNAP). *Psychological Medicine*, 41(3), 619–27.

Coghill, D. (2012) Editorial: Getting the basics right in mental health assessments of children and young people. *Journal of Child Psychology and Psychiatry*, 53: 815–817.

DeJong, M. (2010) Some reflections on the use of psychiatric diagnosis in the looked after or 'in care' child population. *Clinical Child Psychology and Psychiatry*, 15, 589–599.

DeKlyen, M. (1996) Disruptive behaviour disorder and intergenerational attachment patterns: A comparison of clinic-referred and normally functioning preschoolers and their mothers. *Journal of Consulting and Clinical Psychology*, 64(2), 357–365.

Döpfner, M., Breuer, D., Wille, N., Erhart, M., Ravens-Sieberer, U., & Bella Study Group (2008) How often do children meet ICD-10/DSM-IV criteria of Attention Deficit-/Hyperactivity Disorder and Hyperkinetic Disorder? Parent based prevalence rates in a national sample – results of the BELLA study. *European Child and Adolescent Psychiatry*, 17 (supplement 1), 59–70.

Farnfield, S., & Holmes, P. (eds) (2014) *The Routledge Handbook of Attachment: Assessment*, London and New York: Routledge.

Freitag, C. M. (2008) *Autismus-Spektrum-Störungen.* München: Reinhardt.

Frick, P.F., Lahey, B.B., Loeber, R., Stouthamer-Loeber, M., Christ, M.A.G., & Hanson, K. (1992) Familial risk factors to oppositional defiant disorder and conduct disorder: Parental psychopathology and maternal parenting. *Journal of Consulting and Clinical Psychology*, 60, 49–55.

Furman, L.M. (2008) Attention-deficit hyperactivity disorder (ADHD): Does new research support old concepts? *Journal of Child Neurology*, 23, 775–784.

Guttmann-Steinmetz, S., & Crowell, J.A. (2006) Attachment and externalizing disorders: A developmental psychopathology perspective. *Journal of the American Academy of Child and Adolescent Psychiatry*, 45, 440–451.

Henggeler, S.W., Schoenwald, S.K., Borduin, C.M., Rowland, M.D., & Cunningham, P.B. (2009) Multisystemic therapy for antisocial behavior in children and adolescents (2nd ed.). New York: The Guilford Press.

Hill, J. (2002) Biological, psychological and social processes in the conduct disorders. *Journal of Child Psychology and Psychiatry*, 43, 133–164.

Howlin, P. (1998) *Children with autism and Asperger syndrome: A guide for practitioners and carers*. Chichester: John Wiley & Sons Ltd.

Loeber, R., Wung, P., Keenan, K., Giroux, B., Stouthamer-Loeber, M., Van Kammen, W.B., *et al.* (1993). Developmental pathways in disruptive child behavior. *Development and Psychopathology* 5:103–133.

Lord, C., Rutter, M., Goode, S., Heemsbergen, J., Jordan, H., Mawhood, L., *et al.* (1989) Autism diagnostic observation schedule: A standardized observation of communicative and social behavior. *Journal of Autism and Developmental Disorders*, 19(2), 185–212.

Lord, C., Rutter, M., & Le Couteur, A. (1994) Autism Diagnostic Interview-Revised: A revised version of a diagnostic interview for caregivers of individuals with possible pervasive developmental disorders. Journal of Autism and Developmental Disorders, 24(5), 659–685.

NICE (September 2008, last modified in March 2013) [ADHD]. [CG72]. London: National Institute for Health and Care Excellence.

Pliszka, S.R., Carlson, C.L., & Swanson, J.M. (1999) *ADHD with Comorbid Disorders: Clinical assessment and management*. New York: The Guilford Press.

Polanczyk, G., De Lima, M.S., Horta, B.L., Biederman, J., & Rohde, L.A. (2007) The worldwide prevalence of ADHD: A systematic review and metaregression analysis. *American Journal of Psychiatry*, 164(6), 942–948.

Rutter, M., Andersen-Wood, L., Beckett, C., Bredenkamp, D., Castle, J., Groothues, C., *et al.* (1999) Quasi-autistic patterns following marked early global deprivation. *Journal of Child Psychology &Psychiatry*, 40(4), 537–549.

Timimi, S. (2002) *Pathological Child Psychiatry and the Medicalization of Childhood*. Hove: Brunner-Routledge.

World Health Organization (1992) *ICD-10 Classifications of Mental and Behavioural Disorder: Clinical descriptions and diagnostic guidelines*. Geneva: World Health Organization.

Chapter 9

Other dimensions of developmental influences

Not everything can be explained by attachment theory

Margaret DeJong

Introduction

The powerful influence of attachment theory as a fundamental domain of child development has led to a growing awareness of its importance in diverse fields of child care such as residential care, social work and family law. However with the increasing enthusiasm for the ideas has come a tendency to attribute many different kinds of psychological difficulty to deficits in attachment.

The development of this field has been characterised by, on the one hand, a rich and immensely productive output by academic researchers, and on the other by a relative lack of applied clinical research in populations such as maltreated children or children in care, where the concepts have such immediate clinical relevance. This gap has added to an understandable confusion about aspects of attachment theory, in particular around how to apply what we have learned through research to assessments in clinical or forensic settings. There remains an uncertainty around the limits of the theory in explaining parent–child relationships and aspects of child development.

The purpose of this chapter, in a volume devoted to attachment theory, is to attempt to put attachment in perspective in relation to the vast body of scientific knowledge about human social behaviour, child development and relationships. This is a daunting task and will inevitably be restricted to a glimpse at selected examples from the literature with an emphasis on social development in particular. The chapter will look at aspects of parenting and child development which are distinct from, although connected to, attachment processes. It will highlight areas where there remains uncertainty and a need for continued research, and touch briefly on the clinical implications of the findings.

Other affectional bonds and behavioural systems

Mary Ainsworth (1991) reminds us that attachment relationships are only one form of 'affectional bond', considered by Bowlby (1969/1982) and Ainsworth to be social bonds that are significant and involve a degree of emotional commitment. All affectional bonds begin as a relationship with an individual but are thought to become internalised over time as a mental representation of that interaction which is enduring and very meaningful at an emotional level. The special significance of the bond means that it is highly specific and not replaceable; disruption or loss of the bond will cause significant distress.

Attachment relationships have these general characteristics but are also thought to have a specific and vital role in both protecting the species and providing a secure base for emotional development during the complex and protracted stages of infancy and progression towards autonomous functioning in humans. What is uniquely characteristic of the attachment relationship is the biologically ingrained pattern of seeking proximity to the care giver when under threat or in danger, referred to as attachment behaviour. The presence of the secure base in the form of a reliably available and reasonably responsive carer will foster other aspects of development, enhancing emotional security and allowing confident exploration of the external world.

Other affectional bonds and social relationships have important roles to play. These include the social/affiliative bond, the caregiving bond, sexual pair bond, enduring friendship and non-parental kinship bond (Prior and Glaser 2006).

Similarly, attachment is only one of several important 'behavioural systems' that evolve during a child's development and are necessary for survival. This term is derived from ethology, referring to patterns of behaviour which are thought to be biologically driven and which have species-specific organisation, including particular mechanisms for activation and de-activation. Both animals and humans exhibit behavioural systems relating, for example, to fear, exploration and the drive for social affiliation. Behavioural systems interact closely with one another; for example, fear will trigger the attachment system and activation of the attachment system will decrease the drive to explore.

The idea that attachment is embedded in a wider conceptual framework was therefore present from the beginning of its inception as a theory. An understanding of this framework used by developmental psychologists and other researchers helps to place attachment within a broad overview of child development.

Stark evidence of the need to keep a broad perspective, beyond that provided by attachment theory, is provided by the fascinating example of Harlow's research with monkeys (1969) as described by Jude Cassidy (2008). Harlow found that monkeys raised by mothers but with no exposure to peers were seriously impaired in their capacity to mate or parent effectively. Clearly other influences on development are of crucial importance.

Below we consider aspects of another form of affectional bond, the caregiving relationship, which includes but goes far beyond the provision of a secure base for a growing infant's attachment. We consider individual characteristics of the child that influence their development and the child's relationships with siblings and peers. Finally we look briefly at wider social influences that impinge on the quality of all relationships.

The caregiving environment

Parenting tasks

It will be apparent to anyone who contemplates the parenting role that it encompasses far more than promoting attachment. There are myriad parenting tasks that have been subsumed under three broad headings or domains by Hoghughi (1997). They are discussed in Reder *et al.* (2003) as:

- *care* (promoting health and well-being and avoiding harm);
- *control* (setting and enforcing appropriate boundaries);
- *development* (ensuring the child realises their potential, partly through access to education and appropriate social experience).

Achieving these tasks requires deep-seated and stable commitment from parents, an ability to prioritise a child's needs above their own, as well as capability in more mundane everyday tasks, such as providing adequate routines for children and ensuring they attend school.

The concept of the parenting role is socially as well as culturally determined and has evolved across the ages. Maccoby (1992) provides an excellent historical review of the way in which our thinking about parental influence in the socialisation of children has evolved. There has been a gradual decline both in the influence of psychoanalytic models of development and in the more straightforward behavioural models which proved through research findings to be inadequate to explain the complexities of child development and child rearing outcomes. However, the emphasis on early childhood as a formative period and the family as the main vehicle of socialisation has remained.

Grossman and Grossman (1991) carried out a longitudinal study of infants' attachment and other dimensions of behaviour with parents in two community samples, followed up at intervals throughout childhood. Observation of play with both parents showed that in relation to certain play tasks the parent's role as teacher, playmate and caregiver were quite distinct. A child's success in completing a task was related to cognitive development, which was linked to both socioeconomic status and evidence of parents taking a didactic role with their children. The impact of attachment was seen in the children's level of confidence, both socially and in relation to the task, and also in more subtle aspects of emotional development such as the open quality of emotional communication, competence at resolving conflict and reported peer integration. We see in this careful observational research that parental tasks can be separated in terms of their influence, but that all contribute in a closely linked way to a child's developing competence.

These various parental roles – caregiver, disciplinarian, or playmate – will challenge parents in different ways, and parents will show strengths in some areas but not in others. It is also the case that parents might find one stage of development easier than another; for example, the mother who successfully promotes a secure attachment in her infant and toddler but who fails to promote socialisation outside the home. The way in which parents exert their influence will also vary, both according to the task and to the parent's own preferred style.

Parents may be 'teachers', in teaching manners for example. They may serve as role models, where observational learning takes place. They may stimulate their children's imagination through engaging in play or their cognitive development through their engagement with their child's learning. Or they may actively shape their children's development through behavioural management.

The most basic task of the domain of *parental care* is to protect the child's health and well-being and prevent them from coming to harm. A substantial part of our knowledge about this level of parental care comes from analysis of failed parenting, in cases where the care of children is, of necessity, taken over by the state. The risk factors are well known and include socioeconomic deprivation as well as parental criminality, mental health problems or substance abuse.

Belsky and Vondra (1989) analysed factors relating to parenting in extreme examples where it has failed, and children are maltreated. They conclude that a range of factors are relevant including child and parent individual factors as well as the social context, the nature of the parents' relationship and their own developmental histories. The latter can be part of an intergenerational pattern, where succeeding generations of children receive poor parenting and become themselves ill-equipped to carry out this complex task.

Within the domain of *parental control and discipline* an important line of research has focused on the management of aggressive, oppositional and conduct disordered behaviour. There has been an examination of parenting style, including close observation of parent–child interaction. Baumrind (1973) has been very influential in drawing attention to parental style. In applying her work on leadership styles to parenting, she developed a typology of parenting styles, which ranged from authoritarian to permissive. The authoritative parenting style was regarded as optimal, in that it combined elements of warmth, affection and attentiveness to children's needs with very clear expectations of behaviour. Authoritative parents negotiated with children but were prepared to be confrontational. Both elements of this process appear to be important and this view of optimal parental style has been strongly endorsed in the literature.

Patterson and colleagues (Snyder *et al.* 2005) emphasised the role of parenting practices in their work with conduct disordered children. They identified coercive parental styles which were often combined with emotional rejection and lack of warmth. Other parenting styles associated with poor child outcomes were inadequate parental authority or inconsistent management of behavioural difficulties, such as harsh discipline alternating with tolerance of inappropriate behaviour. This and other seminal behavioural work around improving parenting styles and management of problematic behaviour has been influential in the training of teachers and in the plethora of parent training programmes which now exist. What we have learned is that parents need to work jointly, setting clear limits and implementing discipline in a consistent and effective manner.

Fostering a child's development

Current theorising emphasises the importance of a trusting reciprocal relationship between parent and child as the early foundation of child socialisation. Sensitive atunement and predictable parental responses allow the child to develop a coherent sense of the self as distinct from the other and to internalise the capacity for self-regulation. Attachment is thought to have a pivotal role to play in this very early stage of development and is one of the key developmental tasks of this period, as is described in more detail by Fonagy and his colleagues in Chapter 2. For this process to succeed, a parent must have the capacity to prioritise an infant's needs, to interpret infantile communications accurately and to respond sensitively and consistently over the duration of infancy and beyond.

As the child becomes older, the quality of parental conversations with their children appears to have a significant impact (Thompson 2008: 358). Open communication by a parent, discussing everyday occurrences with emotional content, interpreting emotional events and their impact, encourages children to develop the capacity to understand emotion themselves and teaches a vocabulary with which to describe emotion. Conversations can also teach a sense of altruism, awareness of other people's feelings and approaches to moral issues.

With regard to the development of conscience, earlier research focused on cognitive maturation, such as a child's understanding of moral dilemmas and awareness of societal rules which can be surprisingly sophisticated at an early age. In keeping with current trends and building on some aspects of psychoanalytic theory, Kochanska (2002) stresses the development of conscience within the context of the nature of the relationship with the carer. She hypothesised that it may develop in relation to a child's desire to please or maintain a harmonious relationship with the primary carer, finding an association between the quality of the relationship, specifically attachment security, and early signs of developing conscience. Attachment security may be a moderator here, perhaps in facilitating a positive, harmonious relationship between parent and child or an open style of communication. As with all facets of development, research is currently grappling with the way in which the influence of attachment interacts with other developmental forces.

Moving away from the emotional quality of relationships, the instrumental tasks of parenthood include providing appropriate stimulation for children's cognitive maturation and supporting their education. The importance of this is illustrated in the case of parental neglect, where significant delays in language and academic attainment can be seen.

Quality of family relationships

One of the central questions in child development is the extent to which the quality of the parent–child relationship influences aspects of children's social, emotional and behavioural development. It has been argued that the strong focus on attachment has led the direction of enquiry away from other lines of research. The vast majority of the existing literature focuses on the mother–child relationship, partly because of the centrality of this caregiving relationship in psychoanalytic and other developmental theories, and partly no doubt because fathers have been less accessible for researchers to study. More recent research has gone some way towards redressing this balance by including fathers as research subjects.

What is known about the quality of father's relationships with their children suggests that they might interact differently with their children compared to mothers. They might, for example, engage to a greater degree in energetic physical play, providing stimulation in a distinctly different way from mothers (Lewis and Lamb 2003). Some research suggests that fathers may have a uniquely important role in the behavioural aspects of children's development. Both paternal depression and antisocial traits, for example, have been associated with behavioural problems in their offspring.

Patterson's work, cited above (Snyder 2005), found an association between a rejecting paternal stance with low warmth, and conduct disordered behaviour in boys. Ramchandani et al. (2012), in one of the few studies to examine the impact of paternal behaviour on infants, found an association between an observed father–infant interaction characterised as disengaged at 3 months and an increase in behavioural difficulties including aggression observed at 1 year. Interestingly, the association was significant in boys but not in girls, raising the possibility that fathers' influence on behaviour in this respect may be gender-specific. An attempt was made in this study to separate out the effects of maternal caregiving by controlling for maternal sensitivity and depression. It seems quite possible or even likely, however, that family factors including the parents' relationship will influence the father's role with his children.

The Grossman and Grossman longitudinal study (Grossman and Grossman 1991; Grossman et al. 2005) was notable for its inclusion of fathers as well as mothers, illustrating how close cooperation between the two and a shared understanding of a child's needs led to effective parenting with positive outcomes for children's development.

The quality of the marital or partner relationship is known to exert a major influence. The work of Hetherington (1988), for example, demonstrates the damaging impact on children, both short and long term, of exposure to marital conflict. Exposure to domestic violence can lead to insecurity of attachment, modelling of aggression as a way of resolving conflict. High levels of tension within the home and other adverse influences contribute to the signs of emotional disturbance and social development exhibited by child victims (Holt et al. 2008).

Family therapists assess family function in a number of domains such as open and unambiguous communication, emotional involvement versus disengagement, warm and caring relationships versus hostile rejection, and the ability to maintain appropriate boundaries between parents and children rather than enmeshed over involvement or inappropriate parent–child alliances.

Clinically these are known to have important effects on child functioning. There is a large body of research linking various aspects of family functioning to child outcomes, looking both at resiliency factors that can protect a vulnerable child and risk factors. The structure of the modern day family is evolving, with more single parents and same-sex couples. Research is beginning to address these different family compositions as well as taking into account variation across cultures.

It is known that children in the same family can have quite different relationships with their parents. Children are usually acutely aware of this in relation to their siblings; a sense of rivalry, envy or deprivation in relation to perceived differences in the quality of the parent–child relationship is something that is felt acutely by many children, often lasting into adulthood.

It is also known (Dunn 1993) that parents may have a better quality of relationships with their children at one stage of development over another. For example, parents may relate very well to toddlers but find the drive towards autonomy of adolescents very difficult to cope with.

Individual difference

Genetic endowment and constitution

Research on attachment and on influences of parenting styles or family relationships on child development can seem to imply that environmental influence is the main determinant of a child's psychological outcome. However, studies in environmental genetics make it clear that the picture is more complicated. The field of environmental genetics looks at the genetic contribution of what might traditionally be considered an environmental influence. For example, when considering the impact of parental behaviour on child outcomes (Plomin and Neiderhiser 1992), the environmental geneticist will consider whether parental behaviour could be related to parental genetically influenced personality characteristics or whether their behaviour towards a particular child could be influenced by that child's personality characteristics. Genetic differences contribute towards an individual's appraisal or understanding of an experience, and to their actual experience as well (a person with an outgoing personality is likely to have a different life experience than an introverted or shy one). Therefore, genetic differences among individuals can contribute to differences in their experiences.

It is possible through twin studies, comparing monozygotic twins, who share all their genetic material, with dizygotic twins, who share approximately half, to calculate genetic effects on various environmental factors such as parenting behaviour. Adoption studies are also useful in comparing different outcomes for twins who share the same family environment and for those who are raised in different families. Based on these studies, genetic influence is considered to contribute significantly to measures of family environment. In scientific terms a genetic contribution was found in several studies to account for at least a quarter of the variance on ratings of family environment (Plomin and Neiderhiser 1992).

Research can now confirm what has been known through common knowledge: siblings within the same family can have different experiences of family life. This is referred to as the 'non-shared environment' (Scarr 1992). There are many possible reasons for this phenomenon, but certainly genetic personality traits have a large part to play. Children create their own micro-environments to a degree, as their own temperament interacts with the family they find themselves born into. Differences in individual susceptibility will also mean that children will react differently to shared familial stresses.

Influence of child characteristics on parental behaviour

Genetic influence in parent–child relationships is bidirectional, in that parents' responses to children will partly be determined by the child's temperament and other factors such as gender, but the child's response to the parent is equally affected by parental style and personality factors. The degree to which they interact in a way that facilitates the child's development will depend in part on a harmonious meshing of their temperaments and other aspects of 'fit'. Parents might find it easier to parent some of their children compared to others, or find a given child easier at different developmental stages. The environmental influence can therefore change at different ages. Genetic factors will also influence sibling relationships, the emotional and social environment of the home, peer relationships and so on.

Bidirectionality of influence is a feature of much work on family influences in child development. There is an acknowledgement among researchers that securely attached children are more likely to elicit positive responses and encourage the continuation of 'relational harmony' with their caregiver (Thompson 2008). The debate about whether a child's individual characteristics contribute to their attachment security has been most pronounced at the severe end of the spectrum of attachment insecurity, in relation to the classification of attachment disorganisation. Research studies have found that children with a neurodevelopmental abnormality are more often described as having a disorganised attachment (Green and Goldwyn 2002). This, of course, might be due to a child's innate characteristics or psychological states being interpreted as attachment responses. Equally one might consider the impact of the added stress on parental behaviour of managing more challenging children, or perhaps to the parents' unresolved feelings about having a handicapped child. It can be seen that interpretations of these findings are complex and require a multifaceted approach.

Neurodevelopmental and physical impairment

The impact on psychological outcome of having a neurodevelopmental condition affecting brain function is very significant. In large epidemiological studies it has consistently emerged as a major risk factor. In the Isle of Wight Study (Rutter *et al.* 1970) the prevalence of psychiatric disorder was 29 per cent in uncomplicated epilepsy and 44 per cent in structural brain disorders, compared to 7 per cent in a community population sample. The mediating links between the two are likely to involve both direct organic effects on the brain and the psychosocial impact on the child and family (Goodman 1994). Children with other kinds of chronic illness are also at an increased psychological risk although the impact is not as striking at a population level (Offord *et al.* 1992). It is important to recognise that the existence of a neurodevelopmental condition, such as autism, will result in increased psychological risk regardless of parenting expertise and the caregiving environment. However, it also undoubtedly poses an added demand on carers which might over-stretch parental resources.

Other developmental characteristics

In relation to any domain of a child's development, consideration of individual developmental factors will be crucial in assessing the impact of family influences. The field is vast, examining such diverse aspects as temperament, language, intelligence, emotional and behavioural regulation, self-concept, conscience, social cognition, understanding of emotion and development of empathy. The example of conduct disorder and antisocial behaviour illustrates the complexity of aetiological factors in a common condition.

Conduct disorder has attracted the attention of both researchers and policy makers, in an attempt to analyse the underlying causes and possible remedies. A report to the Department of Health and Prime Minister's Strategy Unit (Utting *et al.* 2007) identified the following individual risk factors:

- hyperactivity and impulsivity (strong genetic component);
- low intelligence; cognitive impairment (not understanding consequences of behaviour or misattributing social approaches as hostile);
- chronic ill health, especially involving the brain;
- an attitude of condoning offending behaviour and drug use;
- associating with antisocial friends and peers.

In the school setting these children have low academic achievement, poor commitment to attending, and exhibit aggressive behaviour including bullying. Protective factors include female gender, an outgoing temperament and ability to form positive social relationships, good problem-solving capacity and at least one strong relationship with a protective parent.

What we have here is a list of risk factors associated with the emergence of conduct disorder. Longitudinal studies such as the Dunedin study in New Zealand (Moffit 1993) suggest that it is the interplay of these factors, including child characteristics, family and social environment, which determine the course and severity of the behaviour. These authors identify the capacity to self-regulate and the experience of receiving adequate behavioural regulation by parents and others as being a key predictive element in outcome.

Dodge *et al.* (1984) carried out the original work into distorted cognitions in conduct disordered boys, describing the tendency to misperceive others as inter-acting towards them in a hostile or aggressive manner. Although he noted an association between security of attachment and levels of interpersonal aggression, he concluded that this developmental characteristic was likely to have a diverse aetiology. In other studies the capacity to be aware of the mental states of others has been linked to attachment processes (see Chapter 2). But many other factors influence social development. Attachment is one strand of a complicated picture here and further research is required to elucidate the way in which it interacts with known risk and protective factors, at the level of an individual, family and social community.

The social environment

Relationships between children

Judith Dunn's research (1993), much of which is based on detailed observations and interviews, demonstrates vividly the rich complexity of young children's rela-tionships. She argues convincingly that the attachment perspective is too narrow a focus to explain the wide diversity in the nature of these relationships.

Dunn describes sibling relationships as characterised by rivalry, ambivalence and conflict but also warmth, affection, shared humour and fun. Shared fan-tasy and play is a binding experience and also makes a significant contribution to children's social development. Sometimes close relationships between sib-lings serve as a compensatory mechanism for other stressful experiences in the family.

There can be an attachment element to sibling relationships, which may be a healthy and normal part of family functioning. Typically one thinks about older children and a large age gap, although Stewart and Marvin (1984) found evidence of this in a 1-year-old child's behaviour in relation to his 4-year-old sibling, whose presence seemed to serve a secure base function for his younger brother.

Many dimensions of sibling relationships, such as a sense of close 'connect-edness' in communication, level of involvement and negative affect were found to be quite independent of each other, and from shared fantasy and cooperation, which tended to be linked. This would argue against a unifying theory, such as the quality of early mother–infant relationships, as an explanation.

There is a fascinating diversity in these observations: many very young chil-dren show sophisticated awareness of social context and others appear to lack much mentalisation capacity; some sibling pairs discuss feelings and some never do; some become easily and deeply absorbed in shared fantasy games and others engage in little shared activity at all.

Peer relationships show many of the same dimensions as sibling relationships. Peer relationships promote a very important part of development, in facilitating play and shared fantasy, learning to share and acquire other social skills. In the early years children who are securely attached have a social advantage in that they appear more easily able to negotiate these relationships. However, as Judith Dunn points out (1993), attachment security may be linked to some aspects of peer relationships, such as intimacy or trust, but not to others, such as companionship, shared humour or fantasy.

Wider social influences

The quality of the caregiving relationship can change over time, and will be affected by life events, the quality of social support and other characteristics of the wider social environment. This is very evident in a high-risk poverty sample (Sroufe *et al.* 2005). In a national population study Belsky and Fearon (2002) examined the role of continuity of sensitive care in relation to the lasting protective effects of infant attachment security. They found that the best outcomes at 36 months on a broad range of social and cognitive measures were seen in children who had early attachment security and continuity of sensitive care, while the worst outcomes had insecure attachment at 15 months and evidence of maternal insensitivity at 24 months. Interestingly, the intermediate outcomes showed that evidence of later sensitive care, even with early attachment insecurity showed a better outcome than early attachment security with subsequent insensitive care. The findings also support a link between the mother's ability to provide sensitive care and common stressors such as depression, overstretched family resources and diminished social supports.

Contributing to the quality of the social environment will be the prevalence of violence and criminality, exposure to adverse peer influences such as bullying, aggression or substance abuse, poor housing and poverty. Protective factors such as community support through religious and other organisations, social support via kinships and friendships and the availability of good schools will militate against risk.

Predictors of psychological outcome; what is attachment related and what is not?

A central tenet of child development theory is that the early years are formative and lay the foundations for subsequent development. Although there is strong agreement about this across theorists researching different models of development, there is much less agreement about which developmental processes are most influential and predictive or what the key mechanisms of influence are. Within the attachment field, longitudinal studies have been useful in beginning to tease out these issues. A striking overall finding has been that attachment status in infancy is only a weak predictor of adult functioning. With respect to global social competence at age 19 it accounts on its own for only 5 per cent of the variance, whereas when other aspects of social functioning and parenting are included in the initial assessment the capacity to predict outcome becomes much stronger, at around

50 per cent of the variance (Rutter 2008). This does not negate the importance of the attachment domain, but rather stresses the close interrelationship with other developmental processes.

Sroufe (2005) provides an analysis of a 30-year longitudinal study in the Minnesota Parent-Child Project, involving a high-risk poverty sample. His team's theoretical model of attachment stresses the importance of attachment in organising patterns of behaviour: 'an organizing core in development that is always integrated with later experience and never lost' (Sroufe 2005: 367). They found strong links between early attachment security/insecurity and later self-reliance, capacity for emotional regulation and social competence. However, he stresses the complexity of the developmental model and discontinuities in outcome due to changing family and social circumstances.

The Grossman and Grossman longitudinal studies (Grossman and Grossman 1991; Grossman *et al.* 2005) also found greater confidence and self-efficacy in securely attached children, and a tendency towards more harmonious relationships. Some of these positive effects were continued into middle childhood and beyond, with significant associations between security of attachment and social competence which were most pronounced during the pre-school period and attenuated over time.

The strongest association between attachment status and psychological outcome is in the disorganised attachment group, where there is a clear link to later psychopathology (Green and Goldwyn 2002). As disorganisation is known to be strongly associated with high-risk or abusing families (Green and Goldwyn 2002) it is fair to say that the strongest correlation of attachment status to psychological outcome is in high-risk families where there is poor functioning in the majority although not all families, and a range of risk factors related to parental function.

Implications for child and family assessments

What are the implications for our current state of knowledge in relation to practice on the ground? How much weight should we place on attachment assessments in predicting psychological outcome in relation to other factors?

The attachment process is fundamental to human development, and appears to be particularly important in the development of emotional security. Infants who are not severely developmentally impaired and receive adequate exposure to primary caregivers (unlike some institutionalised children) will form attachments. In large community samples it has been found that approximately 60–65 per cent of children will form secure attachments and the remainder are insecurely attached (Prior and Glaser 2006). As such a high percentage of children in the general population have insecure attachments this cannot be conceptualised as something that is inherently pathological.

What we can say is that children with secure attachments appear to do better in their emotional and social adjustment compared to children with insecure attachments, with the effect being most noticeable in the pre-school period. Insecurely attached infants may be less resilient to adversity, with a complex interaction between attachment status and other variables including individual characteristics. The quality of early attachment relationships may be most relevant to aspects of emotional and social development, influencing the child's developing sense of self and capacity for intimate relationships.

Clinicians, like researchers, need to be open minded about the aetiology of psychological problems and poor social adjustment in children. Comprehensive, careful assessments are needed which consider all domains of parenting, including the capacity to promote secure attachment. Individual characteristics of children should be assessed, both in their own right and in consideration of the way in which they influence parents' and other children's behaviour towards them. We need to bear in mind the evidence suggesting that children within a given family can have very different experiences; observation of their interactions in the family (with parents as well as siblings) could yield important information about why this is the case.

In a forensic setting, where child protection issues are considered by the family justice system, the influence of attachment theory is very apparent. Experts in child psychological development are almost invariably asked whether children have a secure or insecure attachment to their parents, with the implication that this is of enormous significance in evaluating the capacity of the parent to meet the child's emotional needs.

The categorical nature of secure versus insecure and the assumption that insecure attachment is pathological can lead to misunderstandings between lawyers and clinicians. Unfortunately it is in just such a setting, where important decisions are made about the welfare of the child, that the gap between research findings and their real-life applicability is most apparent.

We are not yet at a stage where we can weight a child's attachment status (secure versus insecure) in relation to other aspects of their development to make confident predictions of outcome in individual cases. Our understanding of the nature of a child's relationship with their parents is certainly enhanced by understanding the nature of their attachments. However, this must be considered in relation to the overall quality of the parent–child relationship and to other facets of parenting behaviour.

Conclusions

Many questions remain about the link between children's early relationships and their future psychological adaptation. The dominance of attachment theory in recent years has risked encouraging an over-generalisation about its influence.

Attachment has provided child development with a deep vein of rich and important material, but there is still a considerable amount of untapped material to explore in other aspects of relationships. Key pieces of research using other models need to be integrated with attachment theory to give us a better understanding of the mechanisms of impact on development.

References

Ainsworth, M. (1991). Attachments and other affectional bonds across the life cycle. In C.M. Parkes, J. Stevenson-Hinde and P. Marris (eds), *Attachment across the Life Cycle* (pp. 33–51). Routledge, London and New York.

Baumrind, D. (1991). The influence of parenting style on adolescent competence and substance abuse. *Journal of Early Adolescence*, 11, 56–94.

Belsky, J. and Vondra, J. (1989). Lessons from child abuse: the determinants of parenting. In D. Cicchetti and V. Carlson (eds), *Child Maltreatment: theory and research on the causes and consequences of child abuse and neglect.* Cambridge University Press, Cambridge.

Belsky, J. and Fearon, P. (2002). Early attachment security, subsequent maternal sensitivity, and later child development: does continuity in development depend upon continuity of caregiving? *Attachment and Human Development*, 4(3), 361–387.

Bowlby, J. (1969/82). *Attachment and Loss, Volume 1: Attachment, Second Edition.* London Pimlico.

Cassidy, J. (2008). The nature of the child's ties. In J. Cassidy and P.R. Shaver (eds), *Handbook of Attachment, Second Edition* (pp. 3–22). The Guilford Press, New York.

Carlson, E.A. (1998). A prospective longitudinal study of disorganised/disoriented attachment. *Child Development*, 69, 1970–79.

Dodge, K.A., Murphy, R.R. and Buchsbaum, K. (1984). The assessment of intention-cue detection skills in children: implications for developmental psychopathology. *Child Development*, 55(1), 163–173.

Dunn, J. (1993). *Young Children's Close Relationships: Beyond attachment.* Vol. 4, Individual differences and development series, Sage Publications, London.

Goodman, R. (1994). Brain disorders. In M. Rutter, E. Taylor and L. Herson (eds), *Child and Adolescent Psychiatry: Modern approaches* (3rd. ed., pp. 172–190). Blackwell Science Ltd, Oxford.

Green, G. and Goldwyn, R. (2002). Annotation: Attachment disorganisation and psychopathology: new findings in attachment research and their potential implications for developmental psychopathology in childhood. *Journal of Child Psychology and Psychiatry*, 43(7), 835–846.

Grossman, K.E. and Grossman, K. (1991). Attachment quality as an organizer of emotional and behavioural responses in a longitudinal perspective. In C.M. Parkes, J. Stevenson-Hinde and P. Marris (eds), *Attachment across the Life Cycle* (pp. 33–51). Routledge, London and New York.

Grossman, K., Grossman, K. and Kindler, H. (2005). Early care and the roots of attachment and partnership representations. In K. Grossman, K. Grossman and E. Waters (eds), *Attachment from Infancy to Adulthood: The major longitudinal studies.* New York, The Guilford Press.

Hetherington, E.M. (1988). Parents, children and siblings: Six years after divorce. In R.A. Hinde and J. Stevenson-Hinde (eds), *Relationships within Families: Mutual influences* (pp. 311–331). Oxford, UK, Oxford University Press.

Hoghughi, M. (1997). Parenting at the margins: some consequences of inequality. In K.N. Dwivedi (ed.), *Enhancing Parenting Skills: A guidebook for professionals working with parents.* Chichester, Wiley.

Holt, S., Buckley, H. and Whelan, S. (2008). The impact of exposure to domestic violence on children and young people: a review of the literature. *Child Abuse & Neglect*, 797–810.

Kochanska, G. (2002). Mutually responsive orientation between mothers and their young children: a context for the early development of conscience. *Current Directions in Psychological Science*, 11(6), 191–195.

Lewis, C. and Lamb, M. (2003). Fathers' influences on children's development: The evidence from two-parent families. *Journal of Psychology and Education*, XVIII, 211–228.

Maccoby, E.E. (1992). The role of parents in the socialization of children: an historical overview. *Developmental Psychology*, 28(6), 1006–1017.

Moffit, T.E. (1993). Adolescence-limited and life-course persistent antisocial behaviour: a developmental taxonomy. *Psychological Review*, 100(4), 674–701.

Offord, D.R., Boyle, M.H., Racine, Y.A., Fleming, J.E., Cadman, D.T., Blum, H.M., *et al.*(1992). Outcome, prognosis and risk in a longitudinal follow-up study. *Journal of the American Academy of Child and Adolescent Mental Health*, 31(5), 916–923.

Plomin, R. and Neiderhiser, J.M. (1992). Genetics and experience. *Current Directions in Psychological Science*, 1(5), 160–163.

Prior, V. and Glaser, G. (2006). *Understanding Attachment and Attachment Disorders: Theory, evidence and practice*. Child and Adolescent Mental Health Series, Royal College of Psychiatrists' Research and Training Unit, Jessica Kingsley, London and Philadelphia.

Ramchandani, P.G., Domoney, J., Sethna, V., Psychogiou, L., Vlachos, H. and Murray, L. (2012). Do early father–infant interactions predict the onset of externalising behaviours in young children? Findings from a longitudinal cohort study. *The Journal of Child Psychology and Psychiatry*, 54(1), 56–64.

Reder, P., Duncan, S. and Lucey, C. (2003). What principles guide parenting assessments? In *Studies in the Assessment of Parenting* (pp. 3–26). Brunner-Routledge, East Sussex, UK and New York, USA.

Rutter, M. (2008). Implications of attachment theory and research for child care policies. In J. Cassidy and P.R. Shaver (eds), *Handbook of Attachment: Theory, research and clinical applications*, Second Edition (pp. 958–974). The Guilford Press, New York and London.

Rutter, M., Graham, P. and Yule, W. (1970). A neuropsychiatric study in childhood. *Clinics in Developmental Medicine* nos. 35/36. SIMP/Heinemann, London.

Scarr, S. (1992). Developmental theories for the 1990s: development and individual differences. *Child Development*, 63, 1–19.

Snyder, P.J., Cramer, A., Frank, A.J., and Patterson, G.R. (2005). The contributions of ineffective discipline and parental hostile attributions of child misbehaviour to the development of conduct problems at home and school. *Developmental Psychology*, 41(1), 30–41.

Sroufe, L.A. (2005). Attachment and development: a prospective, longitudinal study from birth to adulthood. *Attachment and Human Development*, 7, 349–367.

Stewart, R.B. and Marvin, R.S. (1984). Sibling relations: the role of conceptual perspective-taking in the ontogeny of sibling caregiving. *Child Development*, 55, 1322–1332.

Thompson, R.A. (2008). Early attachment and later development: familiar questions, new answers. In J. Cassidy and P.R. Shaver (eds), *Handbook of Attachment: Theory, research and clinical applications*, Second Edition (pp. 348–365). The Guilford Press, New York.

Utting, D., Monteiro, H. and Ghate, D. (2007). *Interventions for children at risk of developing antisocial personality disorder: Report to the Department of Health and Prime Minister's Strategy Unit* (pp. 9–23). Policy Research Bureau, London.

Index

AAI *see* Adult Attachment Interview
ABC classification system 2, 19–21, 73–6;
  expansion of classifications 76; *see also*
  Strange Situation Procedure; types of
  attachment
ABC + D and DMM model comparison 73,
  83*t*, 85–6; differences: (changes in
  attachment over time 85; continuity *vs.*
  discontinuity 82–3, 84; intergenerational
  transmission 85; 'secure'
  attachment 84–5); similarities 82
ABC + D model 3–5, 7, 21, 76–8, 79,
  96; *see also* ABC + D and DMM
  model comparison; Strange Situation
  Procedure
ADHD *see* attention deficit hyperactivity
  disorder
ADI-R (Autism Diagnostic
  Interview-Revised) 163
adolescence 15, 57–8, 57*f*
adopted children 14, 172
ADOS (Autism Diagnostic Observation
  Schedule) 163
Adshead, G. 40
adult attachment 3–4, 4*t*, 12; CC
  unresolved/disorganised (cannot
  classify) 3, 66, 79, 99; D dismissing 3,
  4*t*, 32, 33, 79; DMM model 57–9, 57*f*;
  E preoccupied-entangled 3, 4*t*, 32, 33,
  79; F secure-autonomous (Free) 3, 4*t*,
  32, 33, 79; HH hostile-helpless 99–100;
  and mentalisation 36; U unresolved 3,
  4*t*, 32–3; *see also* Adult Attachment
  Interview; DMM-AAI
Adult Attachment Interview (AAI) 3, 24,
  52, 59, 78–9, 97, 98, 114, 116, 130;
  DMM-AAI 59–61, 65, 67, 79, 99;
  M&G-AAI 78, 98–9

Adult Attachment Projective 65
affect 52, 53, 58, 113
affectional bonds 166–7
Ainsworth, M.D. 2, 3, 49, 50, 99, 166;
  see also ABC classification system;
  Strange Situation Procedure
Allen, J.G. 64, 65
AMBIANCE *see* Atypical Maternal
  Behavior Instrument for Assessment and
  Classification
anger 53
antisocial personality disorder (ASPD) 111
anxious-avoidant attachment *see* insecure-
  avoidant attachment (type A)
anxious-resistant attachment *see* insecure-
  ambivalent attachment (type C)
Arnsten, A.F.T 114
Arsenian, J.M. 17
ASD *see* autistic spectrum disorders
ASPD (antisocial personality
  disorder) 111
Asperger's syndrome 153, 162
assessment of attachment 5–6, 66–7,
  177–8
attachment 11–12, 26–7; development
  of 12–13; effects of 31–3; no critical
  period 14; over the life course 14–15,
  85; phases of development 13; and
  psychological outcome 176–7; theory
  overview 1–5; *see also* individual
  differences in attachment
Attachment and Human Development 89
attachment behaviour 167
attachment network 23–4
attachment strategies 114, 114*f*, 115*t*;
  attachment deactivation strategies
  115–16, 117; attachment hyperactivation
  strategies 114, 116, 117

attention deficit hyperactivity disorder
    (ADHD): causation 156, 158;
    characteristics 155–6, 159*t*;
    comorbidity 154, 158; prevalence 155;
    as a social construct 156–7;
    treatment 156
Atypical Maternal Behavior Instrument
    for Assessment and Classification
    (AMBIANCE) 38, 100–1
Autism Diagnostic Interview-Revised
    (ADI-R) 163
Autism Diagnostic Observation Schedule
    (ADOS) 163
autistic spectrum disorders (ASD):
    Asperger's syndrome 153, 162;
    and attachment 14; Atypical
    Autism 153; causation 149,
    154, 158; characteristics 152–4,
    159*t*, 174; comorbidity 153; high
    functioning autism 153, 162; and
    hormones 136; Infantile Autism 153;
    interventions 155; prevalence 154
autobiographical memory 78
autonomic nervous system 131–2
Avinun, R. *et al.* 136

Baird, G. *et al.* 154
Bakermans-Kranenburg, M.J. *et al.* 22, 89,
    95, 100, 102
Baltimore Study 17–18
Bateman, A.W. 112
Baumrind, D. 169
Beebe, B. 129–30
Begley, S. 128
behavioural systems 168
Belsky, J. *et al.* 34, 50, 169, 176
Biven, L. 138
Blatz, W.E. 15–16, 17
Bokhorst, C.L. *et al.* 23
borderline personality disorder (BPD) 40,
    66, 95; and childhood abuse and
    neglect 41; diagnosis 149; and
    hormones 136; and mentalising 41–2,
    110–11, 118–20
Bowlby, J. 1–2, 3, 6, 7, 12, 13, 14, 16, 23,
    33, 36, 42, 50, 51, 52, 62, 73, 127, 128,
    166
brain 31–2; cerebral hemispheres 138–
    40; cortical midline system 112;
    Default Mode Network (DMN) 141;
    Dispositional Representations 51–3;
    effects of stress on 140; emotion

and empathy 138–40, 141; glia
    cells 141–2; growth and change 140–1;
    hope or hopeless? 140–2; language
    development 141; and mind 42,
    51; mirror neuron system 112, 138;
    neuroplasticity 128–9; self–other
    distinction 112, 170; triune brain 130–1
Bretherton, I. *et al.* 96
Bronfman, E. *et al.* 101

CAI *see* Child Attachment Interview
CAMHS (Child and Adolescent Mental
    Health Service) 150–2
caregiving environment: disconnected
    caregiving 100; family
    relationships 170–2; fostering child's
    development 170; looked after
    children 12, 14, 136, 154; parenting
    tasks 168–9; *see also* parenting
Carlson, E.A. *et al.* 34
Casement, P. 130
Cassidy, J. *et al.* 60, 158, 167
CBT (cognitive behavioural therapy) 64
CD *see* conduct disorder
child abuse and neglect 65; and
    attachment 14; disorganised
    attachment 24, 94, 95; early
    neglect 136, 154; effects on the
    brain 140; investigation of 6; and
    mentalisation 38–40, 101, 119–20;
    and personality disorders 41; sexual
    abuse 33, 41, 56
Child and Adolescent Mental Health
    Service (CAMHS) 150–2
Child Attachment Interview (CAI) 94, 97,
    113
child behaviours 5, 96–7, 159*t*
Chisholm, J.S. 7
Coghill, D. 160
cognition 42, 52, 54, 56; *see also*
    information processing; memory; social
    cognition and attachment
cognitive behavioural therapy (CBT) 64
conduct disorder (CD): causation 157–8,
    169, 171; characteristics 157,
    159*t*, 174–5; comorbidity 158;
    prevalence 157–8; treatment 158
connotative language 63
coy behaviour 56
Crittenden, P.M. 3, 7, 8, 50–1; *see also* ABC
    + D and DMM model comparison; DMM-
    AAI; Dynamic-Maturational Model

culture 4, 7–8, 11
Cyr, C. *et al.* 25

DA *see* disorganised attachment
Damasio, A. 51–2
danger *vs.* security 7–8, 50
Darwin, C. 12, 50
DBT (dialectical behaviour therapy) 64
De Wolff, M.S. 22
depression 60–1, 154
desire 53
diagnosis 148–9; behaviours 159*t*; case
    example 150–2, 160–2; in clinical
    practice 149–52; dilemmas 158–9;
    discussion 159–62; possible differential
    diagnoses 152–8; conclusions 162–3
dialectical behaviour therapy (DBT) 64
Diamond, D. *et al.* 114
Disconnected and Extremely Insensitive
    Parenting Measure (DIP) 100, 101
disconnected caregiving 100
disinhibited attachment disorders 90, 91
Disinhibited Social Engagement
    Disorder 90, 92, 92*t*, 95
disorders: terminology 149
disorganised attachment (DA) 3, 55,
    76–8, 92–5; characteristics 21, 93*t*,
    159*t*; child behaviours 96–7; and child
    maltreatment 24, 94, 95; identification
    and assessment 96–7, 98–101;
    intervening factors 98–9: (disconnected/
    insensitive caregiving 100–1;
    measures 100–1; unresolved trauma and
    loss 98–100); interventions 101–2; and
    mentalisation 101, 116; neurobiological
    and biochemical explanations 52, 95;
    and personality development 33–4;
    prevalence 93, 94; *vs.* reactive
    attachment disorder 5, 89, 103; risk
    factors 25–6; during SSP 21, 32–3, 96
disorientation 61, 63
Dispositional Representations 51, 80; of
    attachment 51–2, 68n2; transformations
    of information 52–3, 61–4, 62*f*; *see also*
    internal working models
dissociation 131
DMM *see* Dynamic-Maturational Model
DMM-AAI 59–61, 65, 67, 79, 99
Dodge, K.A. *et al.* 175
domestic violence 26, 171
Döpfner, M. *et al.* 155
Dozier, M.K. *et al.* 65, 94–5
DSM-IV (*Diagnostic and Statistical*

Manual of Mental Disorders) 90, 92,
    148–9, 155, 157
DSM-5 90, 91, 91*t*, 98, 149
Dunn, J. 175, 176
dyadic developmental psychotherapy 101
Dynamic-Maturational Model
    (DMM) 3, 4–5, 49–50, 79–82, 81*f*;
    assessments 66–7; attachment trauma
    and posttraumatic stress disorder 60,
    65–6; cognition and affect 52–3, 58;
    Dispositional Representations 51–3,
    61–4, 62*f*, 68n2, 80; implications 64;
    lack of resolution of loss and
    trauma 60; memory systems 61–4,
    62*f*; modifiers 60–1, 66; strategies 53,
    64: (adolescence and adulthood 57–9,
    57*f*; infancy 53–5, 54*f*; preschool and
    school age 55–7, 55*f*); concluding
    comments 67–8; *see also* ABC + D and
    DMM model comparison; DMM-AAI

Emerson, P.E. 17
emotion 138–40, 141
empathy 113, 138–40, 141
environment of evolutionary adaptedness
    (EEA) 50–1; and attachment 12–
    13, 23, 31, 42–3, 68n1; inclusive
    fitness 68n1; and mentalisation 40,
    42–3; security vs.danger 7–8, 50
episodic memory 63
explicit memory systems 63, 129
expressed somatic symptoms 61

'false self' 56
family relationships 36, 170–2, 175; *see
    also* parenting
fear 7–8, 35, 36, 53
Fearon, P. 176
Fearon, R.M.P. *et al.* 94
Ferenczi, S. 56
fight-flight response 7, 52, 53, 131–2
Fonagy, P. *et al.* 8, 37, 59, 101, 112
Fraley, R.C. 99
Fredrickson, B.L. 116
Freud, S. 127
Fries, A.B.W. *et al.* 136
Frightening/Frightened (FR) scales 100

genetic influences 23, 172–3
George, C. *et al.* 25–6, 65; *see also* Adult
    Attachment Interview
Gerhardt, S. 134
Gleason, M.M. 89, 90, 91, 92, 98

Goldwyn, R. *see* M&G-AAI
Goossens, F.A. 23
Gray, J. 8
Green, J. *et al.* 97
Grossman, K. 168, 171, 177
Grossman, K.E. 168, 171, 177

Hamilton, C.E. 15
Handbook of Attachment 158
Harari, D. *et al.* 65
Harlow, H.F. 17, 167
Hebb, D.O. 128
Hesse, E. 15, 25, 65, 66, 76, 93, 100
Hetherington, E.M. 171
Hinde, R. 56
Hodges, J. *et al.* 97
Hoghughi, M. 168
Homer 11, 12
hormones and opiates 133; cortisol 12,
   21, 95, 133–4; dopamine 138;
   epigenetic effects 137; oxytocin 134–6;
   serotonin 137; testosterone 137–8;
   vasopressin 134
Hrdy, S.B. 23
Hurry, A. 130
Hypothalamic-Pituitary-Adrenal (HPA)
   axis 95, 133

*ICD-10 (International Classification
   of Mental and Behavioural
   Disorders)* 148, 149, 155, 157
imaged memory 63
implicit memory systems 62, 63
INAs *see* intrusions of forbidden negative
   affect
incest 58
individual differences in attachment 22;
   genetic endowment and constitution 23,
   172–3; influence of child characteristics
   on parental behaviour 173;
   neurodevelopmental and physical
   impairment 173–4; other developmental
   characteristics 174–5; parenting 22–3
Infant and Toddler CARE-Index 66, 67
information processing 51;
   transformations of information 52–3,
   61–4, 62f; *see also* memory
inhibited attachment disorders 90
insecure-ambivalent attachment (type
   C) 19, 22, 42, 52, 54, 75–6; C+ 53,
   57; C1–2 20, 54; C3–4 56; C5–
   6 56–7; C7–8 58–9; and personality
   development 34; in SSP 32

insecure-avoidant attachment (type
   A) 19, 22, 32, 42, 52, 74–5; A+ 53,
   55, 57, 58; A1–2 20, 54; A3–4 55–6;
   A5–6 57; A7–8 58–9; and personality
   development 34; during SSP 32
intergenerational transmission 85
internal working models (IWM) 14–15,
   31, 33, 77, 113; *see also* Dispositional
   Representations
interventions 6–7, 64
intrusions of forbidden negative affect
   (INAs) 59, 61

Jacobvitz, D. 93, 99–100
Joubert, D. *et al.* 65

Kim, H.S. *et al.* 136
Kim, S. 34
Kochanska, G. 34, 170
Kogan, A. *et al.* 135
Koren-Karie, N. 37

Lachmann, F.M. 129–30
Landini, A. *see* DMM-AAI
language development 141, 170
LeDoux, J. 64, 141
Lewin, K. 6
London Parent–Child Project 37
looked after children 12, 14, 136, 154
Lord, C. *et al.* 163
Lorenz, K.Z. 13
loss, unresolved 60, 99–100
love 35
Lyons-Ruth, K. *et al.* 24, 26, 93, 98,
   99–101

MacArthur Story Stem Battery (MSSB) 96
Maccoby, E.E. 168
McCrory, E. *et al.* 95
McGilchrist, I. 139–40
MacLean, P.D. 130
Main, M. 15, 25, 38, 65, 66, 78, 93, 94,
   100; *see also* ABC + D and DMM
   model comparison; ABC + D model;
   M&G-AAI
Manchester Child Attachment Story Task
   (MCAST) 97
M&G-AAI 78, 98–9
Marvin, R.S. 175
Mayes, L.C. 114
measuring attachment *see* Strange
   Situation Procedure
Meins, E. *et al.* 37

memory 61–2, 62*f*; autobiographical memory 78; connotative memory 63; Dispositional Representations 51–3, 68n2; episodic memory 63; explicit memory systems 63, 129; imaged memory 63; implicit memory systems 62, 63; neuroscience 129–30; procedural memory 62, 63, 129–30; semantic memory 63; source memory 63; working memory 64
mentalisation/mentalising 5, 8; and adult attachment 36; and attachment 37–8, 42–3, 107–8, 120–1; and attachment strategies 114–17, 114*f*, 115*t*; and borderline personality disorder 41–2, 110–11, 118–20; dimensions 108–9: (automatic *vs.* controlled mentalising 109, 110; cognitive *vs.* affective mentalisation 112–13; internally *vs.* externally based mentalising 110–11; self-oriented *vs.* other-oriented 111–12); and disorganised attachment 101, 116; distortions of 59; and environment of evolutionary adaptedness 40, 42–3; interventions 111, 121; and maltreatment 38–40, 101, 119–20; relationship-specific mentalising 113–14; and secure attachment 37, 38, 52, 116; when mentalising fails: pre-mentalising modes 118
mentalising profiles 109, 109*f*
Mikulincer, M. 98
mind 42, 51
mind-mindedness 117, 138
Minnesota Study 15, 34
Minnis, H. *et al.* 89
Moffit, T.E. 174
Moran G. *et al.* 65
motivation 52
MSSB (*MacArthur Story Stem Battery*) 96

narcissistic personality disorder 111–12
National Scientific Council on the Developing Child 95
neglect *see* child abuse and neglect
nervous systems: autonomic nervous system 131–2; parasympathetic nervous system 132; 'smart' vagus nerve 132, 133; stress response 131–2, 133; sympathetic nervous system 131–2, 133; triune brain 130–1

neurobiology 35–6, 42–3, 127–8; disorganised attachment 52, 95; dopaminergic reward system 35; epigenetic effects 137; HPA axis 95, 133; memory 129–30; oxytocinergic system 35; vagal tone 132, 133; *see also* brain; hormones and opiates; nervous systems
neurodevelopmental impairment 173–4
neuroplasticity 129
'non-shared environment' 173
non-verbal behaviours 61

obesity 34
Object Relations Interview 114
obsessive-compulsive disorder (OCD) 41, 154
opiates *see* hormones and opiates
Oppenheim, D. 37
oppositional defiant disorder (ODD) 157, 159*t*; *see also* conduct disorder
Out, D. *et al.* 100, 101

PAA *see* Preschool Assessment of Attachment
Panksepp, J. 138
paranoid personality disorder 111–12
parasympathetic nervous system 132
Parent Development Interview (PDI) 37–8
parenting 168–9; care 169; control and discipline 169; disconnected caregiving 100; effects on attachment 22–3, 24, 25–6, 37; fathers 171; fostering development 170; influence of child characteristics on 173; and mentalisation 37–8; sensitivity 22, 23, 26, 34, 100; *see also* family relationships
Patterson, G.R. *et al.* 169, 171
PD *see* personality disorders
PDI (Parent Development Interview) 37–8
peer relationships 175–6
Perry, B.D. 129
personality development 31–2; and styles of attachment 33–4
personality disorders (PD) 2, 34, 39–42; antisocial personality disorder 111; and childhood trauma 41; definition 40; narcissistic personality disorder 111–12; obsessive-compulsive disorder 41, 154; paranoid personality disorder 111–12; *see also* borderline personality disorder

physical health 34, 174
Pinker, S. 128
Porges, S. 131
posttraumatic stress disorder (PTSD) 60,
    65–6, 133, 134
predictors of psychological
    outcome 176–7
Preschool Assessment of Attachment
    (PAA) 60–1, 66, 67
pretend mode 118
procedural memory 62, 63, 129–30
psychic equivalence mode 112, 118
psychopathology 58, 94–5
psychosis 111
psychosocial treatments 121
PTSD see posttraumatic stress disorder

Radke-Yarrow, M. et al. 49
Ramchandani, P.G. et al. 171
Reactive Attachment Disorder of Infancy
    and Early Childhood 90, 95
reactive attachment disorders (RAD)
    90–2, 94; characteristics 91t, 159t; vs.
    disorganised attachment 5, 89, 103;
    identification and assessment 95–6,
    98, 154; intervening factors 98;
    interventions 102–3; prevalence 89–90;
    see also Disinhibited Social Engagement
    Disorder; Reactive Attachment Disorder
    of Infancy and Early Childhood
Reder, P. et al. 168
Reflective Functioning Scale 113
reorganisation 61
Robertson, J. 2, 16
Rutter, M. et al. 154, 173–4

Sagi-Schwartz, A. 7
Sahhar, N. 58
Sarkar, J. 40
Scarr, S. 173
Schaffer, H.R. 17
School-Aged Assessment (SAA) 66–7
Schore, A.N. 129, 139
Schuengel, C. et al. 25
Schwartz, J. 128
Scott, S. 90
secure attachment (type B) 19, 22,
    42, 52, 54, 75; ABC + D and DMM
    models 84–5; B1–4 20; hormones 136;
    and mentalisation 37, 38, 52, 116; and
    personality development 33; during
    SSP 32
security vs. danger 7–8, 50

self-harming 58
self–other distinction 111–12, 170
semantic memory 63
sensitivity 22, 23, 26, 34, 100
sexual abuse 33, 41, 56
sexual arousal 58
Shah, P. 90
Shaver, P.R. 98, 99, 158
Shemmings, D. 94, 100
Shemmings, Y. 94, 100
sibling relationships 175
Siegel, D.J. 131
Simpson, J.A. 50, 68n1
Slade, A. et al. 37
social cognition and attachment: romantic
    and maternal love 35; secure and
    predictable relationships 35; threat and
    fear 35, 36
social environment: peer
    relationships 175–6; sibling
    relationships 175; wider influences 176
Solomon, J. 25–6, 65, 94; see also ABC +
    D model
source memory 63
Sroufe, L.A. et al. 15, 34, 76, 177
SSP see Strange Situation Procedure
Stewart, R.B. 175
'still-face' experiments 129–30
Stockholm syndrome 58
Story Stem Assessment Profile
    (SSAP) 96–7
Story Stem Completion 94, 96–7, 140–1
Strange Situation Procedure (SSP) 2,
    26–7, 32; A, B & C 19–21, 73–6;
    ABC + D 21, 32–3, 96; origins of the
    SSP 15–18; SSP today 18, 74t
Strathearn, L. 136
stress: effects on brain 140; hormones 12,
    133–6; and mentalising 39, 110,
    114–15, 116–17; responses to 19, 35,
    131–2, 133; toxic stress 95; see also
    affect; posttraumatic stress disorder
sympathetic nervous system 131–2, 133

Target, M. et al. 97, 101
teleological mode 118
theory of mind 37, 39, 113, 138, 153
Thompson, R.A. 173
Tolstoy, L. 68
Tourette's syndrome 154
transference relationships 130
transformations of information 52–3,
    61–4, 62f; see also memory

traumas 41, 60, 65–6, 99–100, 140; *see also* posttraumatic stress disorder
Tronik, E. 129
Tuberous Sclerosis 154
twin studies 23, 172
types of attachment 2, 3–4, 4*t*, 8n1, 19–21; *see also* adult attachment; disorganised attachment (DA); insecure-ambivalent attachment (type C); insecure-avoidant attachment (type A); secure attachment (type B)

Utting, D. *et al.* 174

vagal tone 132, 133

Van IJzendoorn, M.H. *et al.* 7, 22, 23, 78, 89, 94, 95, 99, 100
video-feedback parent–infant interventions 111
violence 26, 40, 171
Vondra, J. 169

Waters, E. *et al.* 15, 76
Weston, D. 76
Winnicott, D.W. 55, 56
Woolgar, M. 90
working memory 64
Wu, N. *et al.* 135

Zeanah, C.H. *et al.* 26, 89, 90, 91, 92, 98

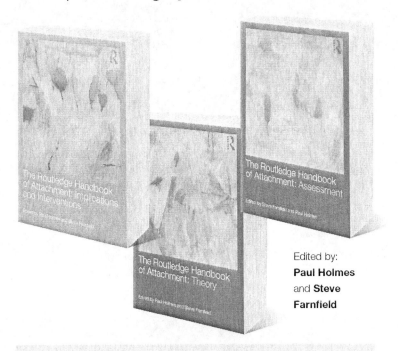